International yearbook of education

VOLUME XLIV – 1994

DEVELOPMENT, CULTURE AND EDUCATION

Prepared for the
International Bureau of Education

by L.F.B. Dubbeldam
*Centre for the Study of Education
in Developing Countries (CESO);*

T. Ohsako
International Bureau of Education;

Lê Thành Khôi
University of Paris V, France;

P. Dasen, P. Furter, G. Rist
University of Geneva, Switzerland;

P. Batelaan
*International Association for
Intercultural Education;*

S. Churchill
*Ontario Institute for Studies
in Education;*

K.P. Epskamp
CESO;

F.M. Bustos
University of Valle, Colombia;

G.R. Teasdale
Flinders University, Australia.

CESO

Published in 1994
by the United Nations Educational,
Scientific and Cultural Organization,
7, place de Fontenoy, 75700 Paris, France

ISBN: 92-3-103038-8

Printed in Switzerland by Presses Centrales S.A., Lausanne.

Preface

This book is a major publication of the IBE on education and cultural development, following the forty-third session of the International Conference on Education (ICE) the theme of which was 'The contribution of education to cultural development' (Geneva, 14-19 September 1992).

Unlike the preceding volumes of the *International yearbook of education*, written by a single author, this volume has been prepared on the basis of contributions from several specialists representing different disciplines in education and cultural backgrounds. Several of these specialists were, prior to the forty-third session of the ICE, requested to submit papers on various priority themes of the Conference for distribution as information documents to its participants. The contents of the various chapters of this book are therefore mainly based upon expanded versions of these information documents presented at the Conference.

It was Leo F.B. Dubbeldam, Director of the Centre for the Study of Education in Developing Countries (CESO, The Hague, The Netherlands), who accepted to be the editor of this book, to accommodate the challenge of the new approach to the material, as well as the intellectual and cultural diversity of its authors. The IBE is very much honoured to work with him and is grateful to Dr. Dubbeldam for his intellectual contribution to the volume. His skills and efforts to co-ordinate the necessary tasks and diversified viewpoints of authors bringing to fruition the publication of this book are very much appreciated by the IBE. Furthermore, the IBE acknowledges the financial contribution of CESO without which it would not have been possible to bring this project to fruition.

The focus of the book is on the interplay of education and culture and is designed to stimulate educational decision makers and educational practitioners in their attempts to maximize educational contributions to cultural development. The book also invites all people from non-educational sectors, such as the community and the media, to join with educators in order to make the process of education more dynamic, creative and relevant to the requirements of cultural development. It is also designed to stimulate current concerns of education in areas such as multicultural-ism/interculturalism, cultural identity as well as cultural change.

Finally, and most of all, the IBE is very grateful to all the authors for their insightful contributions to the various chapters of the book and for their close collaboration with the editor and the Bureau leading to the completion of this work.

Readers are reminded that the ideas and opinions expressed in this work are those of the authors and do not necessarily represent the views of UNESCO. Moreover, the designations employed and the presentation of the material throughout the publication do not imply the expression of any opinion whatsoever on the part of UNESCO concerning the legal status of any country, territory, city or area, or of its authorities, or concerning the delimitations of its frontiers or boundaries.

Contents

CHAPTER I

What are development, culture and education?

Leo F. B. Dubbeldam

WHAT IS THE CONTRIBUTION
OF EDUCATION TO CULTURAL DEVELOPMENT?

The main theme of the International Conference on Education in Geneva in 1992 was not whether education contributes to cultural development, but rather how education contributes to cultural development. This implies two assumptions: one is that there is something called 'culture' that develops; the other is that there is something called 'education' that contributes to the development of culture. Here are two concepts about which very different opinions and ideas exist. What is culture and what is education? Somehow the two are inherent to human beings, because other living beings, apparently, do not need them for the survival of the species. Salmon spawn and die even before their young ones are hatched. There is no communication between the two generations. Yet the young ones behave like their elders. Here mechanisms of nature are at work ensuring the survival of the species. Other animals have to learn, for example, how to hunt from their parents. Animals also learn from experience. The question is to what extent one can speak of a conscious and planned teaching/learning process. Human beings, once born, will be unable to survive if not raised by their parents for a very long time. This is where 'education' comes in.

   Then there is that other dimension called 'culture', something that not only enables human beings to survive but also enables them to influence nature and their chances for survival. If one wants to give an answer to the question posed at the conference, one has to come to an understanding of what is meant by 'culture', by 'education' and by 'development'.

DEVELOPMENT

Through the centuries, the way of life of the world's population has changed drastically. Changes have come in waves, sometimes fast, sometimes slow, unequal in different places.

During the last fifty years three major changes have occurred in the global political texture. The first one was the dismantling of colonial empires, resulting in the foundation of a large number of new, independent States. The second change was the breakdown of the communist bloc, also resulting in a number of new independent States and a change in the relations between nations in the world. We cannot speak of a First, Second and Third World anymore. Thirdly, as a result of these two major changes, a new awareness of both intercultural relations and of cultural identity among national and sub-national groups has arisen.

For a long time development was measured and assessed in terms of income per capita, in other words, by economic growth. Lately, views on development have changed. The criterion now is to what extent the quality of life has improved. In addition to gross national product per capita, the human development index is being used to indicate degrees of development.[1]

To what extent developments have been for the better or the worse may be disputed. The fact is that mankind is still struggling with many problems that have a negative influence on development, in the sense of the quality of people's lives.

In order to illustrate these problems, which are in many ways interrelated, a list of them is given below.

Population growth

In the second half of this century the world population has grown from 2.5 thousand million in 1950 to an estimated 6.2 thousand million at present, the majority of whom live in low-income countries. For education this means that the number of learners, and especially of children, has grown immensely. In Africa, Asia and Latin America young people in the age-category 0-14 years form about 40% of the population. In North America and Europe this figure is less than 25%. In addition, there is widespread migration from rural areas to cities. While in 1950 two-thirds of the population lived in rural areas, today the reverse is true in Brazil, Colombia and Mexico. It is estimated that by the year 2000 more than twenty cities, most of them in developing countries, will have more than 10 million inhabitants and some more than 20 million inhabitants (Mexico and São

Paulo). In many cities, thousands of homeless children are trying to survive on the streets.

These demographic developments have serious consequences for the provision of educational services, especially in the poorer countries.

Economic stagnation

During the 1970s and 1980s economic stagnation has set in, affecting most countries, among which the poorer countries once again have been hit most seriously. The last fifteen years may be characterized by the terms 'debt burden' and 'adjustment programmes'. These developments have resulted in decreased budgets for education and cultural activities.

Unemployment

The two issues mentioned above have resulted in an increase in the number of unemployed people. This raises questions about the curricula of formal education: What basic qualifications do young people need to survive and meet the demands and opportunities of society? The search for paid employment and a better life still forces many people to move to urban centres, a growing number of which are becoming metropolises with populations numbered in millions. Many of the people in such cities live in great poverty, with few or no employment opportunities and beyond the reach of the social services, among which figures the formal school system.

Growing economic disparities

The economic disparities between countries and between populations groups within countries seem to be growing larger rather than smaller. Some developing countries have actually been able to improve their economies, while other find themselves facing even more serious poverty than before. Economic policies and practices within some countries also tend to stimulate a concentration of wealth and to increase social inequalities.

Violence

Many countries suffer from occupation and civil wars, lasting many years, and leading to the deaths of many people, the destruction of facilities like schools, and apathy among the survivors. The education system breaks down and one may wonder what the prospects are for the children who have suffered so much, both physically and mentally. Many other countries report an increase in criminality and school violence. What can education do, given the many other, powerful, political or economic interests that foster violence for their own particular benefit and at the cost of others?

Cultural inequalities

There still exist large inequalities between the opportunities available for members of different groups based on gender, ethnicity, religion, social status or language. In some countries there is a strong revival of nationalism of an ethnic character, such as racist incidents and ethnic cleansing now occurring in the European region. Furthermore, some cultures of sub-cultures appear to dominate others, even to the extent that the very survival of the dominated culture is threatened.

Here is a challenge for education to contribute to increased mutual understanding and tolerance. If education can be instrumental in this process, what immediate and long-term actions could be taken?

Migration

As a result of economic disparities and violence, huge numbers of economic migrants and refugees have moved from one place to another, many without much hope in the future. Resistance against the flow of immigrants is growing in many countries, leading, among other things, to a revival of racism. Yet, history shows that many cultures have been enriched by the skills and values of immigrant groups.

Environment

The fast growing population, industrialization and the use of scarce energy sources have given rise to discussions about the preservation of the natural environment. Educational programmes have picked this issue up and introduced it in the classroom, but it seems that more should be done to achieve adequate results.

Health

In many countries the health of people especially children is threatened by poverty, the lack of or inadequate distribution of food and medical services, and violence. In addition, certain diseases like AIDS have spread widely and threaten millions of people the world over, while other diseases which were labelled as 'under control' have reappeared (malaria, cholera), partly because of poverty situations and partly because the carriers of the diseases have become immune to existing remedies.

Government

Democracy and respect for civil rights are a growing cause for concern. The benefits of governmental services and protection of the law are in many places limited to small, privileged groups.

THE DISCUSSION ON EDUCATION AND CULTURE

It is within the framework of these circumstances that one has to discuss the relationship between education and culture with a view to development. Some of the issues mentioned before may facilitate the role of education; others make it very difficult for education to bring about any positive result. Under particular circumstances, one may even question whether formal education is still a priority or even useful.

Yet, partly as a result of the developments and problems mentioned above, the discussion on education and culture has acquired a new dimension. The means of communication have increased tremendously during the last few decades. New technologies bring many of them financially within the reach of more and more people, but there are still wide discrepancies in the degree to which people have access to the products of the new technologies. Furthermore, as a result of migrations within and over national boundaries, larger numbers of people are brought into close contact with other cultures. In the past this had been impossible, or possible only for a certain types of people, for example, merchants, scholars, diplomats, etc. Thus, people are now meeting each other under very different circumstances, which often determines whether the contact will be positive or negative. It cannot always be foretold whether people will build up close relations with each other and mutually learn from each other or will carefully keep their distance or even enter into conflict. In all cases there is (or should be) the question of: 'How to deal with the others'. As a result, questions are being raised about 'intercultural' relations (interaction between cultures of different countries) and 'multicultural' relations (interaction between groups of different cultures within one country). This development has been shown to have tremendous consequences in cultural, political, economic, social and educational terms.

During the preparation of the forty-third International Conference on Education in September 1992 and in the working sessions, the representatives of UNESCO's Member States reported on and discussed particular issues which they believed to be important, given their particular situation. In addition, a number of experts from different countries were invited to contribute a paper on specific issues. Some of these were invited to contribute to this issue of the *International yearbook of education* since their particular subject of interest was considered to have been significant in the discussions during the Conference.

Since the participants in the discussions held very different interpretations of both the concept of culture and of education, attention is paid to this point in the following chapter. The individual authors were not forced to follow the definitions given in that chapter, especially if their interpretations do not essentially deviate from them. The basic idea is that education is the main carrier for cultural development. On the one hand, education may preserve culture, on the other, it can be instrumental in cultural change. Education is described as a total, lifelong learning process. The school as we know it now is an important part of educational supply, although in terms of cultural development, it may not always be the most important. For education to be harmonious, it is a must that the various actors in education should operate in close harmony. Through examples, different forms and functions of education for cultural development are illustrated. Attention is paid to the concept of networking as an instrument of learning, which is especially useful in multicultural and intercultural education. An example of this is UNESCO's Associated Schools Programme.

Chapter III attempts to highlight the issues that were brought up during the discussion.[2] It also tries to place the agenda of the meeting in the context of earlier conferences and debates on the same or closely related subjects. The concept of culture has played a major role in the United Nations, and in UNESCO in particular, from their very inception, not only in terms of the preservation of the cultural heritance, but also in the discussions on essential issues such as 'freedom', 'human rights', respect for each others' value systems and efforts in international and intercultural understanding, as instruments for the harmonious coexistence of the world's peoples. Initially, most attention was given to culture in a national or local context. More and more themes, such as 'multicultural education' and 'intercultural education' are placed on the agenda of meetings on education. During the World Decade for Cultural Development (1988-97) special attention is given to culture. In the following chapters (IV to X) much room is devoted to issues concerning multicultural and international education.

Particular themes, essential for cultural education, are dealt with in the various chapters. Language, for example, plays an important role since it not only reflects people's ways of thought and their values, but also because it is an essential instrument for mutual understanding between people of different cultures. It is a fact that the curriculum of schools is often built on and permeated by the values, norms, language and so forth associated with one, dominant (sub)culture. Culture is an important factor in the process of democratization, but may encounter barriers erected in the name of dominance and centralization (chapters III and V).

Education plays an important role in people's artistic and aesthetic development. It serves to familiarize people with their cultural inheritance and in developing their creativity (chapters III and VIII).

The new view on cultural education has its effects on the content of the curriculum. But even more on the role of the teachers. New subjects, teaching methods, teacher attitudes and the use of a wide range of sources of information have their consequence for teacher qualifications. Specifically, in the chapters V, VI and VII this topic is dealt with in different ways, though issues concerning teachers recur throughout all chapters.

In various chapters (e.g. V, IX and X) community involvement and participation are discussed as essential elements in cultural education. In this context it becomes clear that education is not the monopoly of the school, but a society-wide process of learning in relation to development and change.

New technologies have brought about an increase and wide variation in sources of information and means of communication. The media strongly influence educational processes both in the schools and in society as a whole. In addition to the use of the 'new' media, there is a rediscovery of the 'traditional' media for educational and cultural purposes, such as storytelling, theatre, dance and other forms of expression (chapters VIII and IX).

The discussion on culture and education reveals a number of ambiguities. There are, for example, tendencies towards something that could be called a 'world culture' and counter-movements to foster and preserve 'local cultures'. Developments in one direction may be detrimental to developments in the other. The formal curriculum of the school may differ from the informal, the 'hidden' curriculum and what is learned, for example, in the home environment. While religions teach values that aim at teaching people to live together harmoniously, it also occurs that they divide people and hamper multicultural and intercultural understanding. Furthermore, there is a discussion on the contrast between tradition and modernity (chapters II and V).

In the final chapter (X), the case of small indigenous cultures is discussed, illustrated by examples from Australia and New Zealand. In a UNESCO-sponsored seminar for the Australia-Pacific region held in Rarotonga (1992), one of the recommendations stated that 'indigenous cultures must own all aspects of the education of their people'. This principle, stated in relation to the specific region, has a global significance. 'Top-down' solutions do not work. The motivation and determination must come from the indigenous peoples themselves. Educational activities should include the traditional forms of education, using the indigenous language and with the involvement of various members of the community. There are some crucial questions to be answered, for example the use of modern processes of teaching and learning in schools for Australian Aboriginal children will be destructive of at least some traditional values and beliefs. A solution may be to teach the children both the traditional and the modern way ('two-way learning').

Various chapters highlight particular issues from various angles. Together they emphasize the need for cultural, multicultural and intercultural education. It appears that there are still serious problems to reach the goals of international and intercultural understanding. But the discussion is still going on and getting even stronger, while quite a few promising initiatives and results can be noted.

NOTES

1. 'Development and the environment', *World Development Report, 1992*. Washington, DC, World Bank, 1992.
2. See the *Final report* of the International Conference on Education, forty-third session, UNESCO/IBE, Geneva, 1992; and the issue No. 5, November 1992, of *Communicación/Communicación*, Geneva, UNESCO/IBE, 1992. (Ninth Series)

CHAPTER II

Development, culture and education

Leo F. B. Dubbeldam

CULTURE

At present the world is inhabited by over 5 thousand million individuals. While these 5 thousand million people are all different, there are many similarities, not only physically, but also in the way they act and think. It appears that people behave not only according to rules of nature, but also to other rules, based on particular norms and values, while they also have the capacity of creativity and thought – something that differentiates human beings from plants and animals. This brings us to the concept of culture.

However, there are at least 100 definitions of culture. For a discussion about the effects of education on cultural development, a choice has to be made. The term is often used to distinguish culture from nature.

Herskovitz (1952:625) defined culture 'as the man-made part of the environment, culture is essentially a construct that describes the total body of belief, behaviour, knowledge, sanctions, values and goals that make up the way of life of any people'.[1] In this definition environment refers both to the natural as well as the social environment. In this way culture 'includes all the elements in man's mature endowment that he has acquired from his group by conscious learning or, on a somewhat different level, by a conditioning process – techniques of various kinds, social and other institutions, beliefs, and patterned modes of conduct'. However, Herskovitz points out that there are some 'seeming paradoxes':

1. Culture is universal in man's experience, yet each local or regional manifestation is unique.

2. Culture is stable, yet culture is also dynamic, and manifests continuous and constant change.

3. Culture fills and largely determines the course of our lives, yet rarely intrudes into conscious thought (Ibid.:18).

15

Linton (1964:21) defines culture as 'the configuration of learned behaviour and the results of behaviour, the component elements of which are shared and transmitted by the members of a particular society'. This definition stresses some other issues (Dubbeldam, 1991).
- The component elements of a culture are shared by a group of people, which determines the identity of the group.
- Elements of culture are transferred from one generation to another.
- His definition refers to learned behaviour. Children have to learn in order to survive and become adults.
- The component elements are closely interrelated, they form a closely knit configuration. This implies that changes in one element usually imply changes in other elements of the cultural network.

History and even today's events show that changes in the natural environment – such as droughts, floods, diseases (e.g. AIDS) and earthquakes – do influence the way human beings behave. Also individuals, because of their capabilities of thought, ideas and creativity, can manipulate their natural environment and change culture. Through curiosity, planned experimentation and invention people can bring about far-reaching changes in their daily life.

These definitions somehow ignore the fact that, for human beings, their 'universe' is more than life on this world. There is the supernatural sphere – the spiritual environment. The existence of people, and the *raison d'être* of their existence is often anchored in the spiritual world. Many of the social rules and modes of behaviour have, in a distant past, been determined and ordained by ancestors, spirits or gods. While people's the existence is protected by the supernatural, the latter can be threatening to people who neglect their obligations. It seems that people would sooner resist mundane rules than disobey the supernatural commandments. In many societies this plays a crucial role in socio-political issues. Those in power may enforce their mundane rules by calling upon a mandate or norms set by a supernatural authority.

It is not just a question of the natural, inherited capacity to survive and multiply the species. There is a specific added value, namely the knowledge, skills, attitudes, norms, ideas and creativity that determine behaviour towards other people, nature and the supernatural, and that may lead to development in the sense of an improvement of daily life.

Individuals grow into what they are partly through hereditary factors, but this is not enough to survive. Equally important is that people should keep on learning, through the transfer of knowledge and ideas by other members of society, be it older people, peers or younger ones (Dubbeldam, 1990, p. 25).

In preparation for the forty-third session of the International Conference on Education, a questionnaire was sent to the Member States of UNESCO.[2] For the purpose of this questionnaire, the following concept of culture, proposed during the World Conference on Cultural Policies (Mexico, 1982) was adopted:

The Conference agrees: that in its widest sense, culture may now be said to be the whole complex of distinctive spiritual, material, intellectual and emotional features that characterize a society or social group. It includes not only the arts and letters, but also modes of life, the fundamental rights of the human being, value systems, traditions and beliefs; that it is culture that gives man the ability to reflect upon himself. It is culture that makes us specifically human, rational beings, endowed with a critical judgement and a sense of moral commitment. It is through culture that we discern values and make choices. It is through culture that man expresses himself, becomes aware of himself, recognizes his incompleteness, questions his own achievements, seeks untiringly for new meanings and creates works through which he transcends his limitations.

This definition sums up a series of features of what culture is, rather than defining the essentials. Furthermore, one may question, for example, the critical judgement or the sense of moral commitment of many human beings. Not all people are aware of themselves nor recognize their incompleteness or question their own achievements, and seek untiringly for new meanings. In some cultures such forms of behaviour are encouraged, in other they are not. The elements of sharing and transmission are missing.

These two aspects are especially important in defining culture in relation to education.

Considering the various characteristics and aspects mentioned in the definitions presented above, the following definition of culture is suggested as a useful instrument for the present paper:

Culture can be defined as *the configuration of ideas and learned behaviour and their results whose component elements are shared and transmitted by the members of a particular society, in a continuous process of imitation and intended transfer of knowledge about society, nature and the supernatural, as well as through adaptations to and alterations in society's changing environment and through its members' creativity.*

SUB-CULTURES

One of the problems is that, even though one might speak about the culture of a particular society, it appears upon a closer look that not all elements of a particular culture are shared by all its members. For example, one does speak of a Dutch culture. Yet there is a noticeable difference between farmers in the North of the country and the football supporters in The Hague: in the way they behave, dress or speak. They all speak Dutch, but they use different words, idioms and grammar. Their ideas about social values differ widely. Apparently, there are within society various sub-cultures. What makes it even more complicated is that individuals belong to different sub-cultures, people may be grouped together around a particular profession, religion, age-group, interest, political viewpoint or some other matter. Each of these social groups has its own particular sub-culture. The rationale for the existence of each of these and the purpose for their togetherness is obviously different. In each of these social groups a particular attitude and behaviour is expected of the participants. This is visible in, for example, the way they dress, the way they treat each other and in the language they use. As a result, a person behaves differently in his or her varying social roles: in the work situation, in religious meetings, in the family or during leisure time.

Each person belongs to many sub-cultures that sometimes require contrasting or even conflicting behaviours, norms and values (Dubbeldam, 1991, p. 3 and p. 8). Sometimes individuals are free to join a particular sub-cultural group, such as in sports, political groups or a religious society. On the other hand, people may not easily enter some sub-groups or may never be able to do so. It is often difficult for men to become a member of female societies or even to act and behave as a woman; it is quite impossible to change membership of one's age-group; in some societies there exists a strict separation between sub-cultural groups based on factors such as religion, caste, race, sex, wealth or profession. Often one finds a combination of them.

Each of these sub-cultures has its own means of transferring culture. This means that there is in a particular society a multitude of sub-cultural learning circuits.

CULTURAL IDENTITY

All (sub)cultures have a core of concepts, ideas, values, behaviour and purposes with which the members identify themselves and through which they distinguish themselves from non-members. Belonging to a group strengthens the members' feelings of security. This core forms the *cultural identity* of a social group.

Differences in physical appearance or habitat may make people classify 'others' as different. Cultural differences or similarities may aggravate or mitigate such differences. In general, one could say that the unknown is dangerous. Individuals find security within their familiar cultural setting, since they are culturally at a par with the other people they meet. Strangers, who behave differently, are a potential threat as long as one does not know more about them and does not understand them.

As with the concept of culture, there are difficulties with the definition of cultural identity. Often one finds descriptions serving a specific purpose rather than definitions. For example: 'The cultural identity of a people, a nation, is the right inherent in that people or that nation itself to resist and oppose all the assimilationist pressures and levelling forces of the contemporary world', or 'Cultural identity is the highest expression of the fundamental equality of nations and groups coexisting within one nation', or 'Cultural identity recognizes the right to differ, the right of authenticity', or 'Cultural identity is synonymous with freedom, with equality' (Kane, 1982).

In Webster's Dictionary, *identity* is explained as a state of absolute sameness. *Personal identity* is described as 'being the same person from the commencement to the end of life while the matter of the body, the dispositions, habits, thoughts, etc., are continually changing'. This idea holds also for cultures. For example, the German culture of today differs from its predecessor in the fourteenth or fifteenth centuries. Yet for both the early period and for today we speak of a German culture, while the historical elements play an important role in the cultural identity of today's people. We know that there are many differences, yet we see enough similarities to use the same label. There exists a continuity between the past and the present, as well as between people living at different times within the same geographical – usually artificial – boundaries.

This identification with the past is more difficult for immigrant populations that have occupied the territory of another cultural group that has been expelled from the area or has become extinct. In this case, the people have to refer to ancestors who lived in a much more recent past. For example, there is a difference in this respect between the United States and India. But cultural identity may as well be a construct. For example, when a group with a strong ideology comes into power, they may change the way earlier periods, particular commonalities and specific cultural heroes are referred to in order to suit their ideological purposes.[3]

In the process of identification, a person may assimilate an aspect, a property or an attribute belonging to another person and, using it as a model, change himself/herself accordingly.[4] This may happen in the case of people who feel themselves to be in an inferior position to more powerful people in society.[5] But this phenomenon, found in a socio-political context of domination, can also be found in cases where the dominating party copies behaviour from the dominated group. Assimilating cultural elements of other groups often has a socio-political reason.

A group's cultural identity is not only formed by the people belonging to a particular culture. It often is, at least partly, formed by outsiders, often on the basis of visible behavioural features. People are not always aware of the component elements of their identity. They may be aware of and believe in some elements, but be unaware of others that are evident to outsiders. Outsiders observing a society are likely to name a different set of elements to describe that society or its members' cultural identity. Foreigners may tend to identify the Dutch by wooden shoes, windmills, tulips, dikes and cheese, thereby including some items that are now almost out of use in the country. Many Dutch dislike that image; yet, in promoting business abroad, advertisers use these elements to attract their clients' attention.

The concept of 'cultural identity' has a meaning at two levels – the individual and society. These are partly similar (in nature), partly different (in scale and function) and, finally, reciprocal.

At the individual level, *cultural identity is the psychological recognition by an individual of sharing a set of fundamental behavioural elements with a number of other people, with whom a close relatedness is revealed, by which the rightful and appropriate position of the individual in human society is confirmed.*

Similarly, at the societal level, be it macro or micro, we find that the *cultural identity of a particular society is the aggregate of specific behavioural elements which are recognized as representing the characteristics of the fundamental behavioural pattern of the members of that society, thus confirming the rightful and appropriate existence of that society and its members.*

When the elements forming the cultural identity of a particular group of people have an adequate positive unifying value for the members of the society (or group) concerned, one may classify this as positive. However, the situation is different when elements are fostered, sometimes as it were artificially, as a distinction from other people, as something superior, better than that which identifies the others. Cultural identity then becomes, figuratively speaking, an egocentric 'I entity', different and better than others. This implies a potential danger for relations between communities when some groups are exploited or manipulated politically by groups in power, whether in terms of ideology, religion or economy (Dubbeldam, 1984, p. 16).

It is interesting to note that whenever references are made by a social group to its cultural identity, these relate usually to the past, sometimes to the present, but rarely to the (even nearby) future. Yet at least some people must have a vision of the future for their group.

COMMUNICATION

Expression

People have many ways of expressing their feelings and of communicating with each other. They have developed a variety of means of communication by which they can adequately express their ideas, feelings, norms and values, such as physical signs, sound, language, symbols, scripts and graphics. These are used in mime, dancing, theatre, storytelling, literature, radio, television and computerized communication. Through their creativity and particular skills they can mould all types of matter from flintstones to atoms. Through wood, paint, glass, silk, gold and many other materials people have aired their feelings and they have created many objects useful or pleasant to themselves or others.

Physical signs

People are social beings, who have many ways and means to communicate with each other. Physical expressions can indicate joy, fear, approval and other feelings or messages. Through hand movements we can express our feelings. Yet, the ways in which people use their hands differ, for example in the way they greet each other or how one offers something to another person. Through the movements of the body people can pass on messages to each other. This is extended to the way people dress themselves, colour their skin or make up their hair. Colours of dresses have particular meanings: some dresses are appropriate only in specific situations. Some types of haircut give information about the social status of the persons or about their identification with certain sub-cultural groups. Dress may be an indication of conservatism or modernity, of status, of joy or sorrow, of conformism with or revolt against the current social order.

More powerful is the use of sounds and especially the capacity of speech. A hissing sound to attract someone's attention is accepted in some cultures; in others it may be an insult.

Language

Through the use of language people can express their ideas and communicate with other people of their community. Through language people can transfer their knowledge, values and ideas to others and, by doing so, their culture.

Languages reflect the culture of a particular community. For example, where a particular food-crop is dominant in society, the people will distinguish many variations of it, identifying them with different words. Other societies may just have one word for that type of crop. The Dutch have one word for sweet potatoes, some societies have several dozen words for different varieties. The Dutch and English languages have one word for rice, but others, such as Bahasa Indonesia or Kiswahili, have different words for rice in the field, for uncooked and for boiled rice.

There are great differences in the variety of words for family relations, reflecting different behaviour towards particular relatives. Words do not have the same value in various languages, which becomes apparent when one talks about concepts like 'authority' or 'democracy'. The value a word like 'teacher' has in different languages differs widely in terms of respect and authority.[6] But also technological words and terminology used in natural science (such as 'power') do raise misunderstandings in learning processes. As cultures change, the language will adjust to the new situation, some new words are introduced, others become obsolete or disappear altogether. Sometimes changes are fast, but in other cases it takes a great deal of time and effort for words and linguistic concepts to be internalized.

All individuals are socialized in one language – the one used by their parents, relatives and community. With widening contacts within communities, people come into contact with others who speak a different language. Where particular cultures or sub-cultures are dominating, in terms of numbers or power, it becomes a necessity for the individual to learn one or more other languages. This can be done through informal contacts, while it is usually an essential subject in formal education. It can be one of the reasons why children are prevented from participating in school education because they do not understand what is taught. Yet, when they manage to speak and understand the second language, there still is the question whether they can really internalize the cultural values that are inherent to that language. And if they do, to what extent can this lead to a position where the individual has to balance between two cultures or has to jump from one to the other as a particular situation demands?

Here lies a serious problem for intercultural or multicultural education.

Oral communication

Oral communication is the oldest medium human beings have. It is the means of daily communication within the local community. With the widening circles of communication in the world it plays a role in the contacts with outsiders. It is the most important instrument in the socialization process. But, in addition to this, it is the instrument *par excellence* for the transfer of history, values and norms. In almost all societies story-telling plays an important role. It has an element of entertainment, a social activity. Between the story-teller and the audience is a feeling of together-ness. It often has an educational function, since the audience is informed about the nature of things, the mythological past, religion, history or the daily life. In 'oral' cultures one finds a richness of stories that are told over and over again, and memorised, while their messages are internalized. The message and the pattern of the story is usually pre-determined. Yet in many cases improvisations on fixed patterns may be used to comment on social developments, such as the *wayang* performances in Indonesia. People will have an open ear for a message when they can recognize its framework and its meaning, and can identify themselves with the problem sketched or with one of the persons in the story. Unless the message fits in the cultural framework of ideas and experiences of the receiver, it will be lost. Speech, however, has its limitations. One can communicate directly only with people who are physically present. One may, often without being aware of it, address people in different ways at different places or at different times, but one depends in that case on the accuracy in which the story is retold by a sequence of intermediaries.

New media

At present the traditionally known 'oral culture' has partly been merged with or replaced by other media, for example the written word, the radio, television and computer technology. A new mix of communication tech-niques is developing.

The gradual development of various techniques and modern technology has helped people to widen their capacities to communicate with others. The development of writing together with the materials to be used – such as paper, pencils, typewriters and computers, and reproduction techniques – have been of revolutionary importance to mankind. Later instruments, such as radio, television, telephone, telex and telefax, have widened the possibilities and range of communication. Together, these have not only enabled people to send messages to others in distant places, but also to record ideas and information so that they can be preserved and transmitted accurately.

The various means of communication strengthen each other. Move-ments can effectively support words. Radio transmissions can be used as complementary to and in support of written information. They may, how-ever, also replace each other. For example, someone who may call some-body else by telephone, does not have to write a letter. a person who has a radio or television can keep himself/herself informed about current events without having to read a newspaper. Extension officers, school-teachers and professors use pictorial information for passing on a message to their audience.

This has its effect on the use of particular means of communication, such as on the use and need for literacy. For many people oral communication plus audio-visual media fulfil their needs for information. For that reason some people may not feel the need for literacy skills. In other situations where people were taught to read and write, these skills may lapse for lack of exercise, leading to an increased number of new illiterates. The use of literacy depends very much on the cultural context. In this respect, when is someone literate? Does it mean being able to read a newspaper? Write a letter to a friend? Fill-up a tax form? Use a computer? There seems to be nowadays a mix-up of criteria: one of being able to read and write, the other of having additional skills of understanding bureaucratic styles and technological techniques. There also seems to be a difference in the learning attitude and capability between people who are literate in one language and learning another, and people who are learning writing for the first time.

Though there is a significant increase in the potentialities of communication there are serious problems.

– In the internationalization of communication, adequate interpretation of the specific codes, signs and words used is becoming more and more essential. This implies that people, whether sending or receiving messages through the new media, have to learn the meaning of the new codes, signs and words, of the 'language and symbols of communication'.

– The availability of the various media in the world, and especially in developing countries, differs widely. In some countries the daily circulation of newspapers is less than one per 1,000 inhabitants. The number of radios and television sets differs much in various countries. The density of television sets is low in some sub-Saharan countries, and much higher in other countries in the same region. This raises questions as to who are the owners of such sets? Possibly only the more affluent part of the population? There is still a lack of realistic data on the availability and the use of the various media in developing countries.

– The accessibility of information through the various media is also limited because, in many instances, the content is curbed by the authorities, for political, ideological or religious reasons.[7] Many news agencies, television and radio stations, printing companies and other agencies that provide information to the audience are owned and controlled (or manipulated) by governments or political, ideological and religious organizations. International press agencies are often run commercially, but, according to their critics, they also have a particular political and cultural bias. Finally, the selection of information is performed by editors who have their own cultural and personal criteria and interests. It seems that such barriers for the free flow of information can only be solved in situations where the people, the consumers, can choose from various sources and compare the products, like they do with the products in the market place.

– Related to the former issue is the fact that individuals attach specific weight to information that is handed to them by persons in authority. This starts with information from parents and relatives during the socialization process, but continues through life, such as what the teacher says in school, what is written on paper, what leaders in society say. Individuals do not automatically check such information with other sources, even if they are in the position to do so, because even the intent to check information is often socially or politically unacceptable. For example, questioning a teacher is not acceptable in many cultures, which has an influence on classroom behaviour and teaching methods. Similarly, many medical doctors do not appreciate their patients seeking a 'second opinion'. Often children are discouraged from asking questions. They are supposed to listen. When such habits are internalized, learners may have difficulties with the curiosity required in problem solving techniques and natural sciences.

DEVELOPMENT AND CHANGE

Given that culture is transferred from one generation to another, and that all elements of a culture are interrelated, one may expect this to be a conservative process. And, in fact, at least until recently, the socialization process and the associated education tended (or were meant) to be conservative. Parents and other members of the community taught youngsters the ideas, norms, behaviour, attitudes and particular skills as these had been transferred to themselves. Yet all cultures change, sometimes slowly and gradually, sometimes violently and abruptly. History and anthropological studies show a full panoply of variations between these two extremes.

Cultures change, or develop,[8] as a result of various causes:
– There may be alterations in the natural environment forcing people to react. Changing particular forms of behaviour in response to the new situation may imply wider cultural change, because the cultural universe

has to find a new harmony. One finds such a situation in cases where the natural environment has changed in a relatively short period of time or when people had to move from one territory to another, which is the case of refugees.

- Cultures may change because of innovations resulting from the creativity and ideas of individual members. Such change may occur deliberately and fast, as well as inconspicuously and slowly.
- There may be changes in the cultural configuration as a result of contacts with other cultural groups. This may occur slowly, or rather imperceptibly. For example, the Kapauku in the Central Highlands of West-Irian used the cowrie shell as their medium of exchange. As the people in the highlands lived in isolation, the influx of new shells was very sporadic. Each shell, however, was treated and handled so frequently that it acquired a specific form and texture. During the first half of the century, through the arrival of expeditions, relatively large quantities of new shells were imported. At first the people noticed the difference between new and old shells, so the imports did not affect the value of the *mere*, the old shells. But new ones eventually wore out by use and people found new techniques to turn new shells into old-looking shells by using newly imported chemicals. As a result, only after a few decades even the experts in that society could not distinguish the newly imported shells from the really old ones. With the result that the cowry-shell devaluated and, with it, the power of the leaders in society (Dubbeldam, 1964). When, at that time in the 1950s, new items were introduced that implied a revolution in daily life, such as iron axes to replace the stone axes, and the introduction of paper money, culture and social life reached a critical and revolutionary point.

In contrast, a particular people may be violently overrun by another one, such as happened in the conquest of the Americas and Australia, but also in comparable migrations, conquests and wars which have taken place in Africa, Asia and Europe. In such cases the changes can be called neither subtle nor gradual. In the case of physical annihilation of a particular population, it is clear that the chances for cultural survival are very slim. In the case of dispersion of a particular cultural group, the chances for cultural survival are greater. The question is to what degree a culturally alien power can really change the culture of the population subjected by it.

During the early 1960s a team of researchers at Michigan University studied the effects of the modernization process in Uzbekistan. In this case, we find a foreign power with a powerful ideology ruling a people with a strong religious tradition. Here was a country with an old and imbedded Islamic tradition, which one would expect to provide resistance to modernizing policies. It had some of the largest and most strategic (politically and economically) urban concentrations in Islamic Middle Asia. It possessed the best all-round posture for economic development in the whole region, including a rich delta and valley country for industrial agriculture. By 1956 the educational institutions of Uzbekistan had produced an intellectual, scientific and political elite that was numerically significant compared to other Islamic countries. The non-native element in Uzbekistan's population in 1959 was no more than 19% (the Russians themselves only 13%). Mass education similar to that of industrialized European countries was being practised at all levels of society. National identity and consciousness in the area appeared to be on the increase rather than on the decline. The question was whether this rapid transformation from mediaevalism just 'happened', or was it the result of deliberate policies designed to bring about fundamental changes in Muslim society? (cf. Medlin, 1969, p. 120-121).

Decision-making in all areas of society was politicized. Soviet economic policy aimed at resolving the contradiction between rural and urban models of production in order to rationalize and modernize the economy. This policy embraced regional specialization and the creation of nationality areas, but within the framework of a total Soviet economy. To conduct the economic and educational policies on a mass scale required extensive participation of the indigenous population in political processes and administration. This implied a native or local nationality consciousness, distinct in Central Asia from the non-native or Russian nationality. The evidence suggested that there was a viable cultural identity, especially in Uzbekistan, that ran parallel to the Russian element and that related in certain ways to distinctly Uzbek political institutions (ibid., p. 125).

Education and youth organizations played an important role. The 'golden thread' running through the entire Soviet effort at educational reconstruction since 1917 has been the attempt to make learning of practical value, and to fashion the school as a gateway to the world of economic specialization and material production. Teachers were asked to relate schooling to work experiences. They were expected to inculcate ideological loyalty and Soviet patriotism. Schools would also serve as community centres to promote adult literacy and cultural programmes. They were to emphasize a materialistic and scientific curriculum aimed at providing manpower resources (ibid., p. 127-28). The Soviet modernizers established policies that both built upon older practices and legitimized new functions of the school in Uzbekistan. In the Soviet native school, similar teaching functions were maintained as in the past, but the content and methods of the roles themselves had been altered somewhat. The same authoritarian relationship between teacher and pupil was expected in the Soviet classroom as in the *maktab* (ibid., p. 131). That the national language was used certainly played an important role, since it enabled the teachers to make references to aspects of cultural identity. By using the native language, a teacher can refer to basic concepts with the traditional connotations and framework of thoughts. The research indicated that reading books used in school showed a relatively high content of items which supported and reinforced native identities, which the skilled teacher could use to advantage.

In a paper based on the original research report (cf. Medlin, 1971, p. 230-33) the authors tried to make a few predictions. The continuous emphasis on educational opportunities could lead to a modification of communist ideology. They expected a continued rise of meritocracy based on educational achievement, an increased manifestation of leadership among native Uzbeks and an increased stratification of the social order based on educational criteria. Maybe, in the same line of thinking, there would be a rise in disaffection and independent attitudes toward Russian domination. A society in which some social groups shared a strong cultural heritage over many centuries can hardly accept radically new policies imposed by foreign invaders without generating some feelings and patterns of behaviour that tend to alienate it from the newly dominant system. Interesting are their observations on the influence of voluntary ethnic groups in the streets, restaurants and places of entertainment and urban segregation in housing. Elementary textbooks and radio programmes produced in the Uzbek language and in cultural manifestations (e.g. national dress) showed a considerable recognition of many traditional customs. Finally, they expected a rise in national consciousness and assertiveness. Later developments showed that they were quite right.

Apparently this was a case where no efforts were made to construct what we call now multicultural education and to raise mutual understanding, but rather one dominant culture simply being imposed on another, ignoring the forces of cultural identity that perpetuated the dominated culture. As it were, two parallel systems in one classroom.

EDUCATION

Education is the process through which a newborn individual becomes an integrated member of his or her community. It is the main agent of transfer of a culture through generations. It guarantees the continuation of a culture. At the same time, by stimulating and developing intellect and creativity, education promotes the development of culture that may lead to change (Dubbeldam, 1990b, p. 106).

Through education, members of a society acquire the factual knowledge, normative systems and analytical framework which they need in order to live in their particular society. Human beings have become increasingly dependent on learning. They have to learn a variety of things, such as:

– adequate reactions to their natural environment, to master particular aspects of it, and skills in using particular materials;

– to behave as members of their community in various circumstances;

– the general and specific intellectual and physical skills needed for particular activities;

– appropriate understanding of the natural and supernatural phenomena, laws and powers basic to existence; and more recently

– understanding of and ways of coexistence with people of different cultures.

Since culture is a configuration of particular elements, education, described as the main agent of culture and reflecting culture, is – at least in theory – basically a composite, an integrated whole as well. The physical, intellectual and ethical integration of the individual into a complete man is a broad definition of the fundamental aim for education (Faure, 1972, p. 156).

Education, consequently, has a wide variety of forms, contents and methods. Through *informal education* people learn from others, in personal contacts, ad hoc, the content being determined by the momentary situation. There is no end to this type of learning. It lasts throughout a person's life. It is perhaps the most integral type of learning. Maybe this is its strength in the formation of personalities and in the transfer of culture.

At a time, different for various societies, there arose a need for more organized and specialized forms of education. The school came into being, groups of children taught by professional teachers, who were supposed to teach their pupils specific skills. Originally the emphasis was on religious, philosophical or vocational education, but gradually it moved into more secular, basic skills, such as reading, writing, arithmetic and other academic subjects. This led to what we name now *formal education: national systems of educational institutions, with a fixed curriculum taught by professional teachers, offered to children and youth in special buildings. The curriculum is usually determined by a national authority and uniform for the nation.* Its strength can be that it may offer, systematically, a variety of subjects in an integrated curriculum to its pupils. There are, however, many reservations about its objectives, relevance, quality and effectiveness.

As an alternative for this formal type of education, all kinds of *non-formal education* programmes have come into being. These are organized forms of education that have specific objectives, but are more geared to the needs and expectations of the learners. The subjects taught may be specific vocational or professional skills, but also other social, cultural or recreational subjects.

Such a distinction is never absolute, as practice shows that there is considerable overlap. For example, teachers have to implement the curriculum prescribed by the authorities. Their degree of freedom to teach something other than what is prescribed are limited. One reason being the final examinations. At the end of a fixed time the teacher must have completed a number of subjects. If he or she does not reach that target, negative results will backfire on the teacher. Especially in countries where appropriate diplomas are a requirement to get a particular job, the atmosphere in the schools is dominated by what has been labelled the 'diploma disease'. This prevents the school from dealing with themes of local interest, i.e. to insert subjects that have a local relevance, either in the classroom or after school hours. However, even though there is little room for teachers to insert additional subjects into the curriculum, they still have ample opportunities to insert their views, values and criticism on social or political events. Teachers are in day-to-day contact with the students. During the lessons they may convey their attitude, through bias or from small remarks. In contacts with students outside the classroom they may find ample opportunities to air their ideas, and communicate with the learners. This is an example of informal education within the formal education system. The study of Medlin, previously mentioned, showed that the teachers can still use the prescribed curriculum to their (cultural) advantage. Also, the way a teacher functions in the classroom, whether he or she stimulates a critical attitude with the children or not, are important for the overall education of the children. But there are limitations to this as well. When children report at home what the teacher has told them in school and when this conflicts with what the parents expect of the teacher's norms, beliefs and attitudes, the teacher may enter into conflict with the parents and the community, if not with the authorities.

There is a never-ending discussion on what school education should offer. Many scholars agree that it should build a complete personality. Politicians want the school to teach along their lines of thinking and ideology. Parents want their children to get something useful for a further career, to become decent citizens or just to be happy. The question of what 'basic education' means confuses not only educationists but also politicians.

At present school systems in the world seem to develop along uniform lines. It is stated that this is 'Western' education.[9]

In terms of format or organization, maybe it is, but there is no such a monopoly as 'Western' education in terms of objectives and pedagogical ideas and techniques. Furthermore, there has always been a debate about the objectives, the methodology and the content of education. The discussion may get out of hand if it is undertaken from the point of view of religion or ideology. The result may be that the discussion is not so much about the technical aspects of, for example, the methodology, ideological, religious or other principles. For example, one reads that the Western system of education considers the child 'as an object undergoing a treatment and not as an active learner' (cf. Altaf Gauhar, p. 75-76).

Many educationists will strongly disagree with this statement, since for decades many pedagogues and educationists in the 'West' have been seeking for methodologies to stimulate the learners' active participation. In many cases their ideas have been implemented to various degrees. The argumentation used seems to be more an attack on the evaluation and examination procedures leading to 'a rigid class structure that has made people subservient to numbers'. The author attacks the importance attached to the examination marks, the subsequent ranking of pupils and its consequences for further studies or employment, which is a point for discussion indeed! But further questions raise some problems. They are posited not from an educational point of view but from a religious, ideological or maybe ethical point of view:

What do the Western modes of examinations aim at judging? Since the system has no clear goal, an assessment is made of a student's capability to: (1) observe, (2) raise questions, (3) explore, (4) solve problems, (5) interpret findings, (6) communicate verbally, (7) communicate non-verbally, (8) apply learning. All these are given certain numbers and each number is kept in an isolated cell – the total personality of the student is taken as an aggregate of these numbers. There is nothing in the system to enable a teacher to find out whether a student who may have collected the highest aggregate will behave honestly or dishonestly, fairly or unfairly, justly or unjustly, kindly or unkindly towards others.

The points mentioned are indeed aspects taken into account during examinations. They are so because they are vital elements in the didactics that, in contrast with what the author writes, aim to prevent children from becoming 'objects undergoing a treatment'. Also values such as 'just/unjust', from a particular point of view, can, if well indoctrinated, be used as 'instruments for treatment'.

If one considers education as a lifelong learning process, and if one wants to promote the idea that learners use the various educational opportunities, such as the school, the media and the people from the community, then the points listed above are useful instruments for learning.

A further point for discussion is the question of whether, and to what extent, subjects should be taught other than arithmetic, languages, history, geography, sciences, biology and the arts, the assumption being that school education should contribute to the formation of a complete personality. What about religion or ideology, as a separate subject or as part of social sciences or philosophy?

The answer lies partly in the conceived complementarity of school education and other types of education, socialization, informal and non-formal education and the media. If (school) education is an integral part of a particular culture, there is no need to force into the school curriculum all kinds of things that could be dealt with even better through any of the other channels. For example, honesty should be taught to children long before they enter the school system and it will be measured and dealt with by the members of the community in various ways. Part of this is the way that teachers and peers will react to dishonesty by one of the pupils, even though it is not a subject in the curriculum. It belongs to the realm of informal education as a built-in element in the formal education system.

The teaching of values, be it religious or ideological, in education usually raises a lively discussion. The first question is, whose values? Those of the authorities, the teachers, the learners, their parents or others in the community? One must admit that no teaching/learning situation is entirely without values, if not in the subject matter, then in the presentation or the informal sphere of communication between teachers and learners. Yet there are differences in the way values are made part of the curriculum.

Much of the discussion concerns religious education. The argument for religious education as a fundamental part of the curriculum, all elements of which have to be related to it, is that education is an essential and integral element of culture. Therefore its content should match the most valued aspects of culture. If these are determined by religion and the values and social behaviour derived from it, then this should be reflected in the teaching/learning situation. It is considered essential in developing a society and in maintaining its identity, in keeping out alien ideas and elements that might direct it in the wrong direction.

The arguments against religious education are that it indoctrinates the pupils, and that it suppresses their intellectual, critical and social development. Besides, it promotes social segregation, since it stresses the core values of a dominating group against the interests of all others.

Religious education is found usually in countries where there is one dominant religion. It is then often made an integral part of the curriculum. Most teachers will belong to that particular religion. If, however, there are in the country people belonging to other religions, it may have a negative effect on their access to school education, since pupils may either be refused enrolment or be frozen out by the attitudes of other pupils and teachers.

There are only a few countries where 'religion' is taught as a subject, explaining a number of religions to the pupils in order to promote their understanding of other people in their own country or elsewhere in the world. If one wants to design a multicultural education curriculum, the place of religious education, an important instrument to convey values to pupils, has to be assessed very carefully. Is it meant to transfer particular values or is the aim to bring about mutual understanding?

A serious problem is that people with a strong value system and, consequently, a strong feeling of cultural identity, belonging to a particular religion, ideology or ethnic community, tend to ignore or reject the ideas and beliefs of others categorically, without any efforts to understand the 'others'. Arguments against the others or in support of their own group are more often than not based on cultural beliefs rather than on rational arguments. The issue becomes even more complicated when arguments derived from basic cultural values are used in economic debates.

Discussions on education are often based on value systems, religious or ideological doctrines, and too little on what the learners need to know now and in the future. For example, in a discussion on the influence of education on society Basheer El Tom (1981, p. 31) writes:

That Mannheim should refuse the tenets of Christianity as the ideological basis of the reformed West is not indefensible; for the Christian article of faith is both obscure and unsound. Despite repeated attempts at reformation, the Christian religion has become somewhat obscurantist and esoteric, and therefore incapable of impinging on society as an educative social force. It has become static, and therefore, lost relevance to a changing and progressive environment.

There is a multitude of examples in which people have labelled others, with different faiths, as pagans or heathens, ignoring their beliefs or condemning them. History shows that many people have been socially rejected and even physically eliminated because of different religious beliefs. Examples are found in colonial history and in today's newspapers. In this way many valuable cultural concepts and ideas, and educational methods and processes have been destroyed or at least have been ignored so that they could not contribute to the development of the people concerned or to the international body of knowledge and ideas. Much of what is called indigenous knowledge and education is, as a consequence, unknown to the wider community. Only recently growing attention has been paid to this type of knowledge and wisdom, from the point of view of its usefulness, out of respect or because of scientific interest.[10]

Better insight in the indigenous learning systems of (sub–)cultures may help in formulating educational programmes for such groups of people, which is especially important if, for one reason or another, they have no access to the national formal education system. It also helps in understanding the way children and adults learn so that the methods used in the classrooms may take this into account. Specific programmes may help to bridge the gap between the culture of the school and the culture of the people and, in this way, contribute to their cultural development.

A problem in education is that breaches of values by 'others' are often described extensively, both in school and in daily conversations, while such behaviour by the 'own' group is denied or ignored. Examples can be found, for example, in an issue like racial discrimination. Practically all (sub–)cultural groups will deny any racial discrimination, yet it can be found almost everywhere. The same holds for gender discrimination. Few people will admit that they think or act against equality of the sexes. Yet practice shows that it exists the world over.

The consequence is that in order to solve this kind of social problem the first step to be taken has to be to raise people's awareness about the problem tactfully, as well as their own ideas and behaviour. This is an essential element in both multicultural and intercultural education.

EDUCATION AND CULTURE

Already in the 1960s the question whether, and to what extent, education influences culture was the subject of research. For example, studies at Harvard University researched the question of whether education makes men 'modern' (Inkeles, 1969 and 1975). Their answer to the question was not an unqualified 'yes': 'Education is the most powerful factor in making man modern, but occupational experience in large-scale organizations, and especially in factory work, makes a significant contribution in "schooling" men in modern attitudes and in teaching them to act like modern man' (Inkeles, 1969, p. 208). One conclusion is that, if attending school brings about substantial changes in fundamental personal orientations, the school must be teaching a good deal more than is apparent in its syllabus on reading, writing, arithmetic and even geography (ibid., p. 213).

Even though we can establish that both the length of schooling and the quality of the school are important in shaping the modernity of the child, we must nevertheless acknowledge that these factors explain only part of the variation in individual modernity scores among young people. Obviously much depends on personal influences which are, to some degree, quite independent of the effects of schooling *per se*. Notable among these personal influences are the characteristics of the child's parents and his school peers (Inkeles, 1974, p. 2).

The research took place in a period when development was seen as a process of 'modernization', of change much along the lines of development in the North Atlantic capitalistic world of the time. Furthermore, much attention was given to formal education, but too little to the wide variety of non-formal and informal learning networks, both outside and inside the school.

Schools always operate in societies that are in a process of development, whether slow or fast. Through formal education pupils learn new knowledge and skills. Part of this can be applied in life. If not, learning opportunities in the community other than through the school are lost. These new skills, leading to new opportunities, but also to disappointments, together with other developments in society, lead to changes in daily life. In principle, new knowledge and skills give the children access to wider communication networks. The two, changes in daily life in society and exposure to information from wider cultural networks, may lead to new ideas, enhance adaptation to the changed environment and stimulate creativity leading to further innovations – which in turn may cause further changes in cultural elements, generating new learning needs that have to be inserted in the school curriculum. During the whole process, however, children, youth and adults, participate in numerous informal learning situations. Important in this respect is the work situation, but others, like social groups, may also be of great influence on personal development. What is learned in the formal setting of the school may be strengthened or weakened by the content of the informal learning processes. It seems, therefore, that the contribution of education to culture will be strongest and most effective if the two are mutually reinforcing. This can be stimulated by close relations between the school and the community, for example, by allowing part of the curriculum to be directed at the community's needs and making use of members of the community as resource persons.

DECENTRALIZING FORMAL EDUCATION

Issues related to the concepts of sub-cultures and cultural identity and to the curriculum of school education are in the midst of the discussion of centralizing or decentralizing the education system.

At a certain moment parents were unable to take care of the education of their children in all aspects of life. Teaching of particular intellectual or

35

manual skills was then delegated to professional teachers. As long as the teachers were nominated and supported by the community, the community could have a say in school organization and in the curriculum. In other cases, however, the programme was organized by a sponsor or by an organization. In all cases, the teaching/learning process was initially a 'sub-cultural' affair. But, in the course of time, education gradually drifted away from the influence of the local community and was formalized.

Chinua Achebe (1964, p. 55-56) makes the leading character in one of his novels, a chief priest of a Nigerian village, say to one of his sons, whom he is sending to a nearby school:

'I want one of my sons to join these people and be my eye there. If there is nothing in it you will come back. But if there is something there you will bring home my share.' And, in defending his decision to send one son to school, the father told the mother: '. . . Do you not know that in a great man's household there must be people who follow all kinds of strange ways? . . . In such a place, whatever music you beat on your drum, there is somebody who can dance to it.'

Mass expansion of school education started towards the end of the nineteenth century, almost at the same time as European and American nation States were formed. School education became a major responsibility of the State.

The assumption was that each state had a national culture, even though in reality many states were agglomerations of ethnic entities each with their own cultures. In some cases there were wide differences between these component cultures. In most, the differences were formally obscured. In some countries there has been a change to the effect that local differentiation is recognized and tolerated. In others, it is still against the law, as formulated by the dominating (sub-)cultural group.

Since central governments managed the school system, the curriculum was prescribed by the authorities in the capital city. The curriculum reflected the culture of the 'centre'. The content served the needs of the ruling groups. The (proclaimed) national language was imposed as the language of instruction. Local communities had little say in the curriculum. In some countries religious or philosophical organizations were permitted to run schools within the framework of regulations set by the central authorities. Day-to-day teaching was strictly prescribed, there was little or no room to include subjects that would answer the needs of the local community. Teachers had little room to bring in any extras in terms of subject-matter or ideas. At the end of the prescribed number of years, an examination was taken leading to a diploma or an entrance examination to the next level of school education.

In many (former) colonies school education was first introduced by private, foreign, religious organizations. It may only have been later that colonial governments began to take an interest. Gradually, however, the curriculum became regulated by the central, colonial governments, even though day-to-day management was still in the hands of the private organizations. Usually the local community had no influence on school affairs. The only choice people sometimes had was whether to enrol their children or not. The system and the curriculum were mostly copies of those in the home countries of the colonial governments. In some cases efforts were made to include subjects that seemed in the eyes of the education officials more relevant to the local people. This sometimes met with resistance from the local people – the parents – because they feared that the adjusted curriculum would not lead the children to secondary school or higher levels. Many felt that the time spent on such extra subjects, for example agriculture or handicrafts, was at the expense of the time needed for the 'basics', especially reading, writing, arithmetics and the 'national' language. After independence the formal school systems were continued, even though in some countries efforts were made to nationalize the schools and the curriculum. New jobs, especially in the government administration, paid salaries that enabled people in such positions to live in a seemingly luxurious situation and offered great prestige. Life in the capital seemed attractive. Soon the number of vacancies was saturated and the problem of unemployed school-leavers became of growing concern to the authorities. It was, nevertheless, next to impossible to stop migration to the cities. Here new urban sub-cultures came into existence and the education systems reflected more the needs of the urban sub-culture than those of the people in the rural areas. The goal was to attain the highest possible diploma that would lead to a paid job and, if possible, to continuing education in the country of the former colonial power. The language of the former colonial power remained the language of instruction and the schoolbooks were based on a foreign culture rather than on the national or local cultures.

With declining economies, growing unemployment, decreasing quality in school education and a high population growth rate, less and less young people could find gainful employment in the cities. More and more people in rural areas and groups with a sub-culture different from the one of the ruling group started to question the usefulness of the school education offered and, lately, in some places, school enrolments have tended to decrease. Here again the school does not meet the needs of local sub-cultures, while the school-leavers could not find a place in the 'modern' urban sub-culture. This situation still persists the world over.

In many urban centres one finds people of whom one might say that they belong to the new national culture. Their relations with their original ethnic groups have slackened or become non-existent. They identify themselves with the national culture. They speak the national language(s). Usually they have completed higher levels of school education. The question is, however, to what extent school education has contributed to their cultural exchange. Because there might have been other factors, such as mixed marriages, a long stay abroad, broken relations with relatives or other individual characteristics.

The process and all the social, financial and psychological problems individuals experienced have been described in many novels and stories, especially in Africa. For example, a quote from *Leopard in a cage* by Jacqueline Pierce (1976, p. 2-3):

'Are your roots so bad that you want to escape them?'
'I simply want to rise above the filth here.'
'What's wrong with progress, Uncle Nsa?' Marangu joined in the conversation.
'She's simply talking about the progress. Look at Walter Mtey. He was the first student from Lomo to study at the University. If he had come back here to live and work, people would have been disappointed.'(...)
'The people here like to read about Walter in the newspapers – see his picture from time to time. Then they sit back contentedly and say 'That's our boy. He's from Lomo. They don't care about his skills. They just know that he's their big man in the town'.
'That's foolish.'
'Why is it foolish? When I finish my studies I'll never come back except to visit from time to time. Think of all your classmates. You were the only one to get a chance to study in America. Yet you're the only one without a car, without a house, without even a job. And why? Because you wanted to come back to Lomo.'

Recently the discussion on decentralizing education has intensified. Part of the reason is that central governments are not able to provide universal education for lack of finance and because of organizational difficulties. One looks for resources in the local communities that might contribute, financially, by voluntary labour, in kind or through the specific expertise of individuals. Cultural factors do not figure prominently on the scene. One may question whether it would be possible to recruit new resources at the community level. In many areas, however, especially those in which educational facilities are weak or absent, the people are too poor to contribute financially or in kind.

Before one can decide on a suitable decentralized delivery system and the resources to be mobilized, it is essential that there is a minimum of consensus about the nature and content of basic education. In public discussions and statements it is usually recognized that basic learning needs differ from society to society. Consequently, it seems logical that the basic education offered shows a degree of variety. But is school education allowed to? Education, perhaps because of its assumed influence on culture, and therefore potentially on all aspects of society, including power, is politically highly sensitive. Most politicians, in the centre, think of education as belonging to the realm of the nation rather than of the (local) community. In order to come to a consensus on the nature and content of basic education in a decentralized system, not only a recognition and tolerance of cultural diversity is needed; also a specific look at the concept of 'empowerment', since this concept is often misused by speakers who mean power for a particular group as envisaged by outsiders, rather than self-determination by a community striving for improvement of their daily lives. If one wants to mobilize local resources, one must ensure that 'empowerment' is seen through the eyes of the people in the community, who must be motivated by the fact that the school and other forms of basic education in their midst are theirs.[11]

One example of an effort to build up a system that the people concerned might feel 'as theirs' was an experiment with developing an educational model for the benefit of the Indian population in the Territorios Nationales of Colombia, starting in 1978 as a co-operative project between the governments of the Netherlands and Colombia. In the philosophical and methodological foundations of the project the cultural identity of the target group took a central place (Oltheten et al., in Epskamp, 1984; see also Alfonso, 1988). The concept of cultural identity formed the basis of a plan to design an educational model that would meet the needs of various groups and would be adaptable to their socio-economic and cultural conditions. Within the new educational policy, the first idea was that education was considered to be of social value, an essential element of the population's welfare and no longer a means to attain it. This implied that, within the social policy, the population's welfare was to be regarded as the driving force rather than the outcome of economic growth. Education is recognized as a permanent process that is not restricted to school or to the so-called school age. It is intended for all groups, and 'students' should be accepted as they are, without being compelled to follow a uniform learning process that is similar to a school or is incorporated into a school. It was essential to find a way in which to adjust the education system to the social system, i.e. to the actual needs of the population. The same holds for the population's active participation in defining educational needs and in finding the right answers.

The elements of the educational process were determined on the basis of local workshops, organized by the people with the assistance of project staff. The main objective of these workshops was to initiate a process of participatory exploration of their own reality. Within the exploration process, which in itself may be regarded as a learning method, cultural reality had an essential place. Various questions were raised with respect to origin, religion and kinship, to the production and significance of particular objects, principal historical events and processes, etc. Older people in the community were identified as resource persons: it was they who had the skills and knowledge from the past, who possessed the knowledge of medicinal herbs and who knew recent history, marked by the contacts with immigrants. In short, they were the ones who had knowledge of the natural and social environment.

The contents of the model were therefore concerned with:
- knowledge and understanding of the physical and ecological environment;
- insight into the social structure and the social and cultural development;
- the acquisition of conceptual and technical skills and capabilities in order to understand and to control their particular reality.

The community, in its first and permanent phase of participatory research, should not only be involved in collecting information, but also in its processing, analysis and interpretation. In the consecutive phases of decision-making, or making or rejecting options and their implicit consequences, the community must indicate priorities and select the means and instruments.

As a consequence of the participatory method, teaching aids and other materials have to be created on the basis of factors of the physical and social environment which are related to the language and way of thinking of the target group. The scattered settlements of the population in the project area and the inadequate methods of communication and infrastructure entailed that use of the so-called 'little media' was of primary significance. It was also of vital importance that the villagers took an active part in creating written, graphic, plastic and audio-visual materials. Students of a local teacher training centre were enabled to follow a special programme so that they could participate in the project.

The strength of this project was that it took the cultural identity of the people and continuous participation as its pivot. Furthermore, it was considered essential that materials and methods suited various types of basic education, for children and for adults, including literacy. Initially it was supported by the central authorities. Its weakness was that at a certain stage, when it appeared that it strengthened the cultural identity and awareness of the population regarding their position in relation to the government and the Church, it met with political opposition from the authorities, so that the programme had to be terminated.[12] In the example given above the experiment aimed at developing an educational model parallel to the national system. Material from the local (sub–)culture was used for the curriculum and the teaching methodology. It was hoped that basic skills could be learned by the people, both youth and adults. Their own culture was to be strengthened so that the people would enjoy a stronger position in the national context.

In other places experiments are within the system. The major aim is to use the local (sub–)culture and expertise (both technical and social skills) in the design of the curriculum of the school or for teaching and management purposes. An example was the experiment SEAMEO undertook in the 1970s and 1980s. The experiment was carried out in Indonesia under the acronym PAMONG and in the Philippines it was called IMPACT.[13] The general objective of the project was to develop an effective and economical delivery system for mass primary education. It was essentially an experiment on a management system to see if primary school objectives can be achieved through non-conventional modes, making effective use of available conventional forms of primary education.

At the lower levels, IMPACT used the native language, only later the national language(s). The IMPACT teacher, called 'instructional supervisor', was assisted by itinerant teachers, aides (non-professionals) for the routine activities of the school, tutors-volunteers (usually high-school students), programmed teachers and, last but not least, parents and members of the community as resource persons. This type of programme also anchors the school in the local culture through the involvement of local resources. By stimulating cultural awareness the school may also enhance development of the local culture in a more harmonious way.

Other experiments are aimed at the adult population, at improving technical, academic or social skills. 'Empowerment' is an essential element in the objectives of many. Literacy is an element in quite a few programmes

41

for adults. An example is the Project Delsilife,[14] which was undertaken at a time when there was a growing worldwide realization that the benefits supposed to have been delivered by the schools had not really reached those that needed them most – people in the depressed areas constituting the majority of the population in most of the South-East Asian countries. It focused on people's development. The active participation of the people in decision-making, in needs or problem identification, in planning, implementation and evaluation of learning programmes was an integral part of the method. The educative process aimed at developing awareness of the needs and problems of the community. It seeks to raise the consciousness of the people about the quality of their lives. It means to sharpen their intellectual abilities and skills to change their environment. It aims at enabling the people to make proper choices of actions to improve their quality of life through self-reliance.

In the examples given, the projects do not aim at teaching particular (vocational or technical) skills. Most, if not all, attention is directed at the improvement of life skills, learning techniques, decision making, awareness and self-confidence.

In the discussion about decentralization of education, little distinction is often made of the various elements of education that will be decentralized. This confuses the discussion because (the system) of education is composed of a great variety of very different aspects. It seems to be a matter of subsidiarity. From the point of view of educating children, youth or adults there is the question of who can perform a particular task best? Furthermore, if one looks at education from the point of view of cultural development – and especially in terms of the interests of a multicultural and intercultural development – there are questions about the values held at the national and the various sub-cultural levels.

For example, from a national point of view it is of great interest that everyone speaks the national language (only or in addition to local or foreign languages). It is important that achievement levels throughout the country are comparable, so that a pupil from one area being admitted to the next level of education can be selected on objective criteria. It is normally the central government that can negotiate with donor agencies for loans. Therefore the central government's duty could be – depending on the size of the country – to provide for basic provisions: these could be financial, ensuring a core curriculum, teacher training, higher education or ensuring national values, multicultural and intercultural education. Other tasks could possibly be better fulfilled at lower levels of government, or even at the community level. For example, integrating school education with life in the local community could best be taken care of by the community itself.

Given a particular prescribed core curriculum by the central government, especially defining intellectual or manual skills, the community may be delegated to fill in the remaining school hours, with local history, environmental studies, particular local skills, local language or other local cultural aspects. The central government may prescribe a particular amount of school hours per year. But it may leave the actual decision about when the children go to school to the community. Decentralization should distinguish what aspects should and can be delegated to other authorities (including NGOs) and the local community.

Yet, where are the limits? For example, if a national government advocates equal access to education for all, what should it do when a local community believes that there is no use in sending girls to school, or excludes pupils from a particular ethnic group, class or caste?

Problems concerning decentralization, skills, diploma levels, financing and organization must not be underestimated. Yet the problems in terms of cultural – and especially multicultural – education seem to be more serious, because if no solution can be found to these, the administrative and practical problems cannot be solved.

REGIONAL AND INTERNATIONAL CO-OPERATION: NETWORKING

The contribution of education to international (multi)cultural development necessitates a global approach and strategies of co-operation among different cultural groups. Cultures could show interest with each other both within and across national boundaries.

There seem to be many universal functions, roles and responsibilities of education in promoting cultural development, such as:

1. Education (both formal, non-formal and informal) helps the learner to learn about his/her own culture, other cultures and those elements of commonly shared cultures.

2. Education helps the learner to understand the nature and meaning of culture, how cultures interact with each other and how cultures evolve and change.

3. Education provides the learner with effective ways and means to cope with the cultural roots of social-psychological problems, which are often manifested by cultural misunderstanding, prejudice, ethnocentrism, racism, etc.

4. Education through its cultural dimensions, particularly through learning and teaching programmes on human rights, respect, understanding and tolerance of cultural differences, contributes to the 'culture of peace'.

5. Education has a powerful role to play in regulating, controlling and reducing conflicts (ethnic, racial, religious, etc.), violence and discrimination which are the daily experience of many populations around the world.

The forty-third session of the International Conference on Education (in Recommendation No. 78) recommended increased regional and sub-regional co-operation in the field of teacher training and educational research (in particular pilot projects). It also emphasized international co-operation in educational and cultural exchange (in terms of information and personnel) and the collection, analysis and exchange of innovative projects and experiences and international education materials for inter-cultural or multicultural education.

Networks are quite efficient ways of sharing and exchanging information in the field of education and culture. The network can operate at the national, regional or international levels. According to McGinn,[15] networking is based on the construction of a shared reality, a 'common culture', through the joint definition of goals and possible means to achieve its objectives. Essential to a proper functioning of networks is that the participants believe that they have something worth sharing: there must be a strong self-interest for all participants in the network. Networks can be composed of individuals or institutions. They can be looking for information or support and co-operation in any one of their functions: teaching, research or consultancy. By participating in a network one feels assured of belonging to a wider group upon which one can rely for those things one needs on a normal reciprocal basis. Networks can be non-formal – often they start as such – or formal. In many cases there is a 'focal point' that helps the participants to communicate whenever needed.[16]

Networks can be useful complementary instruments of learning in addition to the curriculum in the school or in training programmes. In the case of new developments in society they may help participants to exchange experience. For example, at a recent conference on 'Education for All' in Warsaw, the problems of teachers facing the new market economy were discussed and refresher courses were suggested. However, some participants reacted from the floor by preferring networking rather than courses to learn from the experience of colleagues. Sharing information and finding solutions together helps teachers in solving their problems.

The first task to promote networking may be to disseminate information on existing networks whose interests are to link education with cultural development. The types of networks in this field would concern international education, multicultural education, language teaching or other fields related to cultural dimensions of education. This first task may enable individuals to join relevant networks. It also makes possible the so-called 'networking of networks', the exchange of information between networks in similar or complementary fields.

The Associated Schools, initiated by UNESCO, are an example of an international network of schools designed to promote international understanding through the establishment of innovative school programmes. It may be very useful to reinforce the dissemination of significant information and experiences through this network. Although networks represent a variety of participants from different countries, their common perception and understanding of mutually defined objectives and modalities of operation among participants and their commitment are essential factors for successful functioning.

In the area of educational research, networks are now in operation in various geographical regions. Most of these are engaged in the exchange of information and documentation, some have started doing research together. Members are usually individual researchers, often with an institutional base, but also policy makers or practitioners. Some publish newsletters and/or reports.[17]

Networking is possibly one of the most effective modalities for regional and international co-operation. The International Bureau of Education (IBE) will continue to encourage the creation and strengthening of national and regional networks for the collection and management of educational information, including cultural and multicultural education, international understanding and peace education.

There are, however, some caveats. The international networks disseminate information in a limited number of languages, which are often the language of the text (source of information). More co-operation is necessary in order to collect data in less widespread national or local languages. In this sense, linking international networks with national networks is an important task. National networks could provide information which is translated from a national language into the official language(s) of an international network. Particularly, educational information dealing with culture requires a wide source of input data from a diversified cultural settings. Such co-operation contributes to a wide coverage of cultural information, thus also broadening the participation of all population groups in cultural life.

Furthermore, beside the coverage by information networks, the usability and applicability of information are crucial factors determining their success. Often bibliographies, provided by educational information networks, are of limited use, partly because of financial constraints. Information data systems or networks may be encouraged to produce more abstracts and annotated bibliographies in order to provide readers in developing countries (who do not otherwise have easy access to information systems or facilities) with usable and practical information. In line with this, means have to sought to make basic documentation accessible to users through community, provincial or national libraries.

Finally, most networking needs some equipment for communication. If participants in the network are not in the same place, they may need a postal service, telephone, telex, telefax, copier, computers and so on. Such tools are not always available because of the costs involved or technical and maintenance problems. In this respect networks are vulnerable.

The networking of networks involved in intercultural contacts requires an inter-sectoral approach dealing widely with education, commerce, international organizations, research institutions, NGOs, youth organizations and others. Thus, cultural and educationally stimulating and interesting experiences, case studies or reports on action programmes can be collected from many parts of the world and disseminated to all individuals or institutions interested in them. Curriculum developers and teacher-training institutions and practising teachers can take advantage of information collected by these networks and can develop learning materials suiting their own needs.

The collection, analysis, production and dissemination of *teaching and learning materials for intercultural education* and their dissemination by international organizations (e.g. UNESCO or UNICEF), NGOs or cultural centres, can stimulate national efforts in the domain. For example, a Swiss-based NGO, 'The School as an Instrument of Peace' produces human rights teaching materials for children and adolescents, and disseminates them widely to schools in different countries. The Asian Cultural Centre for UNESCO (Japan) is another institution which produces children's books, paintings, music materials, folklore, posters, booklets and audio-visual materials for promoting the protection of the cultural heritage. Some of their written materials have been translated into numerous local languages in the region.

It is very likely that there are many other possible ways of strengthening regional and international co-operation to enhance educational contributions to cultural development. This may largely depend upon our willingness and capacity to create new combinations of co-operative links among different networks, bodies and individuals, particularly among those bodies whose interests are traditionally opposed to each other. It also depends upon our capacity to utilize information and the necessary knowledge to mobilize such creative human organizational skills and behaviours through networking.

CONCLUSIONS

In the vast changing world of today people are increasingly aware of their culture. In recent political developments cultural aspects play a more and more dominant role. Though economic issues and interests still tend to dominate the balance of power internationally and economic development does effect culture, other issues like cultural identity are coming more visibly into the arena. Values, either derived from ideological origins, from religion or from other views on existence, play (once more) a political role. In this respect developments in, for example, Uzbekistan, seem to suggest that during the past decades formal education influenced aspects like work, through vocational skills, rather than social life and religion through the values of the 'system'.

On the one hand, such ideas, norms and values stimulate the cultural assertiveness of the people and strengthen their cultural identity. On the other, the effect is that mankind may be more and more divided again in a multitude of controversial groups. A process that might lead to sharp contrasts and serious conflicts.

The role school education can play in this respect is limited. It equips children and youth with particular skills that may help them to survive in society and develop themselves. One may question whether in the past too much emphasis has been laid on academic and vocational skills while social skills and value education have been neglected. In fact, school education has brought about changes in terms of individual and societal cultural development. Often it changed – rather than developed – indigenous cultures.

However, school education is being increasingly confronted with financial problems. If the targets of 'Education for All' are to be reached, new resources have to be found. The new trend is to look for new resources at the community level through decentralization of the education system.

School education can be a useful instrument in the process if it not only teaches its pupils specific skills, manual and intellectual, but also makes them aware of their own values, while, at the same time, informing them in a positive and comparative way about the values of other people. Without making pupils lose their own values, let them understand the values of others, in this way opening the doors for national and international understanding. School education can be functional in this respect only if it is supported by other educational media, by reading materials, radio, television, and by politicians and religious leaders.

Given that governments lack resources, non-formal education programmes may offer an alternative to the school. One may think of training courses or seminars that may teach groups of learners specific skills for employment, or programmes enabling people to develop themselves in social skills and arts. However, this depends upon finding sponsors or on participants being able to contribute themselves to the costs of such courses. As the participants in most of such programmes aim at acquiring skills applicable in new situations, for change, non-formal education has a more direct and stronger influence on cultural change.

Informal education seems to play the strongest role, at least in terms of costs. Many educational experiments seek for community involvement and support. The advantage is not only to be found in lower expenses, but also in tapping knowledge, skills and ideas that otherwise would be overlooked in the formal education system, which is based on the cultural needs and interests of dominating groups at the national level. In this way, relevance of education and cultural development in a particular country may be fed from a wider range of sources.

It appears also that oral communication and personal understanding do continue even under oppressive regimes. These remain important channels of informal education, even surviving dominant formal systems.

While on the one side there is a growing interest in informal education at the community and sub-cultural level, international communication in the form of different types of information through various media and increased mobility of individuals are becoming important instruments of informal education. People meet each other, within wider circles within their own countries and cross over national, political and cultural borders, and in this way they learn from each other. In this context the usefulness of 'networking' is being discovered.

Formal education – the school – can influence cultural development. This depends on whether the skills and behaviour taught are applicable in the non-traditional part of daily life and, in this way, may lead via further informal learning to a change of behaviour, attitudes and ideas, so that people can fully participate in their society. It is essential that teaching in school is supported by the informal education circuits in or out of school. If this is not the case, the official values and skills taught may come off second best compared to what pupils learn in the informal circuits.

NOTES

1. Cf. Kater (1984:20) and Camilleri (1986:8).
2. Survey in preparation for the forty-third session of the International Conference on Education on the theme: the contribution of education to cultural development. Geneva, 14-19 September 1992, ED/BIE/CONFINTED/43/Q/91, Geneva, 12 June 1991.

3. For example, during the Second World War, when the Netherlands were occupied by Germany, much reference was made by the occupying power to the old times where the Germanic roots for both Dutch and Germans could be found and to the heroes of the glorious Dutch maritime period, many of which fought, with success, against the British (see for example the postal stamps of that period).
4. At the subcultural level, identification with 'heroes' or people from particular subcultures is employed, for example, by commercial firms in promoting music, softdrinks and other goods, or referring to types of behaviour to sell their products.
5. Cf. in this respect the publication of a group study by the Ministry of Education in Guinea Bissau (1982, Educafrica no. 8).
6. For example: the terminology used to indicate particular characteristics of other cultures can easily be misleading. A study was made comparing the Thai and the American cultures (Fieg, 1989). In the study, a number of characteristics was identified in which the one culture contrasted with the other. Also certain common cultural features were described. The study shows that it is very risky to stick labels on cultural elements or aspects. For example, even though both cultures could be named individualistic, there still was a great difference. Individualism was generally played down by Thai culture in favour of group harmony, including especially close family ties and smooth interpersonal relations (op.cit., p. 32-33). Therefore, the same word does not cover the same phenomena in the two societies.
7. Cf. Syed Altaf Gauhar (1981, p. 72): 'In the reconstruction of the system of education in the Muslim World, it is the Muslim mind which should determine not only its methods of teaching and training, its courses of study and procedures of evaluation, but also the policy and operations of the mass media including newspapers, news agencies, radio broadcasts, television programmes, films and other audio-visual facilities.'
8. There is little difference between the two words. Change seems to indicate a difference between two situations within a relatively short time, and may be to a better or a worse situation. Development often is understood as a gradual process to a better situation. We believe that also development may be both in a positive and a negative direction.
9. One should be careful in using the term 'western', especially in relation to education. If one looks at the education systems in the 'western' countries, such as in Europe, North America or Australia, one finds fundamental differences. Maybe not in the format, but especially in the objectives, the teaching methods, the style, the subjects taught and the examinations. True, many educationists and pedagogues who influenced the development of the school internationally during the past century lived in those countries, but on the other hand these systems have absorbed many cultural elements from other societies.
10. Cf. for example the publications by Luis Rojes Aspiazu (1980), Dr. Gershom N. Amayo (1984) and Dr. A. Kater e.a. (1988). See also chapter XI of this book.
11. Cf. Dubbeldam, Boeren & Hoppers, 1990, p. 4.
12. Cf. Oltheten et. al., in Epskamp 1984 and L. Alberto Alfonso, 1988.
13. IMPACT: Instructional Management by Parents, Community and Teachers; PAMONG: Pendidikan Anak Oleh Masyarakat Orangtua dan Guru. Cf. Socrates, 1986.
14. The full title of the project is 'Development of a Co-ordinated Educational Intervention System for the Improvement of the Quality of Life of the Rural Poor Through Self-Reliance'. Four countries, Indonesia, Malaysia, the Philippines and Thailand participated in the project. It was not implemented in Malaysia (cf. Socrates, 1990).
15. Noel McGinn, Cultures of policy and cultures of networking (p. 11), *NORRAG News*, No. 13, December 1992.

16. Leo F.B. Dubbeldam. 'Networking and Institutional Development'. Paper prepared for the NORRAG workshop on 'The Policies and Cultures of Networking', Oxford, September 1993, 8 p.
17. For example some international networks are:
    ERNESA: Education Research Network for Eastern and Southern Africa;
    ERNWACA: Educational Research Network for West and Central Africa;
    NORRAG: Northern Research Review and Advisory Group;
    REDUC: Red de Información y Documentación en Educación para América Latina y el Caribe;
    SEARRAG: South East Asian Research Review and Advisory Group;
    SERI: The Southern Educational Research Initiative
    and others, also at the national level.

REFERENCES

Achebe, Chinua. 1964. *Arrow of God*. London, Heinemann. 287 p. (African Writers' Series; no. 16)

Alfonso, Luis Alberto, et al. 1988. *Educación, participación e identidad cultural: una experiencia educativa con las comunidades indígenas del nordeste Amazónico*. The Hague, CESO. ix, 243 p. (CESO paperback; no. 3)

Altaf Gauhar, Syed. 1981. Education and the mass media. *In:* **Khan, M. Wasiullah, ed**. *Education and society in the Muslim world*. London, Hodder & Stoughton; Jeddah, King Abdulaziz University, p. 61-81.

Amoyo, Gershom N. 1984. *Indigenous traditions of early childhood education in Africa: their meaning and relevance*. Paris, Unit for Co-operation with UNICEF and WFP, UNESCO. 11 p. (Child, family, community: notes, comments; N.S. 154; Aids to programming UNICEF assistance to education: preschool education; no. 43; parent education; no. 17)

Camilleri, C. 1986. *Cultural anthropology and education*. London, Kogan Page; Paris, UNESCO/IBE. 171 p. (Educational sciences series)

Dubbeldam, L.F.B. 1964. The devaluation of the Kapauku-cowrie as a factor of social disintegration. *The American anthropologist* (Washington, DC), vol. 66, no. 4, part 2, p. 293-303.

—. 1984. We are we, and they are different: cultural I entity. *In:* **Epskamp, Kees, ed**. Education and the development of cultural identity: groping in the dark. The Hague, CESO, p. 12-19.

—. 1990a. Culture and education: education as the agent of transfer and change *In:* **Boeren, A.J.J.M.; Epskamp, Kees P., eds**. *Education, culture and productive life*. The Hague, CESO, p. 101-17. (CESO paperback; no. 13)

—. 1990b. Culture, education and productive life in developing countries. *In:* **Boeren, A.J.J.M.; Epskamp, Kees P., eds**. *Education, culture and productive life*. The Hague, CESO, p. 25-35. (CESO paperback; no. 13)

—; **Boeren, A.J.J.M.; Hoppers, W.H.L.M**. 1990c. Mobilizing resources for basic education. Paper prepared for the IWGE meeting at IIEP, Paris, 30 May – 1 June. [S.l.: s.n.] 7 p.

—. 1991. Literacy and socio-cultural development. Paper prepared for the International Conference 'Attaining functional literacy: a cross-cultural perspective', Tilburg University, the Netherlands, 10-12 October 1991. [S.l.: s.n.] 26 p.

El Tom, Basheer. 1981. Education and society. *In:* **Khan, M. Wasiullah, ed.** *Education and society in the Muslim world.* London, Hodder & Stoughton; Jeddah, King Abdulaziz University, p. 28-43.

Epskamp, Kees, ed. 1984. *Education and the development of cultural identity: groping in the dark.* The Hague, CESO. 58 p.

Faure, E., et al. 1972. *Learning to be: the world of education today and tomorrow.* Paris, UNESCO; London, Harrap. xxxix, 313 p.

Fieg, John Paul. 1989. *A common core: Thais and North Americans.* Revised by Elizabeth Mortlock. Yarmouth, ME, Intercultural Press. 118 p.

Guinea Bissau. Ministry of Education. 1982. Education and cultural identity in Guinea Bissau. *In: Educafrica* (Dakar, BREDA), no. 8, p. 59-68.

Haar, G. ter. 1988. Religious education in Africa: traditional, Islamic and Christian. *In: Exchange: bulletin of Third World Christian literature and ecumenical research,* vol. 17, no. 50, 86 p.

Inkeles, Alex. 1969. Making men modern: on the causes and consequences of individual change in six developing countries. *In: American Journal of Sociology,* (Chicago, Universtiy of Chicago Press), p. 208-25.

—; **Holsinger, Donald B., eds.** 1974. *Education and individual modernity in developing countries.* Leiden, E.J. Brill. 136 p. (International studies in sociology and social anthropology; vol. 14)

Herskovits, M.J. 1949. *Man and his works.* New York, Knopf.

Kane, M. 1982. Cultural identity: a historical perspective. *In: Educafrica,* (Dakar, BREDA), no. 8, p. 129-36.

Kater, A. 1984. Culture, education and indigenous learning systems. *In:* **Epskamp, Kees, ed.,** *Education and the development of cultural identity: groping in the dark.* The Hague, CESO, p. 20-27.

—, **et al.** 1989. *Indigenous knowledge and learning: papers presented in the workshop on indigenous knowledge and skills and the ways they are acquired, Cha'am, Thailand, 2-5 March 1988.* Bangkok, CUSRI; The Hague, CESO. 137 p.

Linton, R. 1964. *The cultural background of personality.* London, Routledge & Kegan Paul.

Vargas Llosa, Mario. 1990. *The storyteller.* New York, Penguin Books. 246 p.

Medlin, William K. 1969. The role of education in social development: the school as an agent of modernization in a transitional Muslim society. *In:* CESO. *Educational problems in developing countries: papers given at the Amsterdam Symposium, 8-19 July 1968.* Groningen, Wolters Noordhoff, p. 121-42.

—; **Cave, William M.; Carpenter, Finley.** 1971. *Education and development in Central Asia: a case study on social change in Uzbekistan.* Leiden, E.J. Brill, 20, 285 p.

Pierce, Jacqueline. 1976. *Leopard in a cage.* Nairobi, East African Publishing House. 221 p.

Oltheten, Theo; Oowens, Jan; Thybergin, Anton. Participatory education and cultural identity: the case of the Amazon Indians in Colombia. In: **Epskamp, Kees, ed.** 1984. *Education and the development of cultural identity: groping in the dark.* The Hague, CESO. 58 p.

Rojas Aspiazu, Luis. 1980. *Ayni Ruway: the role of indigenous cultural institutions in a development and education process.* [S.l.: s.n.]. 28 p. Paper prepared for the DSE international seminar: 'The use of indigenous social structures and traditional media in non-formal education and development', Berlin, 5-12 November 1980.

Socrates, Jose B. 1986. *IMPACT: instructional management by parents, community and teachers: an alternative intervention system for mass primary education*. Manila, SEA-MEO/INNOTECH. 31 p. (Innotech research monograph series; no. 2, S. 1986)

—. 1990. Improving the quality of life: the Delsilife way. *In:* **Boeren, A.J.J.M.; Epskamp, Kees P., eds**. *Education, culture and productive life*. The Hague, CESO, p. 85-100. (CESO paperback; no. 13)

CHAPTER III

Policy goals and objectives in cultural education

Toshio Ohsako

INTERNATIONAL CULTURAL CO-OPERATION AND THE UNITED NATIONS

When the United Nations Charter came into force on 26 October 1945, the promotion of cultural co-operation took on a new international dimension. The peoples of the United Nations were determined to appeal to international cultural co-operation as a means to achieve a peaceful world.

The charter proclaimed that one purpose of the United Nations was to 'achieve international co-operation in solving international problems' of a 'cultural' character in 'promoting and encouraging respect for human rights and for fundamental freedoms for all without distinction as to race, sex, language, or religion' (Article 1.2 of Chapter I).

The Constitution of the United Nations Educational, Scientific and Cultural Organization (UNESCO), adopted on 16 November 1945, proclaimed that 'the wide diffusion of culture, and the education of humanity for justice and liberty and peace are indispensable to the dignity of man and constitute a sacred duty which all the nations must fulfil in a spirit of mutual assistance and concern'.

It was the Universal Declaration of Human Rights (adopted by the United Nations in 1948), among many other declarations, which paved the way for everyone's 'right to freely participate in the cultural life of the community, to enjoy the arts and to share in scientific advancement and its benefits' (Article 27 (1)). This declaration led the United Nations to adopt an International Covenant on Economic, Social and Cultural Rights (1966) which stated the right of everyone to 'take part in cultural life' (Article 15.1).

Eight years later, in 1974, the General Conference of UNESCO adopted a Recommendation concerning Education for International Understanding, Co-operation and Peace and Education Relating to Human

Rights and Fundamental Freedoms, which emphasized knowledge and respect for different cultures as an essential part of international understanding. Its paragraph N° 17, concerning 'cultural aspects', claims that: 'Member States should promote, at various stages and in various types of education, study of different cultures, their reciprocal influences, their perspectives and ways of life, in order to encourage mutual appreciation of the differences between them. Such study should, among other things, give due importance to the teaching of foreign languages, civilizations and cultural heritage as a means of promoting international and inter-cultural understanding.'

This recommendation explicitly called for the study of different cultures, cultural influences, appreciation of the cultural diversity and specific educational contents which are instrumental in promoting intercultural understanding.

It was in the mid-1960s, when many Member States of UNESCO realized that culture was in part the responsibility of governments, that ministries and departments of cultural affairs were set up. From 1970 onwards, the results of critical reviews revealed the limitations of development based primarily on quantitative and material growth. As a result, UNESCO began to set up intergovernmental conferences on cultural policies.[1]

A most significant intergovernmental conference, which provided a decisive turning point in the cultural policies of the United Nations, was the World Conference on Cultural Policies (Mexico City, 1982). Recommendation N° 27 adopted by that conference emphasized that 'culture constitutes a fundamental part of the life of each individual' and 'development – whose ultimate aim should be focused on man – must have a cultural dimension'. It further proclaimed that 'action to promote culture should be considered in the international perspective, as an imperative of world development conducive to peace.'

In the last year of the United Nations Decade for Women (1976-1985), the World Conference to Review and Praise the Achievements of the United Nations Decade for Women: Equality, Development and Peace, was held, which adopted 'The Nairobi Forward-Looking Strategies for the Advancement of Women' during the period 1986 to the Year 2000. It drew attention to cultural conditions that constrained the advancement of women (paragraph 1) and emphasized women's rights to develop their potential in order to participate in cultural development (paragraph 11).

In 1986, four years after the World Conference on Cultural Policies in Mexico City, the General Assembly of the United Nations adopted Resolution 41/187 and proclaimed the World Decade for Cultural Development, 1988-1997, to be observed under the auspices of UNESCO. It established a Plan of Action for the Decade which centres on the following four main objectives:

1. Acknowledging the cultural dimension in development.
2. Affirming and enriching cultural identities.
3. Broadening participation in cultural life.
4. Promoting international cultural co-operation.

The Plan of Action for the Decade, emphasizing that the ultimate aim of development should be focused on man, placed culture at the centre of development. The cultural dimension in the development process, cultural identities, as well as enriching processes of cultural identity through human creativity and artistic expression, the effective exercise of cultural rights (participation) and culture as an instrument of peace were put forward as the main guiding principles of the Plan of Action.

UNESCO, as the lead agency for the Decade, matched the objectives of the Third Medium-Term Plan (1990-95), approved by its General Conference in 1989, with those of the Decade, by creating a Major Programme Area III: Culture: past, present and future. It was the forty-third session of the International Conference on Education (ICE, 1992), the main inspiration of this present book, which extensively debated the linkage and contribution of education to cultural development.

In March 1990, the World Conference on Education for All (Jomtien, Thailand) was held. The conference, emphasizing basic learning needs, adopted a 'World Declaration on Education for All', which asserted, in its Article 1 (*Meeting basic learning needs*): 'the satisfaction of these needs empowers individuals in any society and confers upon them a responsibility to respect and build upon their collective cultural, linguistic and spiritual heritage . . .'.

A few months later, following the Jomtien Conference on Education for All, the Convention on the Rights of the Child came into force (September 1990). Article 29 of this convention explicitly proclaims education's role to foster the child's cultural identity, languages and values, and respect for his/her cultural background. Article 29 (c) states:

The development of respect for the child's parents, his or her own cultural identity, language and values, for the national values of the country in which the child is living, the country from which he or she may originate, and for civilizations different from his or her own;

Article 30 insists on the right of children of minorities or indigenous populations to enjoy their own culture and to practice their own language and religion:

In those States in which ethnic, religious or linguistic minorities or persons of indigenous origin exist, a child belonging to such a minority or who is indigenous shall not be denied the right, in community with other members of his or her group, to enjoy his or her own culture, to profess and practise his or her own religion, or to use his or her own language.

The Declaration on Environment and Development, adopted by the United Nations Conference on Environment and Development (Rio de Janeiro, 3-14 June 1992) proclaims a close linkage between environmental protection and sustainable development. Principle 4 of the Declaration states: 'In order to achieve sustainable development, environmental protection shall constitute an integral part of the development process and cannot be considered in isolation from it'.

Principle 22 of the same Declaration refers specifically to the importance of the cultures of indigenous people and the need for their co-operation in environmental management:

Indigenous people and their communities and other local communities have a vital role in environmental management and development because of their knowledge and traditional practices. States should recognize and duly support their identity, culture and interests and enable their effective participation in the achievement of sustainable development.

An international conference is an instrument for stimulating and promoting international exchange and co-operation. It is in this spirit that the forty-third session of the International Conference on Education was convened in Geneva in 1992 under the theme: 'The contribution of education to cultural development'. This conference, focusing on the interplay between education and culture, debated how to achieve co-ordinated policies for educational and cultural development, what cultural dimension education should take into account, the role of education in cultural and artistic development, how various potential educational contributors, such as the school, the community and society, could co-operate with each other, and new responsibilities for teachers with regard to cultural and intercultural aspects of education.

This text highlights the debates of the Conference concerning the relationship between education and culture, the cultural goals of education in Member States, co-ordinated policies for educational and cultural development, innovations in cultural and multicultural education and, finally, regional and international co-operation in this field. The sources of information are conference documents (the Recommendation, working documents, plenary speeches delivered by heads of delegations, information and reference documents) prepared for the forty-third session of the International Conference on Education, national reports on the development of education submitted to the International Bureau of Education (IBE) prior to the conference and replies to the questionnaire sent by the IBE on the themes of the conference. When necessary, some relevant external documents (other than conference documents) are quoted to supplement the information provided by the sources of information.

POLICY GOALS AND OBJECTIVES OF CULTURAL
AND MULTICULTURAL EDUCATION

Linking education with cultural development

It was the World Conference on Cultural Policies (Mexico City, 1982) which revealed the limitations of a development concept based primarily on quantitative and material objectives, and declared the importance of 'culture constituting a fundamental part of the life of each individual and each community and, consequently, development – whose ultimate aim should be focused on man – must have a cultural dimension' (Recommendation N° 27). This conference proposed two significant guiding principles – placing culture at the centre of development (development is therefore called cultural development) and defining human factors as the most important ones in planning and defining the strategies of such development.

Participants at the forty-third session of the International Conference on Education described the relationship between education and culture as a reciprocal and mutually influencing process. They agreed that education is not only a main agent of cultural transmission but should stimulate, change and vitalize the process of cultural development through the formation of the individual learner's critical, analytical and creative thinking and the cultivation of their moral values and artistic talents. Mr. Federico Mayor, Director-General of UNESCO, in his opening speech, emphasized that 'the promotion of human creativity is at the heart of the notion of cultural development' and the task of cultural development is promoted by 'the education that promotes such creativity by fostering new ways of thinking and seeing while transmitting a common heritage of knowledge, experience and values'.

Cultural goals of education in a national development plan

The analysis in this section is mainly based on the results of the questionnaire prepared for the Conference seeking information on cultural and educational objectives expressed in the national development plans of Member States as well as on those sections of the national reports dealing with education for cultural development.

On the basis of an analysis of these documents, the following main clusters of cultural objectives and priorities in Member States emerged:

1. Preservation and enrichment of the nation's cultural heritage and identity.
2. Enhancement of individuals' creativity, aesthetic and artistic talents.
3. Participation of all people in cultural activities and support of their cultural diversity and cultural rights.
4. Promotion of human rights, democratic values, moral and civic values, justice, peace and tolerance.
5. Partnership and decentralized strategies in the process of cultural development.
6. Regional cultural co-operation (e.g. Europe).

A further analysis was made in order to find the educational objectives (identified by Member States) corresponding to the above-mentioned cultural objectives. Through this analysis, the following priorities of the cultural dimension of education emerged.

EDUCATION TO PROMOTE INTERCULTURAL CONTACT

This education may require not only that culture is taught cognitively (information, knowledge) but also involves how to live with different cultures and peoples, as one delegate of the conference asserted: 'We must emphasize that learning about other cultures should not stop with mere knowledge or tolerance. These alone are not sufficient. The purpose of multicultural education should be to help individuals appreciate, and positively experience, important aspects of other cultures.'

Education should go beyond providing bookish knowledge about culture and explore the opportunities to expose learners to living cultural contacts, experiences and interactions. Multi-ethnic societies, where several cultural groups live side by side, offer an advantageous position as educational programmes involving learner's direct interaction and communication with different cultural groups are more easily arranged. The countries without such a cultural environment may have to explore other means to make this education possible. A more frequent use of audio-visual instructional media, presenting a variety of cultures and ways of life, may be an alternative for these countries, but cultural learning based upon face-to-face contact between peoples of different cultures cannot be achieved by this method alone. Nonetheless, education designed to promote the experiential aspect of cultural learning is receiving growing attention internationally.

EDUCATION TO PRESERVE AND ENRICH
THE NATIONAL CULTURAL HERITAGE AND IDENTITY

There are two types of cultural heritage – physical (monuments, cultural sites, etc.) and non-physical. The non-physical heritage covers cultural values (local and national), religious values, mother tongues and national languages, cultural traditions (including oral and non-verbal ones), etc. Education more often deals with the non-physical aspects of cultural heritage, although its task involves teaching and learning about the values and attitudes pertinent to the preservation of cultural monuments, sites, artistic masterpieces, etc.

Many conference participants asserted that multiculturalism is a matter of degree and that 'all societies are more or less multicultural and therefore we talk of cultural heritages'. Even countries claiming a 'mono-cultural' society admit the existence of local cultures and sub-cultures. The idea of a 'pure culture' seems an unrealistic notion. It is also interesting to note that predominantly multicultural nations (e.g. Canada, Australia) tend to use the plural word 'cultures' instead of the singular word 'culture' in their national reports.

On the other side of the coin of preserving cultural heritages is the idea of enriching culture. Education must deal with, in this sense, both the preservation and enrichment of cultures. Cultures do change, both negatively and positively. Education can play an important role in bringing about positive changes – stimulation of creativity, critical thinking, problem-solving approaches of the learner and foster attitudes of co-operation, democracy and peace in people's minds.

The national reports also almost unanimously support this dual task of education: the transmission of cultural heritage and the enrichment of these heritages. Many countries asked the question: 'why does education need to adapt itself to the requirements of present and future world changes?' The following factors have been identified by many countries which believe them to be factors affecting the changing role of education:

1. The growing volume of information and knowledge of all kinds and flowing from all parts of the world.
2. The development of science and technology which is one of the major determinants of a nation's economic development.

3. The development of information and communication technology and of international transport making it possible for large numbers of people to communicate and interact with each other.

4. The increased concern and awareness of environmental problems and the worldwide desire for its protection.

5. The growing internationalization of commercial and cultural activities.

6. The growing interest and priorities placed on humanitarian values and their development or enrichment, including human rights, moral education and peace education.

7. The decline of the East-West military stalemate and increased regional co-operation witnessed, for example, by European integration.

The educational implications of cultural identity seem to require a deep analysis of the concept, both socially and psychologically. Both national reports and the replies to the questionnaire indicate that the cultural identity of Member States, particularly traditional values, are being challenged by the rapidly evolving socio-economic and socio-cultural environments in which we live. The factors which Member States think affect traditional values are: science and technology; the mass-media; foreign languages; the influence of other nations' life styles; international travel; study abroad; products of cultural industries (films, magazines, games); and tastes and life-styles encouraging materialistic prosperity.

Many countries point out that young people, minority groups, immigrants and indigenous populations are particularly vulnerable to these influences.

To European and North American multicultural nations, cultural identity is rooted in their recognition of cultural and linguistic diversity within a nation. Several Member States belonging to the European Community, or currently considering their future membership in the Community, and those 'new democracies' in Eastern Europe, indicated the European dimension of education as one of their preoccupations. Evidence for this position can be found in the working paper prepared by the Education Committee of the Council for Cultural Co-operation for the seventeenth session of the Standing Conference of European Ministers of Education (Vienna, 16-17 October 1991). This document, stressing 'how to educate Europeans', put forward the following overall objective of 'closer European unity'.

– To establish lasting peace, co-operation and mutual understanding between the peoples of Europe;

- To foster the common European heritage of political, cultural and moral values which lie at the root of civilized society: human rights, pluralist democracy, tolerance, solidarity and the rule of law;
- To promote sustained economic and social progress, while reducing disparities and safeguarding the environment; and
- To give Europe sufficient weight to fulfil its responsibilities to the rest of the world.[2]

Along with this movement of enhancing the European dimension of education, several Eastern European countries manifested their current educational efforts and role in assisting national transition from a centralized form of cultural policies to that of cultural diversity and pluralism.

For many countries in Africa, the issue of cultural identity seems to be closely associated with national development. The cultural relevance of education is a predominant issue in these countries. The Nigerian national report asserts the intention of making 'our educational system not only academically sound but also culturally relevant'. The United Republic of Tanzania's insistence on the 'promotion of Kiswahili, Tanzania's national language and the development of educational curricula which are Tanzanian in content and organization', bear witness to the reality of the region. As explicitly pointed out by Burkina Faso, cultural identity is a very important educational issue for Africa, not only as an important educational goal but also as a unifying value for national development. Yet, the contribution of education to cultural development seems to have created mixed feelings among African countries. This point is clearly mentioned in the following statement which appears in Lesotho's national report:

> Traditionally in Lesotho there was no difference between education on the one hand and cultural development on the other .... With the advent of Western Education, a visible dichotomy began to emerge between education and culture. It was a programme of education which was not independent from the motives of both the Christian Missions that introduced it, and the colonial administrations that gave it security and legitimacy.
>
> But it was not only altogether autonomous from the socio-cultural milieu of its time; it was actually in large measure opposed to it. Culture was viewed as a symbol of resistance and opposition to progress; and the practice of culture was met with a manifold set of direct and indirect punishments and sanctions. Education and culture became antonyms; and proponents of local culture became enemies of educators. This antipathy has remained deeply embedded in the social fabric of Lesotho society to the present day.

We can see from this example that the relation between culture and education is not always harmonious. Education and culture are sometimes contradictory concepts in African history. In this sense, the decision concerning what aspects of cultural heritage or identity should be preserved is an important and delicate question, particularly in the light of socio-economic reality in the region, where society is facing a great deal of development problems.

EDUCATION TO SUPPORT CULTURAL DIVERSITY AND PLURALISM

Although there is a consensus among Member States who participated in the Conference that all nations are more or less multicultural and therefore the educational content of cultural diversity and pluralism are relevant and respected, the policy priorities arising from this issue depend upon the cultural composition of a nation.

For those so-called predominantly multicultural societies (e.g. Australia, Canada, India, Malaysia), cultural diversity and pluralism are a reality and their multicultural educational policies are geared towards multiculturalism within a nation. Education of cultural and linguistic minorities is a main concern for these countries, whether they are indigenous peoples, long-established minorities, immigrants, migrants or refugees.

The national reports give examples of these cultural minority groups as follows: Aborigines and Torres Strait Islanders (Australia); Frisian-speaking minorities (Netherlands); the Saami population (Norway); Hungarian and German minorities (Romania); the minorities of German, Ukrainian, Byelorussian origins (Poland); Non-German-speaking or Turkish workers (Austria); the Romany minority (Czechoslovakia); immigrants (Belgium, Netherlands, Sweden); Maori and Pacific islanders (New Zealand); native peoples in the Western provinces, the Acadians in the Maritime provinces, the black community in Nova Scotia (Canada). For these countries, which are culturally and linguistically more homogeneous and possess few linguistic and cultural minorities, cultural diversity, though it sometimes refers to local and sub-cultures within a nation, tends to be interpreted as the relation of their culture to those of other nations. In this sense, the notion of cultural pluralism is often associated with the international understanding of the cultures of other nations. However, there is a growing recognition in these countries about the importance of local and sub-cultures.

In multicultural nations, people need not only to learn about cultural diversity but also to live with the reality of cultural pluralism. Daily, people face different languages, different ways of life, and a variety of cultural groups. The children living in multicultural societies are privileged since they are exposed, from an early age, to cultural differences and similarities. Therefore, they have a better chance of acquiring cultural sensitivity, an understanding of cultural diversity within a nation, and communication and interpersonal skills required by the reality of a multicultural nation. However, history also witnesses that close and direct contacts among different cultural or ethnic groups do not necessarily lead to mutual respect, understanding and appreciation – it sometimes invites intergroup conflicts, prejudice and discrimination. It is therefore an important task of multicultural education in these countries to create a good quality of learning and teaching programmes which foster a spirit of tolerance, understanding and knowledge of minority groups, including their historical and cultural backgrounds, and genuine attitudes and skills for intercultural communication and interpersonal relationships. Such programmes have already been created in several multicultural countries and considerable innovations in this area are on the way.

On the other hand, in more homogeneous countries, considerable efforts are being made to promote the learner's understanding and knowledge of other cultures. However, educational programmes in these countries seem to be predominantly cognitive (world history, geography, etc.), while attitudinal and behavioural aspects of multicultural programmes require innovative approaches, since these countries possess less varied populations compared with multicultural nations. The cultural frame of reference in the latter tends more easily to stimulate educational policies, school programmes and public awareness on the need for multicultural education.

EDUCATION FOR ETHICAL AND CIVIC VALUES

Forming an ethically and morally sound individual is a common concern of UNESCO's Member States. For this purpose, the majority of countries responding to the IBE questionnaire report that an ethical and civic dimension of education is provided. However, very few countries report that moral or civic education is offered as a separate subject. The majority of Member States indicate that this type of education is integrated across several subjects, such as 'history, geography, literature, social studies, language teaching, religious education'. For the Islamic countries, moral and civic education are synonymous with Islamic education. Elsewhere (e.g. Lesotho, Costa Rica, Panama, Austria), one of the most popular forms of moral and civic education is religious instruction.

UNESCO seldom discusses the issues of religious education, but an interesting meeting took place two years ago in the Asia and Pacific Region. A Regional Meeting on the Promotion of Humanistic, Ethical and Cultural Values in Education was convened jointly by the National Institute for

Educational Research (NIER, Japan), the Ministry of Education, Science and Culture and UNESCO's Principal Regional Office in Asia and the Pacific (PROAP). The meeting, emphasizing that 'the matter of teaching religion or teaching about religion or religions is for individual Member States to decide', made the following observations :

1. Teaching about religion varies from country to country in Asia. Some teach only their religion. Others teach about religion, as well as other major religions of the world.

2. Some countries do not provide religious education through the State-sponsored system. They, however, do provide all facilities to persons following different religions. They also give equal respect to believers of religions.

3. All religions have commonly-shared moral values and practices.

The following are some specific examples :

– Buddhism states, 'Hurt not others with that which pains yourself.'
– Christianity states, 'All things whatsoever ye would that men should do to you, do ye even so to them; for this is the law of the prophets.'
– Confucianism states, 'Is there any one maxim which ought to be acted upon throughout one's life? Surely the maxim of loving kindness is such. Do not unto others what you would not they should do unto you.'
– Hinduism states, 'That is the sum of duty: do naught to others which done to thee would cause pain.'
– Islam states, 'No one of you is a believer until he loves for his brother what he loves for himself.'
– Taoism states, 'Regard your neighbour's loss as your own.'[3]

The International Conference on Education (ICE) recommended universal values such as: 'respect for human rights, tolerance, dialogue, solidarity and mutual support and education to put these values into action'; 'teachers should participate with their pupils in solidarity activities and assistance for the sick, deprived or socially underprivileged people, the elderly and disaster victims; pupils could also act as organizers, for educational, sports and other activities intended for younger pupils and children not enrolled in schools'. It also recommended that schools 'present learners with examples of moral behaviours' (Recommendation paragraph 19) in keeping with these values.

The Conference also stressed the roles of the family, members of the community and the communication media in influencing children's ethical and moral values. It is the role of the school to foster understanding and organized knowledge on these values. The media also influence the learner's value orientation in an unstructured fashion but it is mainly through the school and family that the learner deepens his/her learning about ethical and moral values. The Conference, while recognizing the contribution of science and technology to the progress of all societies, also emphasized that 'scientific and technological culture' must be linked to ethical and humanistic values in order to maximize its contribution to the improvement of the natural and social environments.

ARTISTIC AND AESTHETIC EDUCATION

One of the traditional goals of artistic and aesthetic education is the development of the learner's technical competence in producing and constructing art forms and products. The development of talents and artistic professionals is a goal closely attached to this objective. Although this kind of goal is still considered important and many countries are trying to improve the quality of the art curriculum in this respect, many other goals are emerging concerning artistic and aesthetic education in many parts of the world.

The diversity of such goals found in national reports can be summarized as follows:

1. The combination of the both artistic and aesthetic aspects of education. In other words, the construction of art forms are pursued together with an appreciation of the arts.

2. Artistic and aesthetic education as an instrument in promoting or consolidating national identity and cultural values.

3. Artistic and aesthetic education as a means to develop the individual's balanced personality, creative expression and sensitivity, particularly artistic and aesthetic education complementary to the cognitive objectives of education.

4. The role of artistic education to promote international and cultural understanding through the arts; the arts being conceived as a a part of culture which carries aesthetic messages.

5. The role of artistic education in promoting popular arts and traditions.

6. Artistic education as a means to promote the productive use of increased leisure time.

7. The role of artistic education in contributing to individual wealth and the local and national economy, for example, through the development or artistic industries.

8. Artistic education using modern scientific and technological methods.

Together with widening and diversified goals for artistic and aesthetic education, there is increasing partnership between educational and cultural institutions in this area. The mobilization of resources from both public and private sectors (particularly local and community resources), in terms of human expertise and material resources for the benefit of each others' activities, is a major development.

There seem to be two main approaches in the partnership of educational and cultural institutions:

Participation in each others' activity and programmes

Schoolchildren's visits are arranged to museums, exhibitions, art galleries, cultural centres, drama festivals, cultural monuments, etc. This is a very popular form of involving schools in the community's artistic activities practised by a substantial number of countries. In France, museums have become an important place for supplementing art education. About 60% of French museums co-operate with schools and 1 million children visit museums every year. Some 30% of these museums are equipped with workshops, audio-visual materials and other informational services which promote the understanding of the art. In Saudi Arabia, the government encourages students to be members of cultural centres or art societies, thereby creating opportunities for students to appreciate art lectures, poetry, music and plays.

The artistic and cultural personnel, such as artists, musicians, film-makers, as well as NGOs, teachers organizations, youth organizations, etc., participate in arts education programmes at school. The Australian 'Artists-in-school' and 'Theatre-in-education' projects are examples. 'Nor-Concert' institutions in Norway organizes 'school concerts', linking them to the teaching of music in school.

The joint development of programmes in arts education

Joint activity brings educational and cultural institutions even closer to each other. It involves joint planning, the creation of mixed programme committees among artists, business men, government officials and others. It also involves the sharing of project outcomes. The Republic of Korea established twelve 'Culture Schools' (Music Culture School, Theatre Culture School, Art Museums Culture School, etc.) involving artistic communities actively in the planning and organization of the project. Tunisia is trying, in co-operation with cultural institutions, to create cultural clubs within the school. Saskatchewan's (Canada) Minister of Education established an Indian and Metis educational advisory committee whose mandate includes the dissemination of cultural information and strategies to both Native and non-Native people in the province. The Gabriel Dumont Institute on Metis Cultural Matters and the Education Department produced a Metis Dance Kit.

The advantages arising from partnership and co-operation in promoting artistic and aesthetic education between educational and cultural development can be summarized as follows:

1. Co-operation provides a wide range of learning opportunities for students in the domain since artistic institutions provide expertise, resources and a variety of ways of organizing learning activities which are not readily available in schools.

2. Cultural institutions can provide students with 'living' cultural contacts and traditions (music, theatre, dance, etc.), therefore students motivation to learn about the arts can be remarkably enhanced through their active participatory learning in the company of professional artists.

3. Teachers are not often professional artists and their organizational capacity and time available to organize artistic activity is often limited, which may be supplemented by available artistic expertise and artistic personnel.

4. Co-operation contributes to the mobilization of resources available in schools, and local and national artistic institutions, thus reducing the cost of education.

5. The cultural institutions and events (concerts, theatre, art exhibition, etc.) often offer an opportunity to expose the learner not only to local or national culture but also to cultures of other nations, thus contributing to his/her appreciation and understanding of the cultural diversity.

Elliot Eisner, Professor of Education and Art, Stanford University, and author of a reference paper presented to the Conference, believes that the most essential task of art education is the 'creation of mind'. According to him, the human mind is malleable and its growth depends largely on the 'culture at large: its language, its art, the symbol systems and forms of representation it employs, the values it embraces, the spiritual interests that permeate it, in fact the entire complex of intellectual, social, religious, and technological features that collectively constitute a civilization'. He recommends that: 'UNESCO's agenda is (...) to expand the array of opportunities through which different minds can be grown.'

LANGUAGE TEACHING

Language reflects the culture of a particular group. Cultures are also expressed through languages. Language teaching, either as a subject or as a medium of instruction, is substantially affected by the cultural environment in which one lives.

The language of a country often reveals the cultural history of a nation and also the cultural make-up of a society. It may reflect the past history of a nation's relationship with other nations or the ethnic structure of the society in a given nation. The answers provided to the pre-Conference questionnaire demonstrate that numerous Member States possess more than one official language (languages prescribed by law): Botswana (English, Setswana); Burundi (French, Kirundi); Spain (Spanish, Catalan); India (English, Hindi); Israel (Hebrew, Arabic); Central African Republic (French, Sango); Sri Lanka (Sinhala, Tamil, English); Swaziland (English, Swazi); Switzerland (German, French, Italian, Romanche), etc.

There is a common claim among Member States with a multi-linguistic society that there should be at least one (sometimes two or three) commonly shared languages to serve as a means of communication across different linguistic groups, be it a mother tongue or even an official language of foreign origin. Some countries claim that having such a language contributes to the solidarity and cultural identity of a nation. Some others think that, from an economic or practical point of view, such a practice is inevitable.

A tension has been observed, particularly among those countries which suffered from colonialism, between the use of the mother tongue as a means of preserving and enriching cultural identity and the use of non-native languages (e.g. English, French) as a medium of instruction. There are cultural and psychological problems associated with this issue. The cultural problem is often expressed as a concern that the use of mother tongues may tend to become more and more unpopular and that an integral part of cultural identity will thereby be lost. The main psychological problem is that the learner assigns a relatively low value to his/her mother tongue in view of its utility, prestige and practicability, especially when a dominant official language (which is not a mother tongue) exists which is considered as an important means to move up to higher levels of education or technological and scientific fields of education. In this situation, mother tongues are used as linkage languages leading to the introduction of official languages (particularly when the latter are of foreign origin). These transitional methods of teaching languages are quite frequent at the primary school level and in adult education. Barbados, Kenya, Lesotho and Namibia, for example, mention them. Some countries, particularly at the post-secondary level, use English or other foreign languages to teach the science curriculum (e.g. India, the Islamic Republic of Iran, Kuwait, United Republic of Tanzania, Turkey).

In literacy training, the choice of language (official language or mother tongue) is an important issue. Lind and Johnston in this respect raised the following crucial questions:

– Does high student motivation for learning literacy in a second (official) language justify teaching directly in this language, rather than starting in the mother tongue and transiting later?

– When is it best to start the transition from mother-tongue to second-language literacy? How long does it take to complete the transition sufficiently? What facilitating factors can be provided in the environment? What methods are best?

– What is the situation of literacy retention in a second language?[4]

Recommendation No. 78 of the ICE also suggests that 'research should be carried out in such fields as educational sciences, linguistics, anthropology and history, and the preparation of teaching materials in the mother tongue should be encouraged' (para 14).

Cultural diversity is very evident when one looks into a complex world situation in the use of languages of instruction. A survey carried out by the Division of Statistics of UNESCO[5] shows that more than half of the countries (fifty-five out of 101) reported a single official language of instruction, thirty-four reported two and twelve reported three languages or more. However, according to this survey, at the world level, a comparatively small number of languages are used in a large number of countries. English, French, Spanish and Arabic are popular languages in one-third of these countries, and either English or French is used in the majority (70%) of them.

Particularly in countries where linguistic and cultural minorities exist, teaching subjects in the language of the minority (indigenous populations, immigrants, refugees, etc.) and teaching minority languages are attracting more and more attention at both local and national levels.

Education in the language of the minority is guaranteed at the elementary and secondary levels in Canada under the Canadian Charter of Rights and Freedoms. For example, it guarantees education in French (where the majority language is English) and also education in English (where French is the majority language – i.e. Quebec). Australia provides, where appropriate, the opportunity of learning twenty-three aboriginal languages.

In these multicultural countries, the choice of foreign languages taught is also becoming greater. Ontario in Canada, for example, provides opportunities for study in at least forty-one different languages at the secondary level (Canadian National Report, 1992, p. 25). Australia, at the primary level alone, teaches thirty-six foreign languages (Australian reply to the Conference questionnaire, p. 18).

The minority language policies and practices of multicultural societies are in harmony with the Recommendation of the Conference (para. 14): 'when choosing the language of instruction, in particular at the level of education, account should be taken both of the efficiency of the educational process and the right of individuals and various ethnic groups to preserve their cultural identity, of which their language is one of the most important vehicles.'

The language policies of Member States are closely related to their cultural policies, socio-economic situations, the cultural make-up of the society, historical relationships of countries with other countries, the socio-economic power of a nation to pursue and improve language policies, and the individual (of a particular culture) person's psychological orientation and readiness to learn the languages. It is a very complex field and comparative research aimed at language policies and language teaching could play an important role in collecting systematic and analytical data in this subject. Such research needs to adapt a multi-disciplinary approach as the issue of language touches upon a wide spectrum of people in diversified cultural settings.

INTERACTION BETWEEN THE SCHOOL,
THE LOCAL COMMUNITY AND SOCIETY

Although the school is expected to undertake numerous activities and functions in promoting cultural development, it cannot do everything – this was the opinion of many participants. Other partners in society – apart from education – have joint responsibility with the school for the cultural development of society. However, many participants also felt that the school can contribute to the cultural development task in raising awareness about the importance of the individual's contribution to the solution of societal problems and creating useful interactive educational programmes between the school and other community-based establishments (e.g. industries, the media, museums, artistic institutions).

In their replies to the Conference questionnaire, a large number of countries reported that schools and adult education centres are engaged in both formal and extra-curricular activities involving students in the cultural life of the community. These countries indicated the following ways of using the community as a curriculum resource for the school:

- Visits by students to cultural sites, monuments, etc.
- Visits by students to local artistic events (local theatres, museums, dance performances, etc.).
- Participation of pupils and students in competitions (sports, games, music, etc.).
- Creation of clubs, hobby groups, artistic groups, youth organizations, summer camps and cultural centres.
- Participation by students in community-based environmental protection campaigns or literacy campaigns.
- Participation of artistic specialists and local dignitaries in the school's work.

UNESCO's Associated Schools Project was frequently cited as a support mechanism for these activities. There are now over 2,350 institutions in 100 Member States at pre-school, primary, secondary and teacher training levels. The main aim of this project is to promote the development of education for international understanding through the networking of institutions. The project publishes and disseminates information on innovative projects concerning pupils' involvement with the community, voluntary activities, visits to cultural sites, campaigns for environmental protection, etc.

One of the most important pedagogical advantages of promoting community/school interaction is that learning can be more directly linked with what takes place in the everyday life of the community. The community is a living culture which presents learners with the challenge of environmental and social problems, and the need to find solutions to these problems. The school alone cannot provide solutions to all kinds of societal problems. However, encouraging learners to learn through interaction with the living culture of the community and developing abilities to apply knowledge to solve community problems is a way of increasing the educational contribution to cultural development.

The participation of community members in the educational activities of the school also influences the attitudes of the community to the school. The community, by forging a closer linkage between the contents of the school curriculum and the life of the community (e.g. health and environmental issues), tends to develop positive attitudes toward schooling and recognize meaningful outcomes on the future prospects of children. It may also be important that the community becomes convinced, through its participation in school activities, about its contribution to education and the development of human resources being worthwhile.

For full-scale school/community partnership and involvement in education, it is necessary for both parties to initiate discussion and consultation in order to clearly define areas of responsibility for education. Such a process seems to require some permanent structures and mechanisms through which discussions and the exchange of ideas can take place concerning the purposes of co-operation, identification of priority areas for co-operation, and the ways both parties can effectively mobilize available resources, as well as continuous evaluation of the partnership to improve future co-operation.

The Conference participants recognized the importance of the media in influencing the educational process. Forming a partnership with the media is a powerful means for education to reinforce its contribution to cultural development. The media can be both a powerful means of multiplying access to education (e.g. distance education) and also of improving the quality of teaching and learning, though some concern was expressed about negative influences.

Most countries which responded to the Conference questionnaire report that 'media education' is not offered as an independent subject but constitutes an integral part of the school curriculum. For example, Norway integrates media education into subjects such as civics and literature. Australia asserts that media studies occur at every level and are designed to develop critical faculties and media literacy. The Republic of Korea provides courses at the middle and high-school level on the way the mass media influence individual student's socialization process and on politics.

The results of the Conference questionnaire also draw attention to the growing trend for co-operation between educational sectors and the media. This is shown by consultative links established by ministries of education and major national television and radio corporations (e.g. Austria, Bahrain, China, Spain, Jamaica, Jordan, Turkey) for the production of educational television and radio programmes. Bahrain reports the existence of joint committees bringing together the Ministry of Education and the Ministry of Information to discuss educational and media matters. Qatar similarly reports the formation of joint committees to follow up and evaluate efforts in the field of education and the media. Some French-speaking 'cantons' of Switzerland (Geneva, Vaud) assign teacher specialists (nominated by and paid for by the Public Education Departments) to prepare and produce educational television and radio programmes. Spain's Ministry of Education and Science co-operates with Tele Madrid for the delivery of diplomas for distance education. An innovative 'Inter-Action Israel' is designed to teach people how to produce educational television programmes. Portugal actively utilizes media information (journals, magazines) in the classrooms and encourages students to write 'school newspapers'.

The Conference, while praising the enormous positive contributions of the media to education, noted the concerns expressed by many countries about the negative impact of the media on the educational process. In this respect, the Conference put forward two strategies to cope with this problem. The first strategy is to reinforce aspects of media education to foster the individual's understanding of the role and effects of the media and his/her formation of a critical capacity to judge and evaluate the message conveyed by the media. The other strategy lies in the hands of the media and its supporting personnel, particularly their self-regulation or their self-censure concerning the possible negative impact of the media message upon its receivers. However, when all was said and done, the participants of the Conference reiterated their support for the freedom of the press, which should be preserved at all costs.

EDUCATION TO ENCOURAGE THE PARTICIPATION OF ALL POPULATION GROUPS IN CULTURAL LIFE

Although illiterate people do participate in cultural activities, their participation is limited through not having access to written and symbolic communication. Literacy and basic education, as manifested by the World Conference on Education for All (Jomtien, 1990), are a powerful means to enrich and broaden the participation of the individual in cultural activities. The Conference maintained that the spread of culture depends to a large extent on the diffusion of literacy and basic education.

Several speakers stressed that the illiteracy rate in many developing countries continues to be high for rural populations, especially for girls and women. Through the questionnaire survey, most countries reported that equal opportunities between the two sexes are constitutionally and legally guaranteed. However, their efforts to improve the reality of inequality were also reported. Some countries have ministries or ministerial units in charge of equal opportunities of both sexes (e.g. Ministry of Women and Culture, Fiji; Division of Women and Girls Education in the Ministry of Education, Austria; a Secretariat for Equal Educational Opportunity, Ministry of Education, Norway). Some countries (e.g. Australia, Canada, Netherlands), are trying to improve the enrolment of women in higher education science and technology courses. Some countries are encouraging the establishment of women's clubs, associations, national commissions and media programmes. Switzerland offers information and guidance services and, in several 'cantons', 'equality bureaux' or a 'women's bureaux' have been established to promote equal educational opportunities for women.

The Conference also recommended the elimination of barriers which prevent various culturally disadvantaged groups (indigenous populations, migrants, refugees, nomads, etc.) and disabled persons from full participation in educational activities and programmes. Several countries report educational measures which have been adopted in this respect. The training of teachers to meet the specific cultural and educational needs of disadvantaged groups is a priority concern for these countries. The teaching of languages (both mother tongues and foreign languages) to refugees, immigrants, migrants and indigenous people is also an important educational priority.

Increased access to cultural and educational opportunities is a first step to realize the participation of all populations in cultural life. The quality of access is another dimension which requires more concerted educational efforts in linking education with the unique cultural needs and aspirations of these groups.

THE ROLE AND TRAINING OF TEACHERS

The Conference asserted that the cultural dimension should be taken into consideration in pre-service and in-service teacher training programmes, particularly a broader and deeper knowledge of cultures within the country and in the world.

More specifically, the Conference recommended the teacher training programme to encompass the importance of media, technology, environment, the skills to develop innovative approaches in intercultural/multicultural education, intercultural communication and some notions of anthropological analysis for teachers to carry out their professional functions within the context of a plurality of cultures. The teacher training curriculum to meet these requirements needs a wide scope of objectives, innovative and problem-solving approaches, encompassing national cultures, cultures of other nations and multiculturalism within national and regional cultural settings.

Such teacher education curricula may address the cultural content of the school curriculum and its instructional objectives, class management (communication, interpersonal relationships, etc.), teaching methods (motivating the student's learning resources, information technology, co-operative learning, etc.), the assessment of culture-related learning outcomes and other organizational aspects of school education.

The cultural dimensions of the teacher education curriculum need to be supported by clear national or local policies. The process of formulating national policies and goals for teacher education designed to promote cultural aspects of teaching and learning requires a collaborative approach involving all the people concerned (learners, teachers, school administrators, the community, policy-makers, the media). Such a partnership approach can more easily secure administrative, financial and resource requirements needed for teacher education in the area and also supports teachers' motivation and responsibilities to further cultural and intercultural education.

CO-ORDINATING EDUCATIONAL
AND CULTURAL DEVELOPMENT POLICIES

One of the main objectives of the Plan of Action for the World Decade for Cultural Development (1988-97) is: 'Broadening participation in cultural life'. To combat illiteracy and promote the democratization of education is, in this sense, an important priority for education. Education is also expected to contribute widely to other areas of cultural development – it could no longer act alone or claim a monopoly in educating people to achieve such a goal. The resources allocated to education are also unable to cover the ever-increasing cultural responsibilities of education. While effectively mobilizing the available resources, education needs to explore additional human and material resources in co-operation with other establishments. The Conference recommended that educational and cultural policies in Member States should be closely co-ordinated with the spirit of mutual participation and co-operation affecting these two sectors in the task of cultural development.

Recommendation No. 78 (para. 9) suggests the following considerations in promoting co-ordinated educational and cultural policies:

1. Increased co-operation between formal and non-formal educational establishments and cultural institutions.
2. Increased participation by staff from cultural institutions in the educational process.
3. A broadening of the network of cultural institutions involved, together with an improvement in the initial and in-service training of the network staff.
4. An increase in educational programmes broadcast by the media.
5. Taking into account, when allocating public and private resources, the reciprocal needs of education and culture.

Co-ordination mechanism

The establishment of *a single ministry* dealing with both education and culture is a way of co-ordinating these two sectors. Replies to the Conference questionnaire indicated that several countries (e.g. Argentina, Chile, Finland, France, Indonesia, Israel, Japan, Kenya, Lebanon, Lesotho, Malawi, Namibia, Philippines, Saudi Arabia, the United Republic of Tanzania, Zambia) have a single ministry dealing with education and culture. Some of these countries report that a single ministry makes co-ordination between educational and cultural programmes easier and results in improved efficiency and cost-effectiveness. At the same time, they expressed some disadvantages. For example, budgetary cuts tend to affect culture alone, while educational programmes always seem to take precedence over cultural ones.

There are also other ways of organizing educational and cultural sectors at the ministerial level. Austria has the Federal Ministry of Education and Arts. India has the Department of Education and the Department of Culture which are both parts of the Ministry of Human Resource Development of the Union Government.

Many other countries report *inter-ministerial co-ordination*, usually through the establishment of a committee or its equivalent structures. Benin has the National Commission of Human Resources playing a co-ordinating role between education and culture. The United Arab Emirates convenes the Committee of Educational Policies which is attended by the senior departments supervising educational and cultural affairs. Japan has an advisory council at the Ministry of Education, Science and Culture composed of specialists in education and culture. Both educational and cultural policies are co-ordinated by the appropriate committees of the Supreme Council of the Russian Federation. France in 1988 established a high committee of artistic education, presided by the Minister of Education and Culture. Argentina's National Committee for the World Decade for Cultural Development, composed of members from several sectors (science, technology, health, culture, etc.), co-ordinates activities related to culture, science and technology and communication. The Republic of Korea co-ordinates cultural and educational policies through the Economic Planning Board. Australia's Office of Multicultural Affairs, in the Department of the Prime Minister and Cabinet, co-ordinates cultural and educational policies and strategies relating to multicultural affairs.

Partnerships

Other ministries or departments are also major partners. The ministries dealing with youth and sports, environment, commerce, economy, foreign affairs, information and home affairs are major partners at the ministerial level. *Local authorities* (provincial boards of education, local government), *universities, the private sector* (business councils, economic federations), *NGOs, associations* (teachers' unions), *community groups* (parents, local leaders, artistic organizations, youth organizations) and the *media* have been reported by Member States as major partners.

Factors affecting the success of partnerships

1. Access to information and knowledge about what potential partners are doing may be a first step informing a co-operative enterprise. The media and networks are helpful mechanisms in locating this information.
2. Equal partnership in the spirit of mutual respect facilitates co-operation and mutual exchange.
3. The involvement of partners in the entire process, from the planning stage to the execution and evaluation of the project, is beneficial.
4. Clearly defined mutual benefits and shared outcomes of a project may be a factor of success in partnership. There should be an agreement by all the parties concerned at the outset of a co-operative project to share responsibility.
5. There should be clearly defined (in terms of tasks and financing) and agreed responsibilities, roles and implications of expected outcomes by all the parties involved.

It seems that there is a multitude of types of partnership which have yet to be explored in making education more relevant and dynamic with a view to increasing its contribution to cultural development. Creativity is required so invent new types of human group organization and relationship.

NOTES

1. *A practical guide to the World Decade for Cultural Development, 1988-97* (p. 15).
2. *Education Newsletter,* 5/91, Council of Europe (p. 3).
3. Final report of the UNESCO regional meeting (p. 45-46), Promotion of Humanistic, Ethical and Cultural Values in Education, Tokyo, 1991.
4. *Adult literacy in the Third World: a review of objectives and strategies,* A.Lind and A. Johnston, Swedish International Development Authority, 1990.
5. *Statistical document on education and culture.* International Conference on Education, 43rd session (ED/BIE/CONFINTED 43/Ref.1), p. 34-35.

CHAPTER IV

Intercultural education

Lê Thành Khôi

THE CASE FOR INTERCULTURAL EDUCATION

One of the major features of the present era has been the growth of relations between peoples and cultures as a result of improved communications. The countries furthest apart on the map are only ten hours away from each other by plane. Radio and television, the telephone and computers bring people all over the world into immediate contact with each other. There have, of course, always been international migrations and transfers between cultures. At times, the former took place on a considerable scale, such as the migrations of nomads across the Eurasian continent or, closer to home, those of Europeans to North America in the nineteenth century. Practically all countries in the world are multicultural in the sense that many ethno-linguistic groups have co-existed there, either for centuries or even millenia, or only during more recent times. The so-called 'domestic' minorities may be distinguished from the 'immigrant' minorities, in that the latter do not enjoy equal legal status with the domestic minorities, which aggravates their problems of integration. In fact, their situations differ in degree and not in nature, since nowhere is constitutional equality sufficient to counterbalance reality in the family, at school, in jobs and in society in general. In the case of the United States, for instance, studies like that of J. Coleman (1966) show that having a single type of schooling, democratic school attendance or 'compensatory' teaching are not enough to eliminate inequalities between ethnic groups, particularly between whites and blacks, because of many mechanisms of differentiation, which may be either apparent or hidden behind supposedly technical criteria, such as the dominant language, the location and types of schools, the resources available in terms of equipment, qualified teachers, study programmes, etc.

Similarly, in the former Soviet Union, where socialism recognized that all peoples were equal, with equal cultural rights and equal opportunities to use their mother tongues, many languages were replaced (in 1990 there were only seventy left compared with 130 at the beginning of the 1930s) by Russian, the language of economic activity, social mobility and political power. On the other hand, neither the spread of Russian nor socialist education managed to quell either nationalism or religion (especially Islam in Caucasia and Central Asia) among the peoples of the USSR.

Western Europe is more concerned with the problem of immigrant workers. Although these existed prior to the Second World War, these population movements were inter-European (such as Poles and Italians in France), which were gradually absorbed into the population. Throughout the long period of industrial growth, which lasted roughly from 1945 to 1970, Europe imported cheap labour from developing countries, chiefly from the Maghreb, Africa South of the Sahara and Turkey. The non-European population now amounts to some 10 million people, most of whom are located in the host countries with their children.

Whether minorities are made up of nationals or of immigrants, they are frequently in a state of tension or conflict with the dominant majority, either for economic reasons (employment) or social reasons (discrimination, racism, etc.). There are also tensions and conflicts between the minorities themselves, often based on historic reasons, which can escalate into a state of war, as has happened in the former Yugoslavia. That tragic case illustrates how socialism failed to eliminate inter-ethnic differences within a country. Having linked nationalism to the bourgeoisie, Marxism thought that it would disappear with the elimination of that social class and the collectivization of the means of production. Events have shown that nationalism is a strong and lasting phenomenon, which is to be found in all social classes. In fact, we are everywhere witnessing the emergence or resurgence of minorities asserting their identity and defending their cultural, social and political rights against the domination of a majority, in other words, against the nation State, in the northern hemisphere as in the south.

For all the above reasons, intercultural education is needed to achieve mutual understanding and peace between peoples. Needless to say, education cannot resolve all problems, particularly those related to unemployment, or the conflict between the political and economic interests of different social classes or states, but at least it can attenuate or eliminate prejudices, by showing that the men and women of all countries share the same needs and the same aspirations, the same joys and the same sorrows, that differences are to be attributed not to skin colour or inherited characteristics, but to history, religion or philosophy, the different problems they have to face as a result of their environment, their production and communication techniques, etc. Intercultural education creates an awareness of the relativity of viewpoints. If people can refrain from judging the thoughts, feelings or actions of others according to their own cultural model, the model with which they grew up and which governs their behaviour, but make an effort instead to put themselves in the place of others, everything becomes clearer and is more easily understood – once ethnocentrism has been eliminated.

Intercultural education will also lead, however, to a rejection of absolute relativism, whereby each culture is unique. Each culture undoubtedly has its own characteristics, but it shares a common basis with other cultures, because men and women are everywhere the same biologically, with the same requirements, the same feelings, and the same basic rational response to the problem of the survival of the species.

For instance, oral cultures for a long time were looked down upon and even ignored because – supposedly – they had no history and had not acceded to science. In fact, every society has a history, which, if not written, is transmitted orally. This oral history can combine fact and myth in different versions, but there is always a kernel of truth and an oral account, just as a written account, can be the subject of internal or external historical criticism, and its facts can be checked by archaeology, historical linguistics and anthropology. As for science and technology, it can also be said that every society has them, since every society must extract from nature what it needs for its subsistence and survival. It is true that writing brought about a qualitative leap in the advance of knowledge. It introduced a huge new capacity for storing, expanding and disseminating knowledge and especially for developing scientific thought. It not only provides a means of recording speech; it also induces a different way of reasoning and knowing. As J. Goody (1978, p. 96-97) wrote: when a statement is put in writing, it can be scrutinized in much more detail; it can be taken as a whole or broken up into parts, manipulated in every way and taken out of context or not. In other words, it can be subjected to a quite different type of analysis and criticism than a purely oral statement. Goody notes that classification by lists (of people, animals, plants, minerals or medicines) and by tables, using graphic techniques, marks a new stage in the build-up of scientific information. The formalization of concepts inherent in writing implies an effort of rationalization which is not possible in the oral tradition. This is particularly obvious in the case of mathematics; even though simple operations can be carried out mentally, this is no longer so for complex operations, which require very abstract procedures. All this means, however, is that the development of science is related to writing and not to any supposed 'primitive' or 'pre-logic' mentality – empty notions which explain nothing.

It may then be wondered why some societies did not invent writing. I am one of those who believe that originally the functions of the human mind were common to all mankind (Boas, 1965, p. 135), that the processes of reasoning and thought are basically the same and include the same logic, that what differ are the concepts, beliefs and values, because each people lives in a different environment and has to face different problems. Writing appeared in an urban society, in Sumer around 3,200 BC, as a result of the growth of trade, crafts, stockbreeding and agriculture, for the reason that a means of expression was needed to keep accounts, to register people and to draft contracts. Similarly, in Egypt, the invention of writing was linked to the growth of population, to the needs of irrigation and Nile control, to the central authority's need to keep accurate accounts of its reserves of food in order to distribute them better in times of famine. On the other hand, the Nubians, whose material culture was equivalent to that of Upper Egypt, did not feel the need for any form of writing, because they were nomads dispersed in less numerous and more mobile groups. South of the Sahara, the Africans did not have any large towns either, because their economies were not sufficiently developed, and because it was not warranted by the size of the population. According to my theory, the absence of writing is to be explained by the smallness of the populations in Africa and not by any sort of 'congenital inferiority' (Lê Thành Khôi, 1991, p. 132-33).

Culture should therefore be given not its elitist connotation of 'intellectual aspects of a civilization' (which tends to belittle oral cultures), but its anthropological meaning. I have proposed to define it as: 'all the material and immaterial productions of a human group in its relations with nature and with other groups, creations which for that group, or for the majority of its members, carry a particular significance, derived from its past or emerging history, a significance which is not shared by other groups' (ibid., p. 31). This definition emphasizes the common significance which men and women, who may be opposed in other respects, attach to their acts as a result of a long history they have lived through together; the significance of an institution which bears the same name will not be the same from one culture to another. The definition also makes clear that culture is not only an acquired heritage; it is constantly being created through the conscious and unconscious effort of all, either impelled by its own dynamics or as a reaction to international influences.

Intercultural education is therefore – or should be – an integral part of cultural development, because every individual participates in the life of his community and because the latter nowadays is constantly receiving messages from outside. If culture is alive, this implies that education must not only transmit a heritage, but must also take account of current changes in knowledge, in ideas and in values, some of which come from outside. In both cases it must be critical, since culture, like any other social phenomenon, comprises both positive and negative aspects, owing to the fact that society is not homogeneous, but includes classes and groups, with interests which may be shared or may be contradictory: what is positive for some is not for others, and what is negative at one time may turn out to be positive, or vice versa.

A further reason in favour of intercultural education is that it offsets the economic and technical bias of the dominant ideology. To take an example, the economic rationality of the capitalist system is an individual rationality based on cost/benefit ratio comparisons, which disregards collective costs in terms of the exploitation of the work of men, women and children (as in nineteenth century Europe and in many so-called developing countries nowadays), of pollution of all kinds, and of destruction of the environment. The pursuit of unlimited growth, driven by profit, focused on all-out exploitation of the planet's resources, which is the corollary of the concept of man as 'the lord and master of nature', has led to catastrophic consequences, such as the disappearance of arable lands and of animal and vegetable species, desertification and health problems. It may be argued that formal and informal education is partly responsible for this process, in so far as it exalts the power of reason without indicating its limits and treats society as a form of work organization by propagating the religion of production and consumption as criteria of civilization and welfare. This remark applies to socialism, which, as practised in Eastern Europe and elsewhere, has been nothing more than capitalism transformed. Even though it adopted different aims (namely raising the material and cultural standards of the population instead of seeking profit), instrumentally speaking it is in no way different, in so far as it has given priority to developing productive forces with the same harmful consequences for the environment.

Other types of society have not shared that philosophy. In Asia, Hinduism, Buddhism, Taoism and Confucianism, whatever their other differences, all stress the equilibrium and independence of the individual through the mastery of desire, the idea that happiness and freedom are to be found within ourselves if we are able to dominate our passions, in a search for harmony with the universe. In Africa, many tales give importance to respect for the environment: hunters who kill not for food but for pleasure, prestige or gain, are punished by the spirits of the forests.

'INTERCULTURALITY' AND 'INTERDISCIPLINARITY'

What are we to understand by intercultural education? I use this term, which implies exchanges, comparisons, confrontations and co-operation, in preference to 'multicultural education', which denotes mere unrelated juxtapositions.

In many countries (such as France), so-called 'intercultural' teaching is intended for the children of immigrant workers in primary school. This means it is designed to help them adapt to the French school system, and to overcome their difficulties, rather than achieving mutual understanding between cultures. Apart from the fact that French culture is not presented as such (being the implied 'model'), the foreign culture is reduced to linguistic and folkloric features (such as cooking, crafts, festivals, etc.) without any attempt to apprehend it in its entirety, that is, without the inclusion of such features within the system of which they are a part and which give them meaning. Nor is the foreign culture situated in relation to world history in terms of exchanges between civilizations, with mutual borrowings and benefits. Also, no mention is made of differences in cultural participation due to differences of social class, age or sex, geographical and ethnic origin. Culture is 'fossilized'. The approach is European in essence.

The 'difference' should be understood dialectically, that is, as an interactive relation between two beings and two cultures, as well as dynamically, that is, subject to change. Every culture evolves in contact with other cultures and education must provide the individual with the reasons and the means to choose knowingly between values he accepts and values he rejects. In other words, real 'intercultural education' should be intended not only for immigrants, but for the population as a whole, both at school and outside school, both for children and for adults; for children because they are at that most impressionable age, a time when they are most deeply impressed with values, patterns of thought and acquired habits; for adults because they are parents, citizens, workers, public opinion and rulers, and because in all these capacities they exert a profound influence on the development of ideas and practice. Among them, teachers and adult instructors must receive appropriate training, if they are to do their job properly.

Thus intercultural values will contribute to cultural development itself, which must or should be the major objective of any form of education, if cultural development is taken to mean the development of the sort of knowledge, values and attitudes which encourage self-fulfilment and creativity (Lê Thành Khôi, 1992, p. 46). In all countries at present, though in differing degrees and with some exceptions, schooling is intellectualistic, in so far as it gives priority to cognitive development and applies authoritarian methods to impose its views, making use therefore of repetition rather than initiative and criticism. There is a resulting imbalance in the personality of the child favouring conceptual to the detriment of imaginary and affective values. Moreover, school education tends to focus on its own culture and makes little allowance for other views of the world and society. Introducing intercultural education can make up for these shortcomings. Our approach is similar to that of all educators, for whom the prime objective of education is to ensure the complete fulfilment of the individual, both physically and intellectually, morally and aesthetically, as well as creatively.

Whatever role the audio-visual media might play, the school remains irreplaceable as an institution offering a structured education to children and young people, because it applies a fairly ordered concept of people and society and employs writing, which, as I said earlier, provides a more efficient approach than the oral tradition to learning criticism, deduction and abstraction. This critical attitude may be directed in the first place at audio-visual messages, which are liable to be manipulated in order to arouse or maintain antagonisms or tensions for the sake of particular political or economic interests. Writing can, of course, also be manipulated. A critical attitude can be inculcated by teaching the child to observe, to deduce, to reason, to compare different opinions with each other and in relation to what the child knows through his own experience, to distinguish between statement and demonstration.

How can intercultural education be put into practice in schools? Should it be introduced as a new 'discipline'? This would not seem advisable, since in most countries curricula are already overloaded and it would only result in extra fatigue for the child, little conducive to development. Intercultural education should not be a separate discipline, but should underlie every discipline, with a double educational benefit, partly awakening the child's interests by opening up new horizons, and partly by applying this 'interdisciplinarity', of which so much has been said and which consists in dealing with a problem by looking at it from different points of view.

The planning of school curricula should be based on the idea that a child's capacity for attention depends on his age and that the timetable available (subject to a maximum determined by the medical profession) should be divided evenly between cognitive, affective and sensory-motor values. Intercultural education covers all three of these areas (for instance, in the case where a foreign play is staged by the children). A further criterion can be adopted in order to limit curricula and not overload children,

85

namely giving priority to an understanding of the world in which the child will be called upon to live, that is, the present, thereby rejecting encyclopaedism and studying the past in so far as it explains the present. This does not mean not studying the past at all, but reducing its importance whenever it takes up too much room (for instance, in cases where some historical periods are studied twice or even more times). While a knowledge of the past is essential for an individual to become aware of his roots, he should also be conscious of the contributions his country has received from other cultures. Moreover, the present is complex and national factors interfere constantly with international ones. Both must be analysed in all their dimensions (political, economic, social and cultural) and their complexity, since there may be contradictions between these dimensions and within them. A critical approach must therefore be adopted. We must bear in mind that intercultural education consists in encouraging a better understanding of different cultures and the contributions of each to world civilization, understanding one's own culture better, and acting in favour of the rights of individuals and peoples and in favour of peace.

We referred above to interdisciplinarity. This concept is not clear, judging by the many terms which are often used synonymously, such as 'multidisciplinarity', 'pluridisciplinarity', 'interdisciplinarity', 'cross-disciplinarity', etc. Leaving aside epistemological considerations and looking at the matter only from the point of view of education, we might usefully take the definitions proposed by the international Colloquy held by UNESCO in Paris from 1 to 5 July 1985 on interdisciplinarity in general education:

Multidisciplinarity is a simple juxtaposition of different disciplines without any apparent interconnection between them.

Pluridisciplinarity is a juxtaposition of disciplines assumed to be more or less interrelated.

Interdisciplinarity is a form of co-operation between different disciplines with regard to problems which are so complex that they can only be dealt with through the convergence and combination of different points of view.

Cross-disciplinarity refers to a general axiomatic system or to a theory which brings together a group of disciplines. It presupposes a conceptual unity or at any rate harmonization. For instance, the concepts of totality, interdependence, change or contradiction are cross-disciplinary (see UNESCO, 1988, p. 8).

Interdisciplinarity therefore implies establishing relations between different disciplines, not unilateral, but reciprocal or possibly systemic, not forgetting that they are also dialectic, that is, sometimes complementary and sometimes contradictory, unlike many 'systemist' authors. Culture is a system, that is, a whole, but all its aspect are not convergent, in so far as some elements can come into conflict with others (for instance, economic aspects with social aspects).

Interdisciplinarity is necessary not only because it is a true reflection of the global or total nature of the world, but also because the latter changes quickly – education must train minds to adapt to change – and because such adaptability is better prepared by means of general, interdisciplinary education than with training fragmented into disciplines. This type of education will counterbalance and complement the increasing trend towards greater specialization brought about by scientific and technological development.

Interdisciplinarity is needed not only within the area of the exact and natural sciences, but also between these and the human and social sciences. Studying, understanding and solving the world's major problems, such as hunger, poverty, ignorance, sickness and the ecosystem, requires interdisciplinarity. Hunger, for instance, is often not due to lack of food, but to poverty, exploitation, the profit motive (the replacement of food crops by commercial farming for export) and to natural disasters (drought, floods, etc.). The solution cannot be found without combining economic and social measures with scientific research (particularly in the area of bio-technology). This example appears to have nothing to do with interculturality. In fact, it is a 'negative'. It shows up the error into which some authors fall when they blame culture for economic backwardness, whether in terms of Rostow's 'long-term fatalism' or Galbraith's 'poverty equilibrium', whereby the poor 'come to terms' with their poverty, since any technical innovation implies a risk of failure which could lead to famine or even death. Yet surveys conducted in Thailand and India have shown that illiterate, poor or outcast (in the case of India) peasants were not the last to adopt new cultural practices (Lê Thành Khôi, 1967, p. 30). And countries which were considered thirty years ago as 'underdeveloped' because their religions (Hinduism, Buddhism, Confucianism) 'hindered' economic growth, have become industrialized with rates of growth, over the last fifteen years, higher than in the United States, France or even Japan. The key to the lasting success achieved by Japan, which was the first non-European country to become industrialized, was sought by many western economists in Zen, the Buddhist doctrine which advocates meditation and concentration to achieve 'awareness' (Lê Thành Khôi, 1992, p. 152-71).

Conversely, health is indeed a cultural problem so long as it is defined not as 'the absence of sickness', but rather as a 'harmonious functioning of

87

the human organism within its environment'. This is why the 'traditional' medical practices of Africa and Asia do not consider sickness or the sick person independently of underlying social and cultural factors and treat them not only with medicines, but also by using symbolic operations which are designed to restore the equilibrium of life forces. Western medicine, which has achieved resounding success thanks to scientific experimentation, has often failed either to cure or to understand a cure. It is above all an 'individualistic' form of medicine, which basically discards the economic, ecological and cultural origins of sickness, and equates health needs with demand for care, that is, with the expenditure an individual can afford according to his income.

In primary school, interdisciplinarity is favoured owing to the fact that there is only one teacher for all subjects. He/she can therefore take a problem and examine it from all its different aspects. In Africa, if rural dwellers are asked what there needs are, three problems stand out: water, food and health. Although the problem of water is less acute in the humid regions of Asia, the last two are common to all southern peasants. They are not only technical, but also social (water rights) and cultural, as we saw earlier in the case of health. The same goes for food: people do not eat any food in the company of anyone and meals are often subject to quite elaborate rituals. The teacher will introduce intercultural aspects by looking at the habits and customs of other peoples, at how they were able (or unable) to solve their problems and why. In Viet Nam, for instance, an author gives the following description of the difficulties faced by doctors in their efforts to spread hygiene in rural areas:

Even with plenty of goodwill, things are not so simple. You realise that before you can convince people to dig a well, they must overcome their fear of the underground dragon; to get them to exterminate mosquitoes, you must convince them that there is no disrespect in powdering the altar of their ancestors with insecticide. You have to tell them millions of times: boil water before you drink it. (In: Lê Thành Khôi, 1992, p. 145).

In intermediate school, some countries already adopt an integrated approach to teaching the natural sciences (physics, chemistry, biology and technology) and even the social sciences (history, geography, economics, sociology), which facilitates an interdisciplinary approach. It is more in secondary schooling and above that this is most difficult to organize owing to its novelty, existing single-discipline traditions, the number of teachers involved and the complexity of the matter.

DISCIPLINES AND INTERCULTURALITY

If we stay in the area of teaching by discipline, let us see how intercultural aspects can be introduced.

Learning foreign languages generally implies studying the civilizations from which they emanate. For small countries, it is worth teaching one or, even better, two widely used languages. A child begins by learning the language of his environment, because it is part of his identity and because he learns better and more quickly than he would in another language with which he is less well acquainted. Once he has mastered the basic mechanisms, he will go on to learn a foreign language. This can provide an excellent form of mental exercise, especially when the structure or the morphology of the foreign language is different from that of the mother tongue (e.g. languages with or without declensions). Also, learning a foreign language provides a better insight into one's own. And lastly, within the culture to which the language belongs, it provides an introduction to logical categories, to moral values, to the social significance of the uses and variations of language, which is beneficial not only for communication, but also for a sense of differentiation, ordering and mastery.

Take for instance the concept of reason. It comes from the Latin *ratio*, which originally meant computation and which has kept this connotation in common language. Reason is the faculty to think and to act not only according to feelings but also according to interest. But *ratio* also conveys the Greek *logos*, which stands for coherent speech, ordered according to universal principles, or universalizable in that it corresponds to 'reality' itself. In Chinese, reason is *li*. In fact, *li* refers to the veins in jade; these are sought by the stonecutter, who follows them with his tool, carving out a square, a disk or a half-moon shape, according to the line of the vein and without following any preconceived model. 'Reasoning is looking for the formal structure of reality, to which action can be adapted' (L. Vandermeersch). It is easy to see the difference between this concept and the European one. It is just as effective for acting on the world if you think of the economic success of Japan, and more recently of the Republic of Korea, Taiwan, Hong Kong, Singapore and China itself, all countries based on Chinese civilization or subject to Chinese influence (Republic of Korea, Japan).

From the point of view of educating the individual, literary studies should concentrate less on the history, criticism and aesthetics of styles and schools than on the human significance of the major works of national and world literature. It is in these that the adolescent will discover the many aspects of human nature, its universal characteristics and its variations in space and in time, and it will be through a continuing dialogue with them that he will deepen and refine his own personality. For this reason, a detailed analysis of a few major works is more profitable than a course in literary history illustrated with selected passages, however well they might have been chosen. Comparing national and foreign texts concerning similar themes can bring an added benefit: the term 'humanism' will acquire its full meaning when, alongside Shakespeare, Molière, Tolstoi, Goethe and Cervantes, will be taught the Indian *jatakas*, Lo Pen's *Lake shores*, the *History of Kieu* of Viet Nam or the oral literatures of Africa.

Literary studies will be combined with those of history, geography and economic, social and political institutions, which help integrate the individual within his environment, then in international society. When he leaves school, the adolescent should know how government works, so that he can fully exercise his rights and his obligations, and so that he has acquired a notion of the major world problems he has heard about in the press, radio and television and which history and geography have already helped him understand. These latter subjects will have to relinquish their event-oriented, nationalistic and even racist approach, which still exists, in order resolutely to adopt a universal outlook, the only one conceivable at a time when the progress of creative and destructive science has developed a bond of solidarity between nations and people.

Geography and history should show the close interdependence of physical and human phenomena, civilizations and peoples. While local examples and regional studies can catch the child's attention because they concern events close to hand, such as the place he lives in, its crops, its industries, even situated within the larger framework of a country, such methods require a lot of time and can lay too much stress on provincial issues at the expense of a global point of view. It is therefore preferable to give more importance to general geography and history, which transcend political frontiers – seen as the outcome of treaties – and take a global look at problems of population, production and consumption, communications, transport and trade, wars and peace, religious and ideological movements and contacts between different civilizations.

Geography and history are usefully complementary, the one being an effort to apprehend the permanent aspects of the way man adapts to his environment (taking account of technical changes), while the other narrates and explains his evolution in terms of his own creations and the contributions of other cultures. While national history develops in the child a love for his country and prepares him for his future role as citizen, it should show him what his country has received from the world just as much as what it has given. In most countries' history books, historical truth takes second place to national pride: contacts between States are reduced to wars, which are blamed on others or which are justified by references to some 'civilizing mission', the 'inferiority' of other peoples or the 'defence of liberty'. It is not a question of denying international wars and conflicts; they need to be explained as objectively as possible, while appropriate stress should be laid on the much greater importance of continual cultural exchanges for the life and development of peoples. For the child to gain awareness of mankind's common heritage, he should be introduced to history as a unit, as a coherent whole, in a logical (i.e. in this case chronological) order, and not as a juxtaposition of individual 'histories' according to the impression given by fragmented curricula.

World history shows that no culture is 'pure' and that the major civilizations have been built up by borrowing from other civilizations, by which they were fertilized. In Asia, Japan benefited from imported writing, Buddhism, Confucianism and political institutions from China via Korea. China was enlivened by Indian Buddhism, just like Viet Nam and the other two countries. Islam took over the Greek heritage and passed it on to medieval Europe, adding its own philosophical, scientific and technical contributions.

In Europe, the two pillars of any advanced civilization – writing and paper – originated in Asia. The Greek alphabet, which was passed on to the Latins by the Etruscans, was adapted from the Phoenicians, which was therefore the origin of European alphabets. Paper came originally from Egyptian papyrus, then from parchment made in Pergamum, before being replaced in the twelfth century by rag paper of Chinese origin introduced by the Arabs. In medical, mathematical and philosophical matters, Greece borrowed a great deal from Egypt, Mesopotamia and India.

What is evident in the world today is the uninterrupted development of science and technology, typified by the media and particularly the computer, which has brought about profound changes in all fields. This has resulted in two demands: scientific and technical education for all and not merely for an elite; and the development of a critical approach, since the flow of information arising from the media is so great that an individual could easily be overwhelmed by it and not know how to use it. The school should teach the individual to be active and critical in order to sort out useful information, to have an opinion on the content of texts and to distinguish the objective from the subjective: a picture shown on a screen is not necessarily 'true', because the opposite picture might just have easily been shown, just as any two or three passers-by will not express the average opinion of 'the man in the street' because they were consciously or unconsciously 'selected' by the presenter.

Many children do not benefit from scientific and technical education since, in many developing countries, it begins only at the secondary level to which they do not have access (due to the heavy drop-out at the primary level and very selective entry requirements to the secondary level). To counteract this, it is necessary to introduce or to strengthen scientific and technical teaching in primary school.

Such teaching should be integrated. Scientific education should not consist of a series of nature lessons dealing with animals, plants and minerals. It should teach the child to observe and understand the surrounding world and present it as a whole, and to study the problems created by this world: why a tree does or does not bear fruit; why it does or does not rain; why there is a drought; why there is pollution, etc. The idea is to bring forth an attitude of observation, critical reasoning and synthesis on the basis of nature study. Some countries give 'nature study' lessons at the primary school, which unfortunately are based more on history and geography than on science and technology. The reason for this is that frequently the qualifications of the teachers and the scientific and technical equipment available to them do not allow it to be otherwise. However, some simple equipment could be assembled from local materials. Some countries have set up scientific equipment production centres (in Africa: Kenya, Nigeria, Ghana and Zambia), an initiative which should be encouraged everywhere.

A common misconception is that technically poor environments do not possess the necessary resources to awaken the faculties of observation, reason and invention in the child. Of course, if all forms are round and no object is square, the child will be unable to imagine a square, unless he is taught to do so by books. In fact, there are always resources available, even if they are limited. I might mention the game (known as *awélé* among the Baoulé, but also found throughout Africa and a large part of Asia), which consists of moving counters in the form of seeds or stones over one or two cyclic paths in the form of two or four rows of boxes carved out of a wooden block or simply marked on the ground. There are thousands of variations of the game. To play *awélé*, players place four counters in each of his/her six boxes and play in turn. A player will take all of the counters from one box and place them one by one in the following boxes, going from right to left. If the opponent's box where he places his last counter also contains two or three counters besides, he takes them all and removes them from the game; he also takes all the counters from the opponent's boxes preceding that one without interruption, if they contain two or three counters. As long as he can, each player must keep supplying counters for the other player. The winner is the player who acquires half the counters (i.e. twenty-four).

This game of strategy, which is as complex as chess or draughts, encourages spatial structuring, logical analysis and mental calculation, in other words cognitive development in general. *Awélé* can be used to illustrate combinatorial analysis, the reduction of a relational graph, the determination of a winning strategy by recurrence and probability calculations (A. Deledico and A. Traore, 1979, p. 36-42).

All educators agree on the educational benefits of the game: it contributes not only to intellectual development, but also to socialization, since playing it means observing rules laid down by the group. Apart from their novelty value, introducing games such as *awélé* in 'northern' schools would also have the advantage of eliminating or attenuating existing prejudice against the scientific and technical spirit of the 'south'.

One concern which is shared by developed and developing countries alike is the environment, or better still the ecosystem, that is, relations between man and his environment. Although the awareness of industrial and urban nuisance is nothing new, it was only in the 1970s that the industrial countries and more recently the developing countries evolved an ecological conscience, whereby this type of nuisance is no longer looked upon as an accident of growth, but in terms of its unavoidable consequences which could lead to the destruction of the world. Ecological education tries to make children and adults aware of this situation and to inculcate in them a sense of responsibility towards the biosphere. Nature is also part of the common heritage of mankind. The lesson must not only be descriptive, however. The teacher must look for the causes of environmental degradation and must examine critically what is reported in the media. Is it due to the number of inhabitants or to the growth of industry? Barry Commoner put together some significant statistics (quoted in *Population*, May-June 1972): in the period 1946-1968, the production of non-organic nitrate fertilizers, insecticides, phosphate detergents, tetraethyl lead and nitrous oxides (in cars), and plastic beer bottles, grew between 267% and 845%, while the population grew between 30 and 42% only. And in the north, the Netherlands, where the population density is as high as 350 inhabitants per km^2, are less affected by pollution than the United States, where the density is 22 inhabitants per km^2.

Lastly education must create an awareness of other kinds of global interdependence (economic, political, etc.). With only a fifth of the world's population, the rich countries consume two-thirds of its resources, of which a large proportion is wasted. This consumption is taken not only from their own territories, but also from those of the south. Thus, soya beans are exported from Brazil to feed European cattle, or meat from Guatemala, etc. to the detriment of the land-holdings of small farmers and

93

for the benefit of a minority of local proprietors and the wealthy in western countries, which are connected through the activities of agro-multinationals. In other words, the poor feed the rich. Any truly international or internationalistic education must convince western public opinion that the latter cannot preach lower population growth in the south without changing its own standard of living (food, paper consumption, etc.), thereby releasing resources to improve the condition of the Third World.

All we have said presupposes some kind of ethical standards. Ethics are an integral part of culture and it is not possible to separate cultural development and ethical development. Are there such things as universal values? All religions have laid down sets of rules, some of which are the same. According to Buddhism, laymen must abstain from destroying life, from taking what is not given, from having unlawful sexual relations, from lying, and from drinking intoxicating beverages (the monks are subject to five extra prohibitions). The Bible, followed by the Koran, commands, apart from the worship of one God, that parents must be respected and that it is forbidden to kill, to commit adultery, to steal, to bear false witness or to covet the property and wife of one's neighbour. In practice, these rules are not always observed, even by the religious community. Their non-observance is sometimes justified by somewhat dubious arguments. In the Japan of the *samurai*, for instance, some opinions held that if you were set upon by an enemy, it was the sword which killed and not the hand holding it, while others justify the act of killing if it saves others from killing (i.e. rather sin than let sin), etc. On the other side of the Pacific, during the conquest of America, the Catholic Church did not consider the Indians as 'men', which justified their killing and exploitation, and contempt for treaties and promises.

Similarly, all the major religions agree on the equality of men and women, which did not prevent the social condition of women being inferior to that of men in practically all societies. The great majority of countries declare that they want democracy and respect for human rights. In the north, as in the south, however, violations of these rights abound. Moreover, the same words can be interpreted in different ways. Does democracy itself carry the same meaning for the ruler and the ruled, the one who exploits and the exploited?

Without being too pessimistic, it seems to me, however, that education can propose a number of values on which there can be a majority, if not unanimous consensus: scientific values such as the spirit of observation and demonstration, and critical reasoning; social values such as democracy, justice, honesty and respect for others (for their persons and their culture), preservation of the environment, or the struggle for international understanding and peace. We should not overlook the difficulties, nevertheless, of moral and civic education, when daily practice belies recommended standards. How can one teach: democracy when the law is ignored? socialism, when the theft of public property is prevalent? respect for human rights in a discriminatory and racist society? Socialism thought it could create a 'new man' by inculcating its ideology in children and young people in the classroom, through the media and in youth organizations. Too many discrepancies appeared in practice, however, between words and facts, and facts were stronger than words. If only a small minority of the population is responsible for violating the law, for discrimination and racism, it may still be hoped that education for democracy, human rights and mutual understanding among cultures will bear fruit. The difference between the sociologist and the educator is that the latter is optimistic.

ARTISTIC AND LITERARY SENSITIVITY AND CREATIVITY

The intellectual concept of culture as heritage has turned the school into an institution for the transmission of knowledge via the teacher rather than for personal expression and creative activities by the child. As the 'object' of teaching, the child is reduced to the role of a receiver of what the adult considers necessary for his/her future social and vocational existence, while the child is in the first instance responsible for his/her own future and is required to participate more and more actively in the construction of the being as he/she develops. Meanwhile, culture, as we have said, consists not only of acquired knowledge but is a dynamic entity which constantly absorbs and interprets all the new objects with which it comes into contact. Just as the school should be open to the national and international environment, it should also leave room for imagination and emotion, to the development of artistic and literary sensitivity and creativity. The teacher will no longer simply be the transmitter of knowledge but a mediator between the child and the world, who helps the child to discover himself/herself to realise all his/her abilities, to live in pleasant surroundings, in harmony with the self and taking the environment into account, and thus to achieve one of mankind's basic needs – joy.

In this joy, art, in its broadest sense (in other words including literature), forms one of the highest sources. Education should not only inculcate good taste and aesthetic feeling, but also creativity, and the capacity to imagine, to express one's self, etc. What is beauty? For a long time now we have ceased to believe in absolute beauty. Beauty is without concept, as Kant said. We cannot define it because taste is always personal. I do not know if the feelings that I have before a work of art are shared by my neighbour; it is purely subjective. According to Valéry, beauty is 'that which drives to despair'.

All civilizations have tried to circumscribe beauty, to lay down the canons of beauty. It continues to be unattainable. Furthermore, it changes because our way of looking at things evolves thanks to artists who have broken new ground. It is often coming into contact with another form of art, or a different way of seeing the world and people, which provokes invention. After Alexander the Great invaded India, Hellenism influenced the arts of Western and Central Asia, particularly town planning and sculpture. Whereas until that time, Buddhist artists had not dared represent Buddha in human form, but used symbols to indicate his presence (such as the wheel or the lotus flower), the school of Gandhara was perhaps the first to model his face on that of the Greek Apollo, except for the smile. With the expansion of Buddhism, the same image came to permeate China, Japan, Korea and Viet Nam.

The adventure of modern European art is familiar. The discovery of Japanese engravings was as decisive for the development of Impressionism as that of African sculpture for Cubism. In the middle of the nineteenth century, painters were in danger of reaching a dead end owing to the emergence of photography. The Japanese engraving brought them solutions, thanks to its absence of realism, its striking, formless colours, its two-dimensional perspective, and its use of flat tones. 'Hiroshige is a wonderful impressionist', wrote Pissaro. In southern France, Van Gogh looked for the equivalent of Japan. He wrote to his brother Theo: 'Here, after a time, your vision changes; it becomes more Japanese and you feel colour differently'. In another letter, he praised Hokusai's lines and drawing techniques. Referring to one of his engravings, he wrote: 'The waves are like claws, and you feel the boat is caught in them'.

At the beginning of the twentieth century, it was Negro art that contributed to the renewal of the plastic arts. Picasso, Matisse and others were struck by its extreme freedom in attaining an essential truth, which is not only that offered by the mere sight of things, but also that imagined, thought or felt by the artist, who abstracts forms in order to convey the idea they express. In the same period, jazz emerged in the United States from American Negro vocal folklore, which combined Protestant religious hymns and popular European themes in its ballads, and then in its 'blues'. It was to spread beyond American society to conquer the world.

All these experiences show that beauty is not entirely relative. People from different cultures can still appreciate the same works which have met with general approval.

While, generally speaking, artistic and literary education provide access to the rich diversity of cultures and to their aesthetic criteria, creativity is a very complicated subject. Despite innumerable studies, there is no agreement on its nature, the way it manifests itself and the manner in which it is carried out, nor on ways of developing it. Most authors link it to four abilities: fluidity ('to produce a large number of ideas'); flexibility ('to give very varied replies arising from different origins'); originality ('to produce ideas not associated with the obvious, the usual and the ordinary'); preparation ('to develop, to broaden and to improve on ideas'). These various characteristics can be found as much in scientific creativity as in artistic and literary creativity, but they may not necessarily all occur in one person, and the way creativity operates is not always comparable depending on the mode of expression (verbal, tactile, sound, etc.) (Gratiot-Alphandéry, 1983).

Even if we do not yet know which is the 'best' form of education to stimulate the child's creativity, there are at least some interesting experiments from several countries which would enable us to gain some insights.

Poetry is the ability of words to recreate the perceived world by liberating language from its conventions and reinventing forms and meaning. How is it then that the child finds it boring rather than attractive? The reason is due to the traditional methods of 'explaining the text' and 'recitation', in which the former becomes a grammatical, semantic and stylistic analysis and the latter a formal exercise employing only the memory. What is really needed is to bring out the deeper meaning of works, the richness of their content and forms, and to resort to imagination and emotion, to arouse in the child the desire and the need to make his own poetry – to read for pleasure and not because he has to. To a certain extent, it is a result of their rejection of school that adults prefer to watch television rather than read. And if they read, they prefer newspapers and detective novels. Yet, whatever proposals were made about the disappearance of the 'Gutenberg Galaxy', the printed word remains the basic instrument of culture since it conveys the legacy of all humanity and leads to confrontation and criticism. Thus, it is the role of the school to teach lively and critical reading, both for the written and the spoken word.

Theatre extends and completes this education. At the same time it represents the real and the imaginary. It brings language to the fore but employs other means: characters, scenery, lighting, movement, colour. All the senses are required to grasp the meaning of the dramatic text. In the traditional school approach, an analysis and an explanation is given by the teacher; even if the latter asks questions, it is through his own approach that the pupils have to understand the author's message. They do not have to participate. On the other hand, an actual theatrical production allows them to express themselves. It not only brings the text alive but restores the rich communication flow among pupils, and between them and the teacher. The outcome is pleasure for everybody which could not have been achieved by a simple reading.

Music opens the child's and adolescent's mind to other aspects of the world, that of sounds and rhythms. The teaching of this subject should encourage expression through singing, playing musical instruments and dancing. This implies active and global methods (firstly practice, secondly analysis) and the involvement of the child in his/her own training. Music has the advantage of transcending linguistic barriers and of communicating directly with the heart. With the present spread of disks and audiovisual productions, there is a meeting and blending of East and West, North and South: the child is brought into contact with all sorts of musical traditions beyond the local one, and enters the universal.

The plastic arts are more difficult to comprehend. Of course, drawing is taught at school, but the ultimate objective of developing the abilities of observation, good taste and imagination may not always be achieved, in the same way that the teaching of poetry kills interest in poetry. Here too, we must have confidence in the child's spontaneity, for whom drawing is a natural way of conveying a personal vision of the world at each stage of development. This does not rule out the teacher's critical observations, not to pour scorn or to restrain, but to encourage creative activity and to draw attention to the beauty to be found in daily life. We know about the remarkable experience of Ramses Wissa Wassef (1914-74), who founded a tapestry school in a poor district of Cairo, where weaving frames were made available to children who were entirely free to create whatever they wanted. The vitality of the artistic tradition among these out-of-school young people led them to create masterpieces, which the world immediately recognized when the tapestries were exhibited in Basel in 1958.

This experience also shows that cultural and artistic education depend less on materials than on an educational approach, which trusts both the child's creativity and the teacher's faith. There is nowhere, even in poverty, where one does not find resources capable of arousing the abilities of observation, logic and invention among children. I mentioned earlier the game of *awélé*. Similarly, the meanings contained in fairy stories and proverbs are rooted in specific socio-cultural and universal contexts.

In conclusion, the school should move away from an exclusively intellectualist approach, which it has so far preferred, and must return to its basic vocation, which is to fulfil the child's abilities by enriching them with all the planet's resources. This is the only way that the school will give children the means of understanding their society and epoch, but also to find their proper balance and to create their own life.

PROBLEMS OF IMPLEMENTATION

Introducing intercultural education as presented above raises many difficult problems.

In school, as we said earlier, it should not constitute an additional discipline, but should permeate all disciplines. This means that the timetable should not be increased, but merely rearranged so that literature, history, geography, the arts, etc., make room for other cultures than the national culture. This rearrangement can be done in the light of an understanding of the present and of a past which explains the present. In classes where several cultures are represented, the teacher should give them most of his attention, using all the written and audio-visual material at his disposal, and making the children and possibly even their parents express themselves. In pre-primary and primary school, the main effort would be to create awareness. This would be continued at intermediate and secondary level with a more in-depth approach to the questions.

Three problems arise: (a) the preparation of teaching materials, especially textbooks; (b) the role of the media; and (c) teacher training.

TEACHING MATERIAL

Alongside teachers' qualifications, the lack of teaching material is the worst problem for poor countries, especially in primary schools. On the other hand, many of these countries, especially in Africa, are multicultural, so that many ethnic groups may be represented in the classroom. The teacher can delve into the rich treasure of popular literature (tales and fables, proverbs and sayings), objects and games, as well as art pictures, to open up the minds of the children to an awareness of others. It is true that Black African culture is very unified, probably on account of the system of technically limited self-subsistence agricultural production and communal land-ownership, whence a certain outlook on the world, a certain way of living, thinking, feeling and educating, which is widespread. Underneath

99

that relative unity, however, there is a great diversity of beliefs and practices. The teacher may compare, for instance, the tales of 'The Spider and the Hare' in West Africa and masks from the savanna and the forest, to draw attention to similarities and differences.

Generally speaking, in order to study any one culture in particular, it is better to refer to internal rather than external sources. It stands to reason that a local author will understand the culture better than a foreigner, because he has been brought up among values and practices, the meanings of which have been given to him by the community. But there are also drawbacks to familiarity: the local author may fail to see the problems or might not have any second thoughts about particular institutions. The stranger, on the other hand, provided that he can overcome any ethnocentrism, can observe with greater detachment and less subjectivity. Furthermore, two people belonging to the same culture may have different opinions according to their social class, their sex, their past experience or their ideology. For instance, here are two different interpretations of sexuality in Islam, one male and the other female. For Abdelwahab Bouhdiba, 'the Islamic model appears as a harmonious synthesis and a constant adjustment of enjoyment and faith ... Social values enhance both the majesty of holiness and the power of the libido ... Islamic life hence shall consist of a complementary alternation between and invocation of the divine word and physical love' (Bouhdiba, 1982, p. 7-8). Fatna Ait Sabbah, on the other hand, holds a quite different opinion. While sexuality is not stated as being opposed to order, 'its most uncontrollable, most versatile human component, which is the richest in potential, namely desire, is identified at the same time as the source and substance of the unlawful ... the incarnation of the forces of disorder' (Ait Sabbah, 1982, p. 189-190). Yet the desire which subverts reason, the foundation of order and the seat of religion, is woman. This is why she is relegated to the home, where her beauty is expressed in silence and obedience. According to a saying from the Maghreb, a woman leaves her home only twice: to go to her husband and to her grave (Driss, 1979: I, p. 66).

One essential task is to revise books and textbooks, whenever the ideas and pictures they contain seriously infringe the truths held by and the respect for others. Two articles published in the UNESCO *Courier* of March 1979 looked at racism in school textbooks. Colonization and disguised forms of slavery, writes the American Beryl Banfield, are presented as so many benefits for the peoples of the Third World, because they have brought them discipline and technical benefits of which they were not aware.

With reference to the Maoris of New Zealand, 'nothing is said of the destruction of their culture, and the use of force to impose another is also justified by the need to keep the peace'. In North America, the culture of the Eastern Forest Indians is presented as inferior to that of the Europeans, whereas 'Indian society was politically more advanced than the European as far as the participation of women in political decision-making was concerned, and more generally speaking, the role of each individual in the life of the community. The organization of the Iroquois Confederation was in fact to serve as a model for the American colonies when they decided to found a new nation'.

Ethnocentrism and racism are by no means exclusively western. They are also to be found in the south, or at least in some parts. In the same number of the UNESCO *Courier*, the Argentine Hugo Ortega considers how the history of America is presented in works recently published in Argentina. Everything is seen exclusively from a 'white' and 'western' point of view. America was 'discovered', which means 'that the continent, its inhabitants and its wealth only acquired value to the extent that they were found and recognized from and by the centre of the world, that is, Europe. It is not surprising, then that civilization (clothes, big ships, white men, the ability to impose names on places and people) should be on the side of America ... The oldest inhabitant of the American continent is depicted pejoratively, half naked, savage, dressed in feathers, irrational and inferior to the European white man ... All this amounts to a denial and a kind of cultural genocide'.

No society, as we have said, is so poor that it is unable to provide some resources for education, including scientific and technical education. Any shortages can be made up with international co-operation, such as the twinning of schools, with one side offering books and other teaching material, and the other side tales, poems, drawings and handicrafts. Teacher and pupil exchanges, while most beneficial for all concerned, are obviously not easy to organize for the poorer countries. In 1953, UNESCO set up a network of 'associated schools', whose aim was to contribute towards international understanding and peace by emphasizing world problems and the role of the United Nations, human rights, the knowledge of other countries and their cultures, people and their environment. UNESCO encourages the development of new teaching programmes, materials and methods on these themes, the dissemination of information, as well as contacts and exchanges between participating institutions, to which it supplies documentation and which it helps to organize workshops and seminars. From thirty-three secondary schools in fifteen countries in 1953, the network had grown by 1992 to over 2,800 establishments at all levels in 114 countries.

THE ROLE OF THE AUDIO-VISUAL MEDIA

The audio-visual media, and especially television, play a considerable part in the life of many children and young people, for the better and for the worse. For this reason, apart from their role as teaching resources, they should be open to guidance and critical study, to enable the individual to sort information, and to use it for his personal development, while avoiding being manipulated. The help of adults is essential for profitable use of the media, providing, of course, that they themselves maintain a critical approach. This critical education should begin in the family, where parents should subject themselves to a degree of discipline in their 'consumption' of television, if only to preserve communication in the home. They should be backed up in this by the teachers, who can organize discussion groups concerning a particular programme or film. Students learn better when they play an active part, such as having to prepare a discussion, look up the necessary documentation and answer questions. For instance, in the case of a documentary concerning a foreign culture, the teacher can ask questions such as: How was it made? Did local people participate? Did they play a part in the programme or film? Who were they (men, women, young people, adults, their social status)? Were their opinions similar or opposed; if so, on what points and why? etc. The teacher might even bring in people who have travelled in the country and are familiar with the culture concerned. A critical spirit will emerge from this confrontation of different points of view, from the observation of possible contradictions within the material and between the latter and other data, from checking whether statements have been properly demonstrated, etc.

Cinema, television and radio can all be very useful in encouraging individuals to discover others, to open up their horizons and to respect differences, by giving accounts of cultural events (art or photographic exhibitions, theatrical tours, recitals), by presenting honest documentaries, films and programmes from other countries, by organizing debates on chosen themes, etc. They should avoid showing countries and groups of population in terms of limiting and inaccurate stereotypes and clichés. The ethics of journalism is not applied everywhere, is not always observed where it does exist or gives rise to different interpretations, and above all excludes any reference to responsibilities towards the international community. The journalists themselves can be manipulated by governments or by economic and financial sources, who stand to gain from 'disinforming' public opinion in order to attain a particular objective.

TEACHER TRAINING

All of the above arguments show how extremely important teacher training is for the success of genuine intercultural education. Intercultural aspects should permeate all the subjects taught in teacher training schools, such as history, sociology, psychology, etc., whereas most of the time they are absent. Comparative education, in particular, is taught in very few countries and is not considered as a priority.

Those responsible for teaching multicultural classes should be given a minimum amount of information concerning the cultures they are dealing with, in order to avoid misunderstanding the values of individual groups and the significance the latter attach to particular signs and symbols. They should know, for instance, that in Asian and African cultures, students do not look straight at the teacher. This conveys an attitude of respect: it is not considered polite to look straight at a person who is older than oneself or in a superior position. Also, in some cultures, 'yes' is conveyed not by nodding the head up and down but by shaking it from side to side.

Knowledge is necessary, but perhaps even more so sensitivity, an open mind, the ability to put oneself in the place of others, all qualities which can be learned as well. For instance, in a Parisian suburb (Nanterre), one of those where racist incidents have taken place, the headmistress of a nursery school, where 45% of the 260 children are of foreign origin, mainly from the Maghreb and Black Africa, has turned her ethnic patchwork into 'a source of wealth, a positive ferment', to use her own expression. An article in the review *Sources*, published by UNESCO (June 1991) describes this experience based on the notions of peace, respect for human rights and awareness of different cultures. Starting from the idea that respect for life means respect for nature, the children there grow vegetables, and keep cats, hamsters, dogs and snails. That gives rise to discussions on the reasons for cages, on life and on liberty. The focus shifts from the vegetable garden to the kitchen, from the kitchen to cultures, but also to writing and arithmetic or recipes. No occasion is wasted for the children to celebrate and every festival of one of the countries from which they come is an opportunity to try out special recipes, for discussions, for looking at the globe and for games. The Chinese New Year is celebrated with jasmine tea and the end of Ramadan with henna make-up. Music and dancing sway from jazz to African rhythms, and the poetry workshop jumps from the French poet Prévert to a Maghreb litany. One course, which has been called 'by the waterside', has focused on the frequent occurrence of this image in world poetry. The school believes in the value of exchanging views. No subject is taboo and if a child announces the death of a grandmother, the news is

103

never met with an embarrassed silence. Even so, the children are initiated 'in respecting the intimacy of others'. A spirit of tolerance in the face of hardship is also learnt through the presence of a number of handicapped children. Besides, the school has made a gesture to the parents, who are regularly invited to attend celebrations and to share their own culture, for instance by telling stories or preparing traditional dishes (N. Michaud, 1991, p. 14).

It is through this kind of experience, if applied, extended and deepened at all levels, that the school can imbue children and young people with the feeling that, to use a Confucian expression, 'the men of the four seas are brothers'.

REFERENCES

Abdallah- Pretceille, M. 1990. *Vers une pédagogie interculturelle.* 2nd ed. Paris, Publications de la Sorbonne.
Abdel Malek, A.; Pandeya, A.N., eds. 1981. *Intellectual creativity in endogenous culture.* Tokyo, The United Nations University.
Ait Sabbah, F. 1982. *La femme dans l'inconscient muselman.* Paris, Le Sycomore.
Banfield, B. 1979. How racism takes root. *Courier* (Paris, UNESCO), March.
Boas, F. 1965. *The mind of primitive man.* Rev. ed. New York, Free Press.
Bouhdiba, A. 1982. *La sexualité en Islam.* 3rd ed. Paris, Presses universitaires de France.
Camilleri, C. 1984. *Cultural anthropology and education.* Paris, UNESCO: International Bureau of Education.
Coleman, J.S. 1966. *Equality of educational opportunity.* Washington.
Deledico, A.; Traore, M. 1979. Apprendre en jouant: les jeux africains, une initiation aux mathématiques. *Recherche, pédagogie et culture* (Paris), no. 40, mars-avril, p. 38-42.
Desmeuzes, J. 1986. *L'action culturelle à l'école.* Paris, Enfance heureuse.
Driss, A. 1979. *L'histoire de l'éducation et les idées pédagogiques en Ifriqiya (depuis Ibn Sahnun jusqu'à Ibn Khaldun).* 3 vol. Paris, Université Paris III. (Thèse de doctorat)
Goody, J. 1977. *The domestication of the savage mind.* Cambridge, UK, Cambridge University Press.
Gratiot-Alphandéry, H. 1983. *Pour une éducation esthétique interdisciplinaire: objectifs, orientation, méthodologie.* Paris, UNESCO. (ED-83/WS-79)
Hainaut, Louis d'. 1986. *Interdisciplinarity in general education.* UNESCO, Paris. (Document: Division of Educational Sciences, Content and Methods))
Lê Thành Khôi. 1967. *L'industrie de l'enseignement.* Paris, Minuit.
—. 1991. *L'éducation: cultures et sociétés.* Paris, Publications de la Sorbonne.
—. 1992. *Culture, créativité et développement.* Paris, L'Harmattan.
—, et al. 1984. Culture et développement. *Revue Tiers monde* (Paris), janvier-mars.
Michaux, N. 1991. L'ouverture à l'autre. *Sources* (Paris, UNESCO), juin.
Ortega, H. 1979. Through other eyes. *Courier* (Paris, UNESCO), March.
Snyders, G. 1986. *La joie à l'école.* Paris, Presses universitaires de France.

CHAPTER V

The challenges to education systems from the contemporary cultural dynamic

P. Dasen, P. Furter and G. Rist

I. SCHOOL CULTURE AND CONTEMPORARY CULTURES

This chapter is intended above all to stimulate a discussion on the relationship between the contemporary cultural scene and educational processes. Certain significant areas of tension can be observed in today's complex societies.

The extension of education systems

First, the extension of school enrolment and, above all, the integration of educational institutions (as well as out-of-school institutions) into 'education systems' has resulted in the reinforcement of the relative autonomy of the culture of these 'systems', which we shall call the school culture. What we mean by this is a system of norms, values and rules of procedure for institutions, laid down by the State in accordance with its social structures, its socio-political and socio-cultural systems, and its history. This school culture manifests itself in the content of teaching (syllabuses and curricula), teaching methods and styles (pedagogy), equipment and classrooms ('educational architecture'), teachers trained according to established methods (teacher training institutions), all of which lead to the development of typical attitudes, behaviour and professional practices (Furter, 1986). The significance of this school culture is evident in the fact that increasingly it tends to reflect only a part of the erudite culture, that part thought to be 'communicable', sufficiently 'indicative' to feature in curricula, even at the risk of becoming a mockery of the cultural dynamic.

Popular culture and school culture

With the increasing stress on industrialization and the services sector, leading to the emergence of a new social structure – the 'programmed society' with its ideas about scientific efficiency – the linkage between popular culture and school culture is changing dramatically. Alongside urbanization, there is the centralization of education and the urbanization of the school culture accompanied by the evolution of other socio-cultural institutions (churches, adult education and cultural activities, vocational training, leisure activities). The 'education system' no longer belongs to the community, making it almost impossible for the local and/or regional authorities to intervene. Such a breakdown reduces the ability of the local or regional community to modify its specific identity, projects and know-how (Furter, 1983).

The culture industry

Finally, the extraordinary modern cultural momentum has multiplied and diversified the agents and institutions involved; the communications media have brought about clashes between cultures that were previously far apart; the sum of these cultures has become a product manufactured by the 'culture industry', sometimes called 'mass culture', such that education only represents one sector – however strategic in the new, modern cultural scene. Culture is no longer created and spread by the institutions of the 'education system' alone. Other institutions (radio and television, religious sects and the military, advertising, the leisure industry and tourism) 'educate', 'train' and 'cultivate' in a more efficient, more continuous manner, and more systematically than all the educational institutions put together – including the out-of-school ones – with their armies of teachers completely overwhelmed by successive crises (Coombs, 1965 and 1985). In addition to the progressive breakdown in all countries of the relationship between culture and the whole of that which we call 'contemporary culture', in the countries of the South there is also the conflict – expressed according to the typical dichotomies beloved of Western thought – between 'tradition' and 'modernity', between (anthropological) 'culture'[1] and 'development'.

CULTURE AS AN ELEMENT IN DEMOCRATIZATION

The modern cultural dynamic has been profoundly affected by the concerns of international organizations and the governments of Member States to define cultural policies and contribute to their introduction in accordance with their means. The concepts of these cultural policies are constantly changing. In the beginning, the question was mainly one of cultural democratization, i.e. the redistribution of the 'benefits' of the dominant culture to a wider public. In this way, artistic creativity and the conservation and distribution of works of art and heritage were encouraged. Then the field of cultural policies was extended to formal and out-of-school education, the culture and communications industry, scientific culture and the popularization of science. Efforts were made to decentralize new institutions and set up better infrastructures (such as the 'Maison de la Culture'). New professions were created with branches for specialized training. Finally, some order was brought to cultural finances and budgets. The fact remains that today the main concern is the setting up of a cultural democracy, through policies that favour the diffusion of cultural property and the democratization of access to works, putting life and strenght into popular culture by placing the collective ownership of institutions, structures and their assets into the hands of the 'users'. In a society increasingly confused by the sheer numbers of its cultural groups, it is essential to ensure the participation of the people in the definition of cultural goals for development. In this way they can prove to themselves and to others that they are equally capable of expressing themselves (Touraine, 1967). This means that priority must be given to daily life in the cultural dynamic, by working to promote sincere human relations, feelings and happiness, to stimulate creativity (and not only creating) and to support communication, confrontation and decentralization (Bassand & Hainard, 1985).

It is not only within cultural policies that the challenge of (cultural) pluralism is evident: the most respectful and attentive understanding together with the awareness that distinct civilizations exist simultaneously – and are in no way convergent – brings into question any reduction of this diversity in order to create 'the' culture. Is the 'loss of direction' experienced by today's societies not related to the great shaking-up of those values we call 'universal', as they are expressed in international law, human rights... and also of 'universal' culture – which does not prevent us from still believing in it – in short, everything which provides the basis for and contributes to that 'universal understanding' still so much desired? Moreover, recent events show that at the very heart of civilizations numerous cultural forms co-exist which, whenn allowed freedem of expression, lead to the breakdown of Nation States.[2]

These events not only call into question the power structures, but they also reveal the vitality of 'cultural survivals' which become cultural activities revealing new identities and calling for the creation of new cultural units. This is true, not only at the level of Nation States, but also within them, since there are communities with neither land nor statehood which today claim their own specific nature and right to exist, either within more democratic and more pluralist States, or as independent States. Let us stress, however, that it is difficult to interpret these movements because the desire for cultural pluralism is accompanied and strengthened by differences of behaviour, attitude and involvement, depending on the socio-economic and socio-professional group.

THE DIFFICULT QUESTION OF LANGUAGE

The choice of language to be used in teaching and the importance of different languages in what can be considered as 'linguistic policies' have, in the past (too), often provoked conflicts, sometimes with tragic results, and great has to be taken to prevent them from spreading, especially with the emergence of nationalist groups. These conflicts arose not only as a consequence of overlooking the significance of language in the process of seeking an identity (see the call for 'mother tongues'!). Rather, they reveal the dilemmas facing such linguistic policies: should 'written' languages systematically take precedence over 'spoken' languages? Should national languages with limited means of diffusion be preferred to 'cross-national' languages which facilitate not only communication, but also the mobility of people? These dilemmas are the result of the exceptional nature of the linguistic factor in the cultural dynamic, or, in other words, its function as an instrument of communication and exchange which is not easily reconciled with its expressive or symbolic function that makes it a particularly efficient instrument in the granting of social status as well as in the cultural integration that goes with the process of seeking identity. In other words, the choice of language may just as easily facilitate communication with foreign countries as it may turn a community in on itself. This also means that language is only one factor among many in the cultural dynamic. But on the other hand it must also be said that symbolically language is an exceptional, specific factor that nothing else can replace.

Even though bilingualism, and even trilingualism, are incresingly recognised by legal and educational authorities, it is still difficult to avoid making minor/major comparisons between certain languages, i.e. the imposition and domination of one language considered as 'superior' with regard to other(s) considered as 'inferior' and destined to become marginal in the long term (Ninyoles, 1977).

It is by no means certain that legal measures will be able to provide solutions (Ninyoles, 1976). Consequently, the surest way of allowing territory to achieve linguistic unit within a pluralist State is by attributing a language to a certain territory. Yet such recognition implies considerable and expensive resources, the effects of which will only be felt in the long term. But, above all, this recognition will not solve the problem of 'migrants', nor will it guarantee human rights. In fact it is this latter principle which will guarantee individuals the services they require in their own language, independent of the place where they happen to be. These are obviously questions which cannot be solved by educational authorities alone, nor by isolated reform or reorganization of the 'education systems'. We are faced here, in fact, by one of the fundamental questions of modern cultural democracy (Petrella, 1976).

The fact is that the language question must be considered in educational circles which, once again, have a strategic role to play. Whatever solutions are envisaged, the fact remains that it is during the years spent at school that the majority, or even the whole of society, strengthens, organizes and absorbs its knowledge, ability and command of the linguistic code(s), at the same time as it is introduced to the values and norms conveyed by that language.

MULTICULTURAL SOCIETIES AND INTERCULTURAL EDUCATION:
AMBIGUOUS ROLES

Here we shall not discuss in detail the recent educational problems caused by consideration of the multicultural nature of all modern societies, nor the attempts to answer those problems with so-called 'intercultural education'. We refer our readers to the excellent bibliography prepared for the IBE by Batelaan & Gundara (1991). Let us simply point out the following important ambiguities:

The ambiguity of words

One must be aware of the differences of definitions used in this field, in particular between those used in English and in French. In the IBE questionnaire sent to member countries in preparation of the forty-third session of the ICE, the following definitions were proposed: 'For the needs of this questionnaire, the term "intercultural" is taken in the sense of interaction between cultures; and the term "multicultural" means mutual coexistence and understanding between various cultures within the same society' (p. 8). In French-speaking countries, the opposite use of these two terms is usual. They speak of multicultural societies, in particular in relation to the co-existence of several groups of different cultural origins, but that does not necessarily imply 'mutual understanding'. In fact, the nature of interaction between different groups depends largely on the attitudes of the host society. In Canada, the use is somewhat different and they speak of the 'policy on multiculturalism' which aims to promote tolerance between individuals and groups.

Of course, in the strict sense, all societies are multicultural, and have always been so: migration and intermixing, including conflicts, are the very essence of history (Camilleri & Cohen-Emerique, 1989). All former colonies, with their ethnic groups within more or less arbitrary borders, and the countries of Eastern Europe which have recently recovered their independence, are eminently multicultural and have, therefore, to face many problems linked to their cultural diversity. Most States seek to promote unity by denying ethnic differences and advocating policies of assimilation; this is the option chosen, for example, by the United States of America (the 'melting pot': *E pluribus unum*) and France (with respect to regional customs).

According to psycho-sociological research, it is possible to argue that this is a bad choice. In fact, even in homogeneous social groups, individuals seek to be different and form subgroups. It appears that the fact of possessing one's own cultural identity and having equal access to resources, in other words when there is the possibility of integration rather than the obligation to assimilate, leads social groups to interact peacefully within a complex society, with respect for and appreciation of its differences (Berry, 1991; Tajfel, 1982; Aboud & Skerry, 1984).

The ambiguity of erudite culture

The basic difference between 'culture' – in the anthropological sense – and erudite culture is important because the role of the latter is ambiguous. Usually it is taken to mean spiritual and intellectual enrichment, thus an improvement of the quality of life. This may often be the case, but ambiguity arises when this erudite culture is imported, imposed or reflects the social domination, whether real or symbolic, of one groupe over another (or one social class over another). If, in addition, the models of erudite culture that are imported are presented as superior to the domestic models, the latter are devalued. Thus, knowing about foreign cultures through the cinema, theatre or music can be, depending on the case, either enriching or, on the contrary, to the detriment of the domestic culture.

The ambiguity of the culture industry

The extraordinary growth of what we can call the culture industry, and especially the development of the mass media (radio, television and cinema) which have invaded the fields of entertainment and leisure, together with other forms of communication such as tourism, has brought about a kind of 'cross-national' culture. This means that nearly everywhere we are listening to the same music, dancing to the same tunes, watching the same television series, smiling at the same cartoons in the newspapers. This 'cross-national' culture, which could easily become the 'world cultural heritage', does not belong to any one society, but forms a kind of hybrid culture, just as certain languages used for international communication (such as English) no longer belong to any one nation. This analogy is significant: just as the development of a lingua franca common to all mankind may be desirable, we may regret the resulting homogenization; just as we may accept the need to speak English, we may feel that this implies external domination and loss of identity.

Moreover, the culture industry, however cross-national it may be, is dominated by certain groups, and in particular by certain economic interests. In this way it is contributing to neo-colonialization and cultural domination.

The ambiguous role of education

Here we use the term 'education' in the usual sense of formal education (or schooling, literacy, etc.). First of all education conveys the erudite culture, and it is often associated with the culture industry in the promotion of cross-national culture. The role of education itself is therefore ambiguous.

The role of education as an instrument of cultural integration has been analysed many times, but the phenomenon must be examined in context. Depending upon the socio-historical context, the conflict between the knowledge and values conveyed by formal education and those conveyed by so-called 'informal' education (in the family, community, etc.), assumes different forms. While on this theme, we could study the 'secondary' or 'perverse' effects of education, which also depend very much on the context: cultural devaluation (e.g. of rural areas, agricultural activities), the conflict between generations, abandonment of the countryside, breakdown of social relations, creation of dominant classes, etc. These effects are well-known, but it is difficult to find the right answer to them.

The ambiguous role of intercultural education

Recently, a lot has been written about 'intercultural' education (Ouellet, 1991; Rey, 1984), i.e. education which aims to promote respect for cultural diversity, mutual understanding and the training of teachers for these purposes. A vast project, not without inbuilt contradictions and traps!

It will, no doubt, figure prominently in the discussions at the forty-fourth session of the ICE. For the moment, let us simply glance at a few of the questions that may be raised in the discussions:

I. Intercultural education is often confused with special arrangements for migrant children: remedial measures, language learning, etc. But these measures are often the expression of assimilation policies, whereas intercultural education should be available to all children with a view to integration.

II. Intercultural teaching is often relegated to peripheral school activities or to subjects which are considered secondary (history, geography, art). A true intercultural education should not consist uniquely of supplementary content, but should be a state of mind that is present in all teaching and throughout the education system.

III. Inconsistency can often be observed between statements concerning intercultural education and the often contrary message which is implicitly conveyed by the institution, which remains essentially monocultural.

IV. Just as often, inconsistency exists between the conciliatory message of intercultural education and the quite different attitudes (ethnocentrism, racism, violence, etc.) conveyed by the family and the media. While education can be a useful vehicle for ethnic values, it remains, nevertheless, dependent on the dominant values of society.

V. Awareness of cultural pluralism does not necessarily lead to peaceful co-existence. Meetings, exchanges, clashes and even conflicts are all integral parts of the cultural dynamic.

TRADITION OR MODERNITY: A FALSE ALTERNATIVE

Even if only for heuristic reasons, we cannot escape the need to return here to the old antinomy of 'tradition' and 'modernity'. In fact, although everybody now agrees that a way round the problem must be found, the invention of the notion of 'cultural development' by UNESCO may prove to be counter-productive because while it claims to protect cultural identity, all it really does is to reaffirm the dominance of 'development' which is considered inescapable, yet necessary and beneficial.

So the important thing is to decide on the meaning of 'development'. The task is certainly just as difficult as finding a definition of 'culture' and the 164 definitions of 'culture' collected by Kroeber and Kluckhohn[3] are nothing compared to the inestimable number of definitions of 'development' that nobody, so far, has collected!

The root of the problem is in the fact that most of these definitions are normative (and say what 'development' should be). It has been said, for example, that 'development consists of all those measures which promote the full bloom of man's potential and make it possible for societies to progress harmoniously', that 'it is concerne not only with economic growth, but also with the well-being of societies', that 'it makes it possible to satisfy basic needs and strengthen cultural identity', that it must be 'humane' or 'long-lasting', etc. This way of presenting 'development' has the enormous advantage of creating immediate widespread agreement concerning its possibilities and desirability since nobody could be against the realization of such generous objectives. But, unfortunately, this type of definition is barely functional because it does not allow concrete identification of the phenomenon to be discussed. This method, in fact, is more of a definition of 'socialism' when it states that it 'abolishes the exploitation of man by man' or that it 'builds a classless society', or even a definition of Christianity when it speaks of 'the religion by which one should love one's neighbour'. If we stick to these formulae – which, incidentally, the followers and believers of these doctrines willingly accept – any outside observer of social reality should conclude that 'development', socialism and Christianity do not (yet) exist anywhere in the world. And yet, there are churches and priests claiming to be Christian, political parties and countries which say (or said) they are socialist, institutions, ministries, banks and plans for 'development'. The misunderstanding lies, therefore, in the manner of defining the concepts, either from the starting point of the values and intentions they are said to possess, or from the facts which are typical of them.

A more sociological definition, then, must be based on observable practices which claim to be working towards 'development', without paying any special attention to those whose intention (which may be presumed, but not necessarily confirmed), consists in working towards the well-being of the under-privileged. Thus, rather than reduce 'development' to a matter of measures of co-operation for development (in the same way as training cannot be confined only to the school system), it should include measures of structural adjustment, the building of infrastructures, modern legal systems, means of communication, the creation of irrigated zones, farmland, the exploitation of basements, employment laws, business relations, etc. Closer examination of these items shows that they are based on a common logic, which leads the various actors in the field of 'development' to act in a variety of ways – which are, sometimes, apparently contradictory

– resulting in a general transformation (and consequently destruction too) of the natural environment and social relations in order to increase the production of merchandise (goods and services) to satisfy creditworthy demand. Any country, in fact, can 'develop' when it creates the means (technical, institutional, etc.) of turning land, water, men and knowledge into 'resources' whose value is determined by the market-place.

Thus, 'development' is above all a real process, a system of practices following a specific logic, far more than an ideal which, according to the UNDP report (from a viewpoint which sounds rather like the old justifications for liberal economy) makes it possible 'to widen the variety of choices available to the individual'.[4]

That being the case, how can 'development' be conceived as a 'cultural' process, unless it is to point out that the only culture conveyed is Western and commercial? 'Development' – conceived as the worldwide extension of a way of organising human relations and man's relations with nature – is, without a doubt – cross-national; this does not imply that it is cross-cultural. Thus, the problem of the relationship between culture and 'development' (or between tradition and modernity) is not solved by creating this 'semantic monster': 'cultural development'.[5]

But if 'development' is historically linked to Western culture and if other cultures cannot benefit from it because it does not correspond to their underlying traditions, should we conclude that we are up against two distinct systems of practice: culture and 'development'? Far from it because, contrary to what is normally thought, 'development' is itself the fruit of a tradition wich it helps to maintain, and any living culture is necessarily a part of modernity. In fact, it is the socio-centric blindness of the West which passes 'development' off as a sort of universal rationality and which describes other cultures as 'traditional' on the pretext that they are against the modernity implied by 'development'. 'Foreigners may have big eyes, but they see nothing' according to an African proverb. In this case it is the Westerners (or the Westernized) who do not understand that the basis of tradition is in all the practices and values which, in any given society, are an integral part of it and that consequently no society – including Western society – can dispose of the shared beliefs which binds its people together as they move towards a common goal, which is made all the more significant by the fact that it is implicit.[6] This misunderstanding leads the Westerner (or the Westernized) to consider only the exotic or folk aspects of traditions, those which are no more than remnants of a past that will be forgotten by the 'march of history'.

On the contrary, in any society, tradition is the mechanism which authorizes and legitimizes change by recording it in history. Once sanctioned by tradition, innovations are accepted as normal, i.e. they join the other things that are just there, since from then on nobody can question their validity. This procedure is true just as much for the introduction of new species of vegetables, as it is for new techniques or new social practices. In the same way, 'modernity' – and in particular all practices involved in economic rationalization which form the hard core of 'development' – is also part of a tradition, embedded in Western history, which considers as obvious the equality of the actors, the utilitarian goal of human behaviour, the legal responsibility of individuals and disenchantment with the world, to name just a few of its characteristics.

By refusing to recognise the overlapping of tradition and modernity, and by reasoning dichotomously, we inevitably fall into the trap of the dominant ideology which obliges all societies to 'respect the requirements of development', provided, however, that it remains 'humane' or 'cultural'. For this reason, even if the Westernization of the world is, in fact, not as complete as some like to think,[7] it has won over such strong voices as those of P.E.A. Elungu in Zaïre, Daniel Etounga Manguele in the Ivory Coast and Axelle Kalou in Cameroon.[8] Their popularity in Northern countries and among certain African intellectuals no doubt resides in their insistence on comparing 'development' with African tradition which they consider to be retrograde. Each in a different way seeks to convert Africa to modernity and confirms the opinion of Lévi-Strauss, who observed long ago that the representatives of 'developing' countries did not blame the Northern countries as much for Westernizing them as for 'not providing them fast enough with the means to become Westernized'.[9]

Setting tradition and modernity up as opposites can lead nowhere. The problem is elsewhere. It is not a question of substituting 'development' for culture, or modernity for tradition, but understanding how two traditions meet, within the limits of modernity.

In remote societies today, these two forms of tradition (one which arises from the cultural heritage of a given society and another which imposes itself, or is imposed) are equally present, but are given different degrees of importance, according to the place, time and people concerned. Reference is made to both, simultaneously when possible, or alternatively when the contradictions are very strong, in accordance with the interests which determine the behaviour of the actors and the type of responses that the different traditions may offer: in fact, even if some people find it hard to accept, their reconciliation as a coherent whole is far from being achieved. Consequently, negotiation tactics with the administration may depend on interpretation that is sometimes 'modern' and sometimes a matter of custom; certain family and social ceremonies may be inspired by ancient customs, yet still include certain 'modern' elements (gifts of money replacing gifts in kind, for example); medical treatment may vary from a stay in hospital to the practice of witchcraft depending on the significance given to the illness and the type of diagnosis that is expected; formal schooling may be a means to social promotion, access to power and honour, which contradicts or reinforces other socially recognised means of achieving the same aims (membership of social networks, age groups, atc.). The reaction of different societies to outside intrusion is not necessarily head-on. They are too subtle to follow the rule of 'all or nothing' because that way they would sooner or later be losing. Like the judo player who wins by using to his own advantage the strength of his opponent, they are cunning and inventive. The 'global village' in which we would all be close is not for tomorrow. Nor is the establishment of 'ethnically pure' communities, in spite of the fanaticism evident today in reaction to attempts at ideological, political and/or religious standardization. Usually, social logic is selective and dependent on relationships, in the same way as the 'informal' sector which only exists because of the relations it maintains – even negative relations – with the sector we can call 'structured'. No doubt the same can be said of education.

Since the beginning, societies have included mixed races and have only survived through borrowing. But while, over the centuries, the slow assimilation of foreign elements assisted cultural synthesis, the wave of colonialization followed by the spread of the 'development tradition' have made mixed race a problem, apart from in those societies which have only accepted 'modernity' in small doses. [10] Thus, due to the speeed and violence of the processes set in motion by modernity, the inevitable mixture is rarely harmonious, whether it be in the North or the South, and may be accompanied by rejection when it does not favour the worst excesses of competing traditions.

However, if we consider the historical phenomenon in its entirety, we observe the emergence, almost everywhere, of 'common cultures' [11] which can be seen in the use – by the same social actors – of various languages, used in different circumstances. Briefly, it can be said that the vernacular is the main language in short, or intimate exchanges, the common language is used for inter-regional exchanges, whereas the official language (frequently of European origin) is used in relations with the governing power and the State. This multilingualism – often badly used, but necessary – is the sign of belonging to several groups within different traditional worlds which nevertheless make up a common culture – however heterogeneous – to the extent that it belongs to everybody and does not allow distinction between one actor and another. From this overlapping of concentric circles emerges the means of mastering one's own destiny, determining the places and values worth conserving, admitting the need to make necessary concessions, avoiding certain duties (particularly State duties) in order to safeguard the survival of the group or the family (which is also built by adapting old rules to new situations).

Administrative procedures, the laws of inheritance as well as school promotion are indicative of these collectively practised shams.

All these cultural tactics make it possible to integrate into the original culture some of the values and practices of the 'development tradition'. However, each social actor is involved in a network of multiple, and sometimes contradictory, allegiances which often make his/her behaviour unpredictable (for the planner and for the 'developer') depending on what he/she considers, according to the circumstances, the best way of promoting his/her own interests or those of the group – or network – leading to the desired social recognition (and which can also be measured in contradictory values). [12]

It is a long time since hard core culturalism was first criticized for claiming to maintain cultures in their original 'authenticity'. It was justified criticism in so far as it attacked the concentration on nostalgia for the past of a culture and, above all, it denounced the political manipulation required to achieve a 'cultural identity' legitimizing the ruling power to the exclusion of all others. Cultures change with time and cannot, therefore, be isolated from modernity.

On the other hand, little has been said about the changes undergone by the 'development tradition' following its contact with other 'exotic' traditions. If cultures (and traditions) change as a result of mutual contact and borrowing, why should we assume that 'development culture' imposes its own laws and codes without being influenced by others? Certainly, the asymmetry of power must be taken into consideration. Economic, political and military strength are undoubtedly on the side of 'development'. Is this enough for it to win the battle over the long term?

Even – and especially? – in Africa which is said to have been abandoned to its own devices or to economic liberalism, the face of 'development' is changing. The success stories registered there dot not necessarily conform to the rules of 'development' as laid down by Western society and the virtues required to achieve it have nothing to do with individualism or economic rationality. It is not, therefore, only 'native' cultures which change. When it comes in contact with them, the 'development tradition' changes direction, imported models are mocked and school culture, so long considered to be the 'key to development', is itself turned away from its utilitarian objective to provide, paradoxically, tools for those who are against it.

Modernity is not fixed eternally in the present, like the eternity of reason. What if the 'development tradition' itself were to be threatened by confrontation with other cultures?

NOTES

1. We shall not got into the complexity of the academic discussion on the concept of 'culture' (Kroeber & Kluckhohn, 1952). Taking as the basis of our discussion the definition proposed by the World Conference on Cultural Policies (Mexico, 1962) and bearing in mind the objectives of our discussion, we consider it useful to distinguish between:
   A. Culture in the sense of erudite culture as found in scientific, literary and artistic 'works' which serve as classical references. This cultural concept is that of minorities ('elites') who dictate the dominant culture. Access to it is restricted and involves an introduction to its codes, only obtainable through education and training. Thus, the school plays the role of 'civilizing influence' in the modern State.
   B. Culture in the sense of anthropological culture on which are based the processes of sociality and identification. It is made up of socio-economic and linguistic heritages, religious and political institutions, a network of relationships between individuals and groups which is exemplified by specific local and regional characteristics: dialects, customs, landscapes, values and specific ceremonies (Bassand & Hainard, 1985). In this situation the role of the school is ambiguous: on the one hand, when it plays a central role in the community, it complements the living culture; but when it is only interested in modernity, it directs the most active young people towards urban centres, thus 'skimming off' local resources.
2. Without going into the vast modern debate on the subject of Nation States, in this document we set out with the idea that modern States define their political organization through all the socio-cultural structures that exist on their national territory. This definition is often called into question today, either because single identity is only apparent (Nation States are in fact made up of several federal, associated or other groups of people), or because the growth of nationalist movements has caused the break-up of 'empires', and even Nation States, into several independent political units.
3. Alfred Kroeber and Clyde Kluckhohn, *Culture: a critical review of concepts and definitions,* New York, Vintage Books, Random House, 1952, 435 p. In fact, if we add up the definitions in the third part of the book, we arrive at the figure of almost 300.
4. UNDP, *Human development report,* New York, Oxford University Press, 1991, p. 2.
5. Cf. Gilbert Rist, 'Des sphinx, des licornes et autres chimères...' in: Gilbert Rist, ed., *La culture, otage du développement?* Paris, L'Harmattan (to be published).
6. Cf. Marie-Dominique Perrot, Gilbert Rist, Fabrizio Sabelli, *La mythologie programmée: L'économie des croyances dans la société moderne,* Paris, PUF, 1992, 217 p. (coll. Economie en liberté).
7. Cf. Serge Latouche, *L'Occidentalisation du monde, Essai sur la signification, la portée et les limites de l'uniformisation planétaire,* Paris, La Découverte, 1989, 143 p. (coll. Agalma); and Jean Chesneaux, *Modernité-monde, Brave New World,* Paris, La Découverte, 1989, 234 p. (coll. Cahiers libres).

8. Cf. P.E.A. Elungu, *Tradition africaine et rationalité moderne,* Paris, L'Harmattan, 1987, 185 p. (coll. Points de Vue); Axelle Kabou, *Et si l'Afrique refusait le développement?* Paris, L'Harmattan, 1991, 208 p.; Daniel Etounga-Manguele, *L'Afrique a-t-elle besoin d'un ajustement culturel?* Paris, Ed. Nouvelles du Sud, 1991.
9. Claude Levi-Strauss, *Race et histoire,* Denoël, Paris, 1961 (1952), p. 52. (coll. Médiations).
10. Cf. Carlos Calderon, 'Nous sommes tous des errants et, en chemin, nous nous rencontrerons. Le cas du Conseil régional indigène du Cauca (Colombie)', *Ethnies – (La fiction et la feinte),* no. 13, spring 1991, p. 21-27.
11. The expression is from Etienne Le Roy; cf. 'L'élaboration des cultures communes comme réponse à la crise de l'Etat', in: *La Culture: otage du développement?* op. cit.
12. On the importance of groups and families, cf. Emmanuel Seyni Ndione, *Dynamique urbaine d'une société en grappe, un cas: Dakar,* Dakar, ENDA, 1987, 179 p.; and, by the same author, *Le don et le recours,* Ressorts de l'économie urbaine, Dakar, ENDA, 1992, 208 p.

REFERENCES

Aboud, F.; Skery, S. The development of ethnic attitudes: a critical review. *Journal of cross-cultural psychology* (Beverly Hills, CA), 1984, no. 15, p. 3-34.
Balandier, G. *Anthropo-logiques.* Paris, Librairie générale française, 1985.
Bassand, M.; Hainard, F. *Dynamique socioculturelle régionale.* Lausanne, PPR, 1985.
Batelaan, P.; Gundara, J. S. 1991. L'éducation interculturelle: bibliographie choisie. *Bulletin du Bureau International d'Education* (Paris, UNESCO), Year 65, No. 260.
Berry, J. W. *Coûts et avantages sociopsychologiques du multiculturalisme.* Ottawa, Canadian economic Council, 1991. (Working doc. no. 24).
Bonnemaison, J. *La dernière île.* Paris, ORSTOM, 1986.
Bourdieu, P. Sytème d'enseignement et système de pensée. *International social science journal* (Paris, UNESCO), 1967, no. 2, p. 367-88.
Camilleri, C.; Cohen-Emerique, M., eds. *Chocs de culture: concepts et enjeux pratiques de l'interculturel.* Paris, L'Harmattan, 1989.
Coombs, P. *World education crisis.* New York, Oxford University Press, 1969.
Coombs, P. *The world crisis in education: the view from the eighties.* New York, Oxford University Press, 1985.
Elungu, P.E.A. *Tradition africaine et rationalité moderne.* Paris, L'Harmattan, 1987.
Furter, P. *Les espaces de la formation: essais de microcomparaison et de microplanification.* Lausanne, PPR, 1983.
—. L'identité régionale et la scolarisation en Suisse. *Les sciences sociales face à l'identité régionale, cinq approches.* Berne, Haupt V., 1986, p. 179-228.
Kroeber, A. L.; Kluckhohn, C. *Culture: a critical review of concepts and definitions.* New York, Random House, 1952.
Le Roy, E. *L'élaboration des cultures communes comme réponse à la crise de l'Etat et aux déséconomies en Afrique francophone.* Geneva, EADI, 1990.
Ninyoles, R. L. *Bases per una politica lingüística democràtica de l'Estat espanyol.* Valencia, 1976.

—. *Cuatro idiomas para un Estado.* Madrid, 1977.

Ouellet, F. *L'éducation interculturelle: essai sur le contenu de la formation des maîtres.* Paris, L'Harmattan, 1991.

Petrella, R. *La renaissance des cultures régionales en Europe occidentale.* Paris, Entente, 1978.

Polanyi,K. *La grande transformation: aux origines politiques et économiques de notre temps.* Paris, Gallimard, 1983.

Rey, M., ed. *Une pédagogie interculturelle.* Berne, Commission nationale suisse pour l'UNESCO, 1984.

Tajfel, H. *Social identity and intergroup relations.* London, Cambridge University Press, 1982.

Touraine, A. *Un désir d'histoire.* Paris, Stock, 1977.

CHAPTER VI

Intercultural education for cultural development: the contribution of teacher education

Pieter Batelaan

INTRODUCTION

Cultural development takes place through interaction. In this communication process the different partners often have different interests: the interests of institutions, such as the State or religious institutions, which aim at the transmission of values; and the interests of individuals, who aim at personal development, liberation, independence and change.

Cultural development is a dynamic process affected by the media, the arts and sciences, commercial activities and technology. Cultural development is not entirely an autonomous process. It can be influenced by cultural policy. Therefore, cultural development is also a concern of national governments. They may be particularly engaged in the development and promotion of the 'national culture', but since the societies in the various States have identified themselves as 'multicultural', the definition of the 'national culture' in a democratic context can no longer be taken for granted. Because the concept of 'democracy' implies the idea of 'inclusive pluralism', the cultural heritage of a country should include the cultures of all its citizens.

Cultural development takes place through the interaction between the different sections of the society, between individuals, between individuals and institutions, and through international exchanges. Without interaction there is no development. Interaction is only possible on an equal basis. As long as minority cultures are referred to as 'cultures of origin', these cultures will remain alien to the 'culture of origin' of the dominant groups (Batelaan & Gundara, 1992). Jacques Berque (Berque, 1985) proposes to speak about contributing cultures (*cultures d'apport*).

One of the aims of cultural policy in a democratic context should be the provision of opportunities to participate in the interaction process.

Education is an important instrument affecting cultural policy. It can be used to promote the cultural values of the dominant majority without any critical reflection; it can also be used to reflect on the multicultural and international character of cultures and to stimulate interaction. In this respect, education can even be regarded as an instrument for cultural development.

In this chapter it will be argued that education has to play an important role in the cultural development of individuals, groups and societies, but that, in general, education has failed to play this role, which is partly due to inappropriate teacher education.

Traditionally education has played an important role in transmitting the culture of the dominant groups in societies, because, in general, the curriculum does not reflect the knowledge and culture of groups who are referred to as 'minorities', or as 'others'.

The contribution of the school to cultural development should go beyond the 'transmission' of values which are taken for granted. The school ought to be the place where students learn to reflect on similarities and differences between cultures, where all kinds of issues can be studied from different perspectives, and where children and students from different origins can (learn to) communicate and co-operate in a secure environment. Cultural *development* goes through interaction and negotiation. Therefore the issue of cultural development is not only concerned with the curriculum but also with the management of the learning process, i.e. the management of the interaction between students and teacher, and between the students themselves. It will be argued that, under certain conditions, co-operative learning methods are an important tool for teachers to achieve the goals of cultural development. One of the conditions is an equal opportunity policy which implies that interaction in the classroom is structured in such a way that all children can participate, and that the contributions and knowledge of all children are appreciated.

This chapter will not address issues of linguistic development, although linguistic development is an important constituent of cultural development. The linguistic competencies of children should be used to facilitate not only the learning of the official national language but other languages as well. The development of multilingualism as such is of crucial importance for the cultural development of individuals and groups in a global society characterized by interdependence. This chapter addresses the issues of cultural development mainly from a European perspective. However, the opinions are based on universal principles as expressed in the relevant United Nations and UNESCO treaties, declarations and recommendations, which hopefully will also make it useful for a wider audience.

EQUAL OPPORTUNITY POLICY AND INTERCULTURAL EDUCATION

As long as children experience alienation in schools, due to teaching and organization based on the tradition of the academic culture (which reflects, in fact, the culture of the dominant group(s) in society), drop-out rates will continue to increase. An equal opportunity policy is a decisive condition if the school has to play an important role in the cultural development of individuals, groups and societies. Intercultural education deals with both diversity and inequality. Diversity and inequality are two sides of the same coin. Many programmes which are aimed at equality of opportunities, including some anti-racist programmes, do not take into account cultural diversity. On the other hand, some multicultural programmes which are aimed at mutual understanding of different cultures ignore social and economic inequality. Promoting the appreciation of cultural diversity includes far more than teaching about 'other' cultures. Equality of opportunities is far more than providing equal access to education. Equality of opportunities includes equal access to participation in the learning process, and the recognition and validation of knowledge and skills (including the language) which children already have.

Intercultural education includes:

- promotion of intercultural and international understanding;
- recognition of and respect for cultural differences;
- issues of human rights and citizenship (human responsibilities);
- the provision of equal opportunities (the education system should be inclusive);
- strategies for equal access to the learning processes in order to achieve equality of outcomes.

In spite of all the documents produced by international organizations, including UNESCO, the recommendations adopted by national governments, and in some cases even despite national legislation, intercultural education is still something marginal to the curriculum in most of the schools of western societies.

One of the conclusions of an OECD/CERI report in 1989 was that:

Despite the importance of the debate on multicultural education, it should be noted that initiatives, experiments and programmes concerning multicultural education have a marginal place in educational curricula and policies, with the possible exception of a few countries, particularly Australia and Canada. (CERI, 1989, p. 65).

Only when educators are completely aware of the functions of education in a cultural and social diverse society will intercultural education become more than a peripheral activity. The implementation of intercultural education requires an in-depth knowledge of what education is about. As is formulated in the Conclusions of the CERI-OECD report *One School, Many Cultures*:

Situated as they are at the meeting point of conflicting educational postulates (individualism or collectivism) and of teaching methods which are also in conflict (spontaneity or artificiality), multicultural education programmes cannot be successfully implanted within education systems without in-depth consideration of the cognitive function of the school and of the mental processes involved in the transmission of culture within the school (CERI, 1989, p. 74).

Where should teachers acquire this knowledge, which is an important ingredient of their professional identity? It will be argued that the marginal position of education for (inter)cultural development and equal opportunities in Europe is partly due to the fact that institutes for teacher education in general do not provide all their students with an appropriate training for intercultural education.

THE PURPOSES OF EDUCATION

What education is about is usually taken for granted by politicians, administrators, interest groups and action groups who want to use education to solve their particular problems. What education is about always includes their concern. It would be better to reflect on the purposes of education before each of these groups charges the school with satisfying any new demand. Why should education be used to prevent AIDS, to counter vandalism, to inculcate good traffic behaviour, to promote peace, to save the rain forest, to prepare children for further education or for the social market, to contribute to cultural development? What can and what cannot be expected from the school system? How can schools, i.e. teachers, respond to the demands of a dynamic society?

The purposes of formal education in democratic societies can be summarized as follows: (a) *economic*: qualification; (b) *social*: education may contribute to democratization and emancipation, both of individuals and of groups; (c) *cultural*: transmission and negotiation of values; (d) *pedagogical*: personal development (which includes creativity and critical thinking skills).

In modern industrialized societies, characterized by labour division and specialization, institutionalized education is a condition for the economic development of society.

Investment in education contributes as much to economic progress as investment in roads, power plants, irrigation canals, or any other physical capital. In fact the economic returns to investment in education, as measured by productivity and income, are often higher. (Constable in World Bank, 1990).

Without education access to many jobs is not possible. A sound education system is essential for the political, economic, social and cultural functioning of a modern industrial society. Education is a condition for qualification. Parents and societies assume that the primary function of the school is the teaching of academics. As a consequence of this thinking, 'the standard measures we use to determine the quality of schools get at academics almost exclusively – and a relatively narrow array of them at that' (Goodlad, 1984, p. 61).

In this chapter the emphasis is on the cultural function of education. The importance of cultural development is implied in Article 1.3 of the World Declaration on Education for All: 'Another and no less fundamental aim of educational development is the transmission and enrichment of common cultural and moral values. It is in these values that the individual and society find their identity and worth.'

However, the cultural function cannot be isolated from the economic, the social and the pedagogical ones. Qualification is important because it is a *sine qua non* to ensure employment and economic development. Without democratization and the emancipation of groups and individuals, culture will be narrowed to the interests of the dominant upper and middle class, which may result in defining it in terms of traditional Western arts and sciences.

Without personal development, people will be at the mercy of producers of popular mass culture. On the other hand, economic development cannot be isolated from cultural development; emancipation includes the empowerment of a person's cultural identity.

Cultural development at all levels depends on the balance of the different purposes of education.

CRITERIA FOR INTERCULTURAL EDUCATION

Intercultural education can be seen as the educational consequence of democratic principles in multicultural societies. Education is intercultural when it deals with issues of both diversity and inequality (including racism and xenophobia). It should therefore be aimed at fulfilling the following criteria:

1. To achieve a balance between the different purposes of education: the economic function the social function, the cultural function, and the pedagogical function.

2. To validate the knowledge and skills of all children, including their language ability, cultural knowledge, and different individual skills and aptitudes (which requires a 'multi-ability approach').

3. A broadly based and accessible curriculum, which reflects the reality of the multicultural society, and which presents knowledge from different perspectives.

4. On the level of classroom organization, it provides equal opportunities for participation in classroom interaction.

5. On the level of evaluation and assessment: fair tests.

These criteria are related to what actually happens in the classroom. Other criteria could be formulated in the areas of personnel management, administration, school organization and grouping, and parental involvement (see Banks, 1988 for a more complete checklist).

THE INTERNATIONAL BASIS FOR INTERCULTURAL EDUCATION

Although the different criteria are not stated explicitly in the different international conventions, resolutions and recommendations, they are derived from the same basic values, which underpin the activities of many intergovernmental organizations including the United Nations, UNICEF, UNESCO, the Conference for Security and Co-operation in Europe (CSCE) and the Council of Europe.

It is always surprising to observe that professionals responsible for the development of education or for their institutional policy hardly ever refer to international conventions and resolutions to which their governments have committed themselves. Therefore, some of this international legislation will be quoted here:

THE CONVENTION ON THE RIGHTS OF THE CHILD:

Article 29. State Parties agree that the education of the child shall be directed to:

(a) The development of the child's personality, talents and mental and physical abilities to their fullest potential;

(b) The development of respect for human rights and fundamental freedoms, and for the principles enshrined in the Charter of the United Nations;

(c) The development of respect for the child's parents, his or her own cultural identity, language and values, for the national values of the country in which the child is living, the country from which he or she may originate, and for civilizations different from his or her own;

(d) The preparation of the child for responsible life in a free society, in the spirit of understanding, peace, tolerance, equality of sexes, and friendship among all peoples, ethnic, national and religious groups and persons of indigenous origin;

(e) The development of respect for the natural environment.

Article 30. In those states in which ethnic, religious or linguistic minorities or persons of indigenous origin exist, a child belonging to such a minority or who is indigenous shall not be denied the right, in community with other members of his or her group, to enjoy his or her own culture, to profess and practise his or her own religion, or to use his or her own language.

The UNESCO Recommendation concerning Education for International Understanding, Co-operation and Peace and Education relating to Human Rights and Fundamental Freedoms, adopted by the General Conference at its eighteenth session (Paris, 19 November 1974), includes cultural aspects:

Article 17. Member States should promote, at various stages and in various types of education, study of different cultures, their reciprocal influences, their perspectives and ways of life, in order to encourage mutual appreciation of the difference between them. Such study should, among other things, give due importance to the teaching of foreign languages, civilizations and cultural heritage as a means of promoting international and inter-cultural understanding.

The Declaration on Race and Racial Prejudice adopted by the General Conference of UNESCO at its twentieth session, Paris, 27 November 1978, includes the following:

Article 5.2. States, in accordance with their constitutional principles and procedures, as well as all other competent authorities and the entire teaching profession, have a responsibility to see that the educational resources of all countries are used to combat racism, more especially by ensuring that curricula and textbooks include scientific and ethical considerations concerning human unity and diversity and that no individious distinctions are made with regard to any people; by training teachers to achieve these ends; by making the resources of the educational system available to all groups of the population without racial restriction or discrimination; and by taking appropriate steps to remedy the handicaps from which certain racial groups suffer with regard to their level of education and standards of living and in particular to prevent such handicaps from being passed on to children.

Article 6.2. So far as its competence extends and in accordance with its constitutional principle and procedures, the State should take all appropriate steps, inter alia by legislation, particularly in the spheres of education, culture and communication, to prevent, prohibit and eradicate racism, racist propaganda, racial segregation and apartheid and to encourage the dissemination of knowledge and the findings of appropriate research in natural and social sciences on the causes and prevention of racial prejudice and racist attitudes with due regard to the principles embodied in the Universal Declaration on Human Rights and in the International Covenant on Civil and Political Rights.

It should be a matter of concern to the Ministers of Education, who are represented in UNESCO conferences and who also discuss and adopt resolutions also in other intergovernmental settings, that these and other recommendations are not at all or hardly implemented by the educational

institutions in their countries. It should also be noticed that implementation goes beyond legislative activities; it is a far more complicated process.
In an evaluation report on teacher education in Sweden (Batelaan et al,
1992), which was compiled by a committee of the International Association for Intercultural Education, it is concluded that, in spite of supportive
national legislation and directives, the intercultural dimension of teacher
education in Sweden is limited to marginal activities. The same is true of
many institutions in the Netherlands, in spite of the legal requirement that
'education should also start from the principle that children grow up in a
multicultural society'.

Governments have to be careful with directives which interfere with
ideas of 'freedom of education' and 'academic autonomy'. On the other
hand, the educational institutions should be more aware of their societal
responsibility, which goes beyond their responsibility for the qualification
of students for jobs and positions in the society.

This does not release governments from their obligations to encourage
universities to implement international agreements and to compare their
own policies with the commitments they made at the international level.
The call, which can be heard in various countries, for a national curriculum
emphasizing 'national values' should be a concern of the international
community. Monitoring of policy development in relation to cultural
development, which does justice to cultural diversity both at the national
and at the institutional levels, should be put on the agenda of forthcoming
ICEs.

INTERCULTURAL EDUCATION AND CO-OPERATIVE LEARNING

Difficulties about implementing intercultural education are not only due
to the (lack of) policies of governments and institutions. On the individual
level, the advocates of intercultural education still lack a sound theoretical
foundation. In many countries the materials which are developed in the
framework of an intercultural or anti-racist project often do not make any
reference to theoretical work. One of the findings of the OECD analysis of
educational programmes states: 'Most multicultural education programmes are not supported by a solid and clear theoretical structure'
(CERI, 1989, p. 63).

Another concern is that intercultural education is seen as marginal. This
marginality is due to the fact that, particularly in Western societies,
'intercultural education' is only seen as a particular pedagogical movement, which has to compete with other priorities including environmental

128

education, peace education, global education, development education; it is not viewed as an ideology which also deals with issues of qualification (see the previous section).

Batelaan & Gundara (1993) advocate an integrative approach, based on the recognition that education has not only the economic purpose of qualification, but is also an instrument for the negotiation of cultural values.

Cultural development through education is more a learning process of negotiation and interaction than of transmission. Intercultural education, as defined in this chapter, is an appropriate framework for the organization of this learning process, because it deals not only with the curriculum, but also with the organization of the learning process. In a recent paper for the International Convention on Co-operative Learning (Batelaan, 1993) I argued that co-operative learning methods should be integrated in intercultural education or that co-operative learning should meet the criteria for intercultural education. What is needed for the development of intercultural education is a comprehensive approach.

Intercultural, multicultural and anti-racist education are traditionally primarily concerned with the content of education, which means concerned with the question *what* to teach, or *what* students should learn.

Co-operative learning is primarily concerned with *how* to teach, or *how* to organize the learning. 'Co-operative learning is an ideal solution to the problem of providing students of different ethnic groups with opportunities for non superficial, co-operative interactions' (Slavin, 1991, p. 35). In most of the work of specialists in co-operative learning, including Slavin and Johnson & Johnson, there is no explicit reference to the consequences of diversity within the classroom. Both aim at better results for the low achievers in traditional teaching/learning situations, but in their work there is no attention to the essence of inequality which exists within the classroom as a result of differences in societal, academic and peer status. 'If status characteristics are allowed to operate unchecked in the classroom, the interaction of children will only reinforce the prejudices they entered school with' (Cohen, 1986, p. 31). Cohen's work is so important for multicultural or intercultural education, because it deals explicitly with inequality on a classroom level. The work of Cohen is also important from the perspective of the theme of this publication, because her work is aimed at the participation of all children, regardless of their socio-economic, cultural, linguistic or peer status, in the interaction which is a prerequisite for cultural development.

CONCERNS FOR TEACHER EDUCATION

To achieve the purposes of education, including the goal of cultural development in diverse societies, conditions have to be fulfilled at the national level, the institutional level and at the level of the classroom. The most important condition is the proficiency and the professional attitude of the teacher. This means that teacher education, both pre-service and in-service, is one of the most crucial factors for the quality of education.

In the evaluation of teacher education in Sweden by an IAIE committee (Batelaan et al, 1992) mentioned above, it could be concluded that, in spite of a relatively supportive government policy, intercultural education has a marginal position in Swedish teacher education. From the experience of the members of the committee, it can be hypothesized that the same applies for most teacher education in Europe. There is no clear commitment to their responsibility to the community and the wider society. Without such a commitment, educational institutions may become subject to the pressures of the educational market. Throughout Europe higher education is being pressurized into becoming more market oriented. The tendency in higher education to become more market oriented is not the result of a fundamental discussion about the purpose of education for the society but results exclusively from economic pressure. The 'market' is here defined by 'clients' who need to 'purchase' qualifications for employers. Hence institutions now need to present themselves as being attractive for students. Some educational 'features' have a higher 'status' than others. The danger of this narrow orientation is that the cultural, the emancipatory and the pedagogical functions of education in a democratic society may disappear or become marginalized, and that only the narrowly defined economic function of education will be served. The challenges for the future of higher education institutions, particularly institutes for teacher education, is to accord greater importance to issues related to the needs of society, including cultural development.

Another important factor is the organization of teacher training institutes. Intercultural education requires an interdisciplinary approach. Universities and other institutions for higher education, including teacher education, are organized in faculties and disciplines. Functionaries within these sections derive their position from their discipline. They have no interest in the development of 'interdisciplinary' courses as long as nobody responsible for the allocation of financial resources complains, and as long as those responsible for quality control ignore the importance of social and cultural diversity in society.

The contribution of education to cultural development as described in this chapter can only be achieved through interaction in the classroom for which teachers are responsible. Therefore the quality of teacher education is of crucial importance.

In this respect some sections of the chapter on teacher preparation, contained in the UNESCO 1974 Recommendation, should be brought to the attention of the managers of teacher education, such Member States are recommended to 'constantly improve the ways and means of preparing and certifying teachers and other educational personnel for their role in pursuing the objectives of this recommendation and should, to this end: (33 e) develop aptitudes and skills such as a desire and ability to make educational innovations and to continue his or her training; experience in teamwork and in interdisciplinary studies; knowledge of group dynamics; and the ability to create favourable opportunities and take advantage of them.'

To improve the quality of teacher education, both pre-service and in-service, it is required that:

– Institutes of teacher education adopt an explicit position with regard to the international commitments which have been made by their governments, including those concerning the International Declaration of Human Rights and the Convention of the Rights of the Child. Governments may require them to be accountable towards society respecting their academic autonomy.
– The intercultural dimension in teacher education should be monitored through all quality control activities. The organizational structures of teacher education in various countries should be evaluated, not only with respect to economic efficiency, but also with respect to the possibilities for interdisciplinary courses and activities.
– The development of an intercultural curriculum and appropriate organization of the learning process which ensures the participation of all children, should be encouraged.
– International networks of teacher education institutes and schools to which they are related should be established. Such networks could be used for the exchange not only of information, materials and methods, but also of staff. Funded international exchange programmes should be supportive of staff development.

What is needed is also an information campaign directed at teacher education. One of the problems is the bureaucratic structure of communication between international institutions such as UNESCO, and national bureaucratic institutions such as governments, and between these national bureaucracies and the institutional bureaucratic level of universities and colleges for teacher education. The result is that the professionals who have to carry out in the classroom decisions which are taken in the conferences attended by bureaucrats are not aware of the relevant information.

Enough recommendations have been drafted by UNESCO and other international organizations for the development and implementation of intercultural education. The problem now is how to implement these recommendations in the schools, and how to make sure that governments who have committed themselves to these recommendations provide the conditions for implementation which include commitment by those who are responsible for the training of teachers.

REFERENCES

Banks, James A. 1988. *Multiethnic education: theory and practice.* Second Ed. Boston, Allynn & Bacon.

Batelaan, Pieter. 1993. Interkulturelle Erziehung und kooperatives Lernen. *In*: Huber, Gnter L., ed. *Neue Perspektiven der Kooperation.* Baltmannsweiler, Schneider Verlag Hohengehren.

Batelaan, Pieter; Gundara, Jagdish. 1991. Intercultural education: a selected bibliography. *Bulletin of the International Bureau of Education* (UNESCO, Paris), vol. 65, no. 260.

Batelaan, Pieter; Gundara, Jagdish. 1993. Cultural diversity and the promotion of values through education. *European journal of intercultural studies* (Stoke-on-Trent, UK). Vol 3:2/3, pp 61-80.

Batelaan, Pieter; et al. 1992. *Interculturalism in Swedish teacher education: an evaluation of the intercultural, bilingual and international dimension.* Stockholm, UHÄ.

Berque, Jacques. 1985. *L'immigration à l'école de la République: rapport d'un groupe de réflexion animé par le professeur Jacques Berque au ministre de l'Education nationale.* Paris, Centre national de documentation pédagogique.

CERI. 1989. *One school, many cultures.* Paris, OECD.

Cohen, Elizabeth G. 1986. *Designing groupwork: strategies for the heterogeneous classroom.* New York, NY, Teachers College Press.

Goodlad, John I. 1984. *A place called school: prospects for the future.* New York, NY, McGraw-Hill Book Company.

Johnson, Davis W.; Johnson, Roger T. 1991. *Learning together and alone: co-operative, competitive and individualistic learning.* Third ed. Englewood Cliffs, NJ, Prentice Hall.

Slavin, Robert E. 1991. *Co-operative learning: theory, research and practice.* Englewood Cliffs, NJ, Prentice Hall.

World Bank. 1990. *The dividends of learning: World Bank support for education.* Washington, DC, The World Bank.

World Conference on Education for All: Meeting Basic Learning Needs, Jomtien, Thailand, 1990. *Final Report.* New York, NY, Inter-Agency Commission for WCEFA.

CHAPTER VII

Teachers as facilitators
of cultural development:
new roles and responsibilities

Stacy Churchill

INTRODUCTION

Teachers are at the heart of the transmission and development of culture
through education systems. Their day-to-day activities shape the environment in which learning occurs and affect the impact of education on the
learner and on the social milieu of the learner outside the school. This essay
takes the position that the starting point for considering their roles and
responsibilities should be the teachers themselves, for their viewpoints and
concerns ultimately determine their role in serving as facilitators of cultural development.

Other portions of this book present an overview of the multifaceted
meanings of terms such as education, culture and development. Accepting
these as background, we shall limit our view in the following text mainly to
the role of teachers who serve in some form of *public education* at the
primary and secondary levels, including practical or vocational/profes-
sional training. The teachers may perform their roles in formal school
settings or in informal ones and their students may be either children or
adults. But the essential characteristic is that their activities are viewed as
being *public*, that is what they teach is controlled or at least regulated by the
State.[1] If this discussion leaves out some highly significant and important
aspects of education, it attempts at least to address the group of teachers
who work in the education systems that absorb almost 100 per cent of the
primary/secondary education budgets of governments in the world.

Writing about culture requires that the author inform the reader about
his own cultural background in order to assist in interpreting his words.
The author of the present article is a university professor in a prosperous
industrialized country. Even though most of his higher education was
obtained in industrial countries of western Europe (France, Finland, the

133

United Kingdom), his outlook was strongly influenced by his first two years in university as an undergraduate in a Third World country (Chile). This article reflects his experience as a researcher and policy adviser who has had the opportunity to visit schools and discuss educational policy and practice with teachers and education officials in dozens of countries in all major world regions. For nearly two decades, he has also been involved periodically with the UNESCO Associated Schools Project, which has pioneered teaching practices that foster better understanding between peoples and cultures.

NEW RESPONSIBILITIES AND INITIAL TEACHER REACTIONS

Most of the practising teachers the author has met would probably raise questions about the title of this chapter. Why should cultural development involve *new* responsibilities for teachers? Is not the fundamental role of the school the transmission and development of culture in its broadest sense? Have teachers not always seen this as the objective and even the justification of their activities?

A second reaction would be to ask whether the word 'new' suggests that there is a shortcoming in teachers' present activities. Does this suggest that there is going to be yet another attempt to load on teachers' shoulders the responsibility to deal with issues that the remainder of society seems to value but does not wish to devote attention to? Is there something new in 'culture' that has to be thrust into the already overcrowded school curriculum? In short, teachers wish to see recognition for: (a) their current contribution to cultural development; and (b) the already heavy demands placed upon their time by the curriculum.

These reactions are, of course, only hypothetical. But they are typical of teacher reactions to proposals for reforms that suggest they or their students can suddenly take on a new set of responsibilities, in addition to what they are already striving to achieve. On the other had, teachers are extremely sensitive to the magnitude of their responsibilities and aware of the limits of what they can achieve, in cultural development as well as in any other aspect of schooling. In fact, they *do* tend to be willing to review their approaches to teaching and to consider proposals for adaptations, provided the suggestions meet minimum criteria for *feasibility*. In other words, they have to face realistically the constraints of their work-prescribed syllabi and examination/selection systems, limited time and material resources, and particularly the needs and expectations of their students and the communities they serve. Moreover, in many areas of the world, teachers are faced with rapid increases in student numbers and changes in the composition of student populations.

But within those constraints teachers usually see considerable freedom for innovation and choice in terms of how they approach the topics to be taught and how they seek to motivate students. Such an outlook is crucial to approaching the topic of cultural development. *Cultural development* – to use an almost simplistic truism – occurs within and through the learners, taken individually and collectively, and may be defined as integrating the school experience into a meaningful whole that supports the learners as participants in various *cultural communities*. Each learner may be visualized as a member of a school cultural community made up of the teachers and other students who share in a common learning environment. But the learner also participates in other cultural sharings with other groupings of people: his/her own family; the society of the surrounding locality – sometimes involving multiple ethno-racial, cultural, religious and linguistic groups – and a broader national or regional culture corresponding to the type of country in which schooling occurs.[2] Viewed from a distance, cultural development in societies involves the sum of the cultural developments in cultural communities, each of which is made up in turn of multiple individuals.

The students' integration of schooling experience into their own cultural frameworks goes beyond formal training in the content of a given subject of teaching, such as mastering the main concepts in a science textbook, and requires that the knowledge be interrelated to the other cultural frameworks that affect the life of the learner. *Teachers understand intuitively that this second stage of integrating learning into cultural frameworks is something that is influenced by the teacher's example and outlook as much as by formal teaching steps.*

As a result, teachers are aware that many of the shifts in teaching required for facilitating cultural development are to a large extent under their own control, thus meeting their criterion of feasibility. This awareness can give teachers, even in very difficult material situations, a sense of empowerment. Students may have great differences in academic performance, as measured in terms of mastering a prescribed subject matter, but strong and weak students alike can be assisted to use what they learn in a culturally meaningful manner for their lives. For the teacher, it is empowering to realize that personal example and attitude conveyed in the classroom can powerfully influence this aspect of every student's life.

Theoretical discussions of culture and the school tend to emphasize two divergent viewpoints: (a) culture as something that is transmitted from one generation to another, in the sense of a cultural heritage; and (b) culture as

135

the shared experience of a human social grouping, its symbolic representation, and the context of its development.[3] The first view tends to inspire discussions of what should be taught in schools and to lead into trying to modify the programmes of study that are laid down for schooling. The second view supports analyses of how teaching interacts with the culture(s) of learners and the larger society and tends to be critical of the results achieved by schooling. Much contemporary theory on schooling dwells extensively upon the encounter between: (a) the school's role of cultural transmission/development; and (b) the interactions and contradictions that arise as this intended curriculum unfolds in a complex learning situation where the learners, the teachers and the very operation of the school as a social institution are all viewed as being embedded in different and partially overlapping cultural frameworks.

When confronted with such divergences, teachers know that they cannot easily choose between these viewpoints. Instead, teachers must live *both* with the framework of what should be taught – the officially prescribed programme of study or 'intended curriculum' – *and* with the fact that results of teaching depend upon the way the school interacts with the culture of the learners and the surrounding society. At the same time, during the last few decades, the rise of critical views of the results achieved by schooling has made progressively larger numbers of teachers aware of their own cultural role, leading to a much greater sensitivity to the cultural needs of learners.

One important dimension of change in the consciousness of teachers has been a growing recognition of *cultural diversity*, even if this recognition is limited to the individual teachers' consciousness and is not reflected explicitly in the intended curriculum. This awareness of different cultural frameworks permits adaptation of teaching in many dimensions. For example, recognizing that the lived cultures of different social classes are widely divergent and that the intended curriculum is often a reflection of only one, can help teachers to meet the needs of different sets of learners. Similar remarks apply to the recognition of needs corresponding to students of varied ethno-racial, linguistic, religious and cultural backgrounds. *In a fundamental sense, the teaching profession is gradually shifting its awareness to realize that the school's role of cultural transmission/development is profoundly inter-cultural: each culture is defined in interaction with and in distinction from, other cultures. If the teacher teaches 'a' culture, the learner 'learns' that culture by integrating it within his/her own cultural framework. This integration modifies the original culture and creates in the learner a 'new' culture. The teacher's message is changed from an objectified external knowledge into a living component of the learner's own identity.*

Perhaps the most visible form of cultural adaptation in many countries has been a move both by teachers and by authorities to give greater prominence to what may be called the *multicultural* dimensions of their country's own populations (including resident foreign workers and immigrants). Depending upon the country and region, the adaptations go under names such as 'multicultural education', 'intercultural education' and 'antiracist education', and they vary from simple acknowledgement of cultural differences in the intended curriculum to active instructional measures to promote understanding and social changes that foster development of different cultural communities.[4] On the other hand, even in schools and countries where heavy emphasis is already placed upon intercultural education, many teachers: (a) feel the need for this as a truly new dimension of the curriculum; (b) are critical of their own efforts in this field; (c) are anxious to receive assistance in improving the effects of intercultural education; and (d) express feelings of being constrained by the official curriculum.

These typical reactions are worth remembering as we examine this topic of new responsibilities for teachers. At every step, teachers must mediate between what is intended to be taught and the pedagogical requirements of teaching students with different cultural backgrounds. Even if the official objectives of schooling and the contents of syllabi for different subjects are fixed in terms of national goals with little place for variability, pedagogy imposes consideration of differences in students' learning abilities, which are fundamentally dependent upon cultural background.

CURRICULUM CHANGE AND TEACHER ROLES

The starting point for teachers' work is the intended or prescribed curriculum, the officially prescribed courses of study that they are expected to teach. Any effort to modify teachers' responsibilities must begin with this framework which defines their activities. But action cannot be limited to the curriculum or to general statements of objectives without follow-through measures. In order for effective change in teacher responsibilities to occur, other support measures are required.

The IBE's preparatory survey of countries for the 1992 International Conference on Education included an item (8c) asking whether 'local educational authorities, school administrators and teachers possess appropriate authority to modify the basic curricula in order to reflect local culture'. The responses confirmed that most countries tend to view the basic curriculum as fixed with little room for local variation. As we have noted, teachers' room for personal innovation is usually limited to adapting their own teaching methods and to choosing support materials for use in the classroom; even the choice of textbooks is only rarely an option. As a consequence, fundamental modifications in teachers' responsibilities for cultural and intercultural aspects of the curriculum require decision-making at higher levels. And, because of the heavy responsibilities teachers already have, such modifications must take into account the issue of practicability. Conversely, teachers who are aware of their cultural roles can – and do – take many practical measures in their daily work to adapt curricula to meet the needs of learners with varied cultural backgrounds, even when this is not officially promoted (and sometimes in spite of official discouragement).

When a higher-level decision is made to emphasize cultural and intercultural aspects of education, teachers are also faced with the fact that superficial changes, such as adding in a unit or two of study in a course or a programme, will have limited impact. In discussions with me in past research, for example in connection with the UNESCO Associated Schools, teachers and other educators in different parts of the world have emphasized the need to consider the *operational meaning of culture* as it is expressed throughout the officially prescribed curriculum, rather than in any single course or unit of study. Depending on the context, they raise different issues:

(a) *National objectives for schooling:* The definition of 'culture' throughout the curriculum is often based on the view that the school is an instrument for nation-building and should emphasize a single national culture or cultural viewpoint. Sometimes this viewpoint is articulated in terms of promoting national economic development, and all schooling is visualized in terms of how its graduates will perform in various job classifications. The responses of some countries to the IBE survey referred to above stated clearly that the main cultural objective of schooling was fostering development of a (single) national cultural heritage or an Islamic cultural heritage. By contrast, in the responses of some 'Western' countries, the assumption of a Euro-centric content is occasionally taken for granted and neither questioned nor stated explicitly. Only a tiny fraction of jurisdictions made explicit mention of attempts to de-emphasize Euro-centric tendencies in the curriculum.

(b) *Content of 'culture' in the official curriculum:* In some educational situations, the curriculum equates 'culture' with teaching about music, 'fine' arts and some aspects of humanities, particularly 'good' literature. While recognizing the value of these aspects of culture, teachers point out that it falls short of being a modern definition.

(c) *Contrasts with traditional cultures:* In many parts of the world, the school represents an element of modernity that contrasts sharply with a surrounding traditional, often rural and/or indigenous, society. The content of the curriculum may be a direct or indirect challenge to the traditional culture(s) of the populations served.

(d) *Balance in emphases:* In teaching groups of students with mixed cultural, ethno-racial, religious or linguistic origins in the same classroom, there is a constant search by the teacher to strike an appropriate balance that recognizes both differing needs of pupils and the requirement to teach within an official curriculum whose main objectives may be to disseminate one national culture or cultural viewpoint. This need for achieving a practical balance in daily teaching continues to exist in situations where the official curriculum endorses multicultural/intercultural education. Legitimating multicultural/intercultural approaches tends to give much greater visibility to teachers' efforts at adaptation and, therefore, to increase their responsibility to search for a balanced approach suitable to groups of students with highly varied backgrounds.

As these examples illustrate, the operational meaning of culture in the curriculum refers to a variety of dimensions that the concept of culture assumes according to different definitions of the curriculum. Simply expressed, 'operational meaning' refers to meaning as inferred from *its impact upon the participants in the schooling experience.* For example, if the school curriculum in a country fails to mention the culture of a given minority group, as if it did not exist, its operational meaning might be considered as two-fold. For members of the *majority* whose culture(s) is(are) represented in the curriculum, the implication is that the minority culture is not important or worthy of consideration in a national curriculum and therefore is not worth their attention. For the *minority(ies)* involved, the neglect of their culture can have a major impact on the way they react to schooling, how they relate to the other members of the national community and, indeed, what benefits they derive from the schooling process.

Characteristically, groups whose cultures are ignored in official national curricula are often those groups who suffer from the most severe forms of disadvantage as measured by the usual indicators of retention/drop-out rates and achievement. Awareness of this differential impact of the operational meaning of a culture has led many countries to review curricula to ensure representation of varied cultural traditions or to eliminate stereotyping of different ethno-cultural or national groups. Such recognition serves to legitimate and reinforce the efforts of teachers to adapt teaching

139

to the needs of students of different backgrounds. (On the other hand, since differential achievement usually results from multiple social factors, changes to schooling alone are unlikely to prove a complete remedy to major causes of disadvantage for cultural groups.)

No observer can fail to notice that the basic structure of the curriculum used in most countries in the world is largely based upon models of public schooling which originated in the European cultural sphere in the nineteenth century. Many of the assumptions of that schooling system remain unchanged, in spite of adaptations for national differences. The traditional definition of culture inherent in the curriculum reflects a view of what, at that time, were important values for middle class and upper-middle class societies of Europe and North America. Culture, as described implicitly (and sometimes explicitly) in many curriculum documents, has often been a 'something' that most ordinary people need to be taught. The 'arts', for example, were defined in terms suitable for the nineteenth-century museum: they included products mainly of leisured males – such as oil paintings – but excluded the products of other groups – such as oriental carpets, weaving, lace and crochet work, carvings – described as 'folklore' or 'popular art and culture'. The exquisite artistic products of women's labour, often serving utilitarian purposes in everyday life, have almost universally been described as 'crafts'.[5] School textbooks often include prints or photographs of 'art', but it is rare that they expose children to the artistic creations of indigenous peoples, of women prior to the contemporary period or of men who were considered craftsmen or artisans.

Many countries have made attempts to rethink curricula in order to enlarge the traditionally narrow definitions of culture. In newly independent countries, most changes have involved introducing elements of national, regional or, sometimes, religious cultural heritage to reduce the Euro-centric content of some topics of study. Other adaptations have sometimes been technology-driven, as in the concern to 'modernize' curricula to deal with the advances of science and technology or to legitimate the study of film and television media. But the traditional definitions of culture in the curriculum remain broadly accepted in the countries using them, and they are an integral part of the way most educators think about the curriculum. These almost unconsciously accepted definitions guide, for example, the choice of authors studied in literature courses. Indeed, most languages now have a word to designate Literature (often written with a capital letter in some languages), which is distinguished from other types of writing by its 'cultural' content. The most far-reaching redefinitions of curriculum objectives and content to accept more popular definitions of culture have occurred within the context of efforts to reach groups that, heretofore, have remained marginal to the formal public education system, as in the many popular education efforts similar to those of Paolo Freire.[6] It is, nevertheless, rare to find cases where such redefinitions have fundamentally shifted the curriculum structure of formal education beyond the primary years.

The discussion of underlying assumptions in official curricula points to *a fundamental responsibility of national educational authorities.* Because their decisions provide a framework and set constraints for the activity of teachers in facilitating cultural development, it is important that national authorities[7] consciously structure their curricula (including determining textbooks and teaching resources to be used) in ways that support the roles and responsibilities of teachers in cultural development. In the discussion that follows, frequent references will be made to areas where the official curriculum of a given jurisdiction may constrain or limit teachers' roles as facilitators of cultural development. These references are deliberate and intended to provide a set of guideposts to areas where educational authorities may review the coherence of their decisions with the goal of promoting cultural development.

Our brief review has also served to illustrate the fact that cultural and intercultural aspects of education include a great variety of topics with overlapping and sometimes partially contradictory meanings as they are reflected in the curricula of different nations. It would be futile in this article to spend time on the multitude of definitions given to culture in the contemporary world. Such abstract discussion will not eradicate the fact that most teachers, in their everyday work, are faced with the task of dealing with culture in all its aspects.

For the purposes of the following discussion, we shall attempt to stay close to an 'operational' meaning of culture as it affects teachers and shall distinguish between teachers' roles and responsibilities in: (a) disseminating and making known a national cultural heritage, usually a core objective of the official curriculum; (b) developing artistic and aesthetic talents of pupils, often in connection with instruction in the fine arts and in literary disciplines; (c) relating the school curriculum to the development of the ongoing culture of a country, particularly the cultural development of the communities whose members are directly served by the individual school; (d) providing education that promotes intercultural awareness; and (e) adapting education to meet the needs of groups whose cultures or lifestyles are divergent from the majority, mainstream or dominant cultural group of the country.

Teacher roles tend to vary significantly depending upon the subject matter being taught. On the other hand, it is important to capitalize upon possible convergences between different subjects to ensure harmonious development. In primary school, where one teacher is responsible for a variety of disciplines or subjects of study, the opportunity often exists to use the teaching of one subject to reinforce the learning acquired in another. Subject-matter specialization of teachers at higher levels of education renders such co-ordination difficult, but the impact of such mutual reinforcement across curriculum areas can be significant.

TEACHER RESPONSIBILITIES:
THE NATIONAL CULTURAL HERITAGE

In almost all countries, teachers are given a primary role for ensuring that citizens are acquainted with the broad outlines of the nation's cultural heritage and the main aspects of knowledge considered useful to being a citizen. Such knowledge ordinarily includes literacy in one or more official languages, awareness of the country's contemporary social structure and customs, and basic abilities in academic disciplines considered relevant for successful participation in community life. By and large, this knowledge constitutes an officially-defined 'national culture' which is the central component of teachers' work in all countries. To this extent, it does not constitute a 'new' responsibility.

The 'new' responsibilities of teachers within this narrower definition of cultural aspects of education may arise in a variety of ways. The primary responsibility appears to be keeping the schoolroom in touch with rapid social evolution. There are few societies, if any, which are not touched by accelerating social change. Even within a rigid and fixed curriculum, such change provides a great challenge to teachers at multiple levels: maintaining adequate knowledge of recent developments and changes, reviewing how such changes require them to adapt the content of their teaching, and monitoring how children and youth in their classes are affected by social change. A key aspect of ensuring contact with evolving reality is to develop among teachers an awareness of the role of media – that is, the role of mass communication media – in shaping the daily reality of cultural heritage. This awareness needs to be translated into daily concern to understand its impact upon children and youth as well as into more focused programmes of instruction in the official curriculum aimed at ensuring among learners at least a minimum understanding of the role of media and a critical stance permitting intelligent critical reactions to the cultural images they transmit.[8] Whereas so-called 'media literacy' has been a focus for teaching mainly in more industrialized countries, the greatest need for it probably exists in settings where large-scale broadcast media are relatively recent innovations; it is in such settings that particularly young people and rural populations need to develop critical awareness of the cultural implications of media messages.

Some nations structure the school curriculum to recognize multiple languages and cultures as part of the core national heritage which the school transmits. In actual practice, this ordinarily involves the teacher in delivering a teaching 'message' that is intercultural, i.e. in promoting better understanding between different languages and cultures. We shall return to this topic shortly.

TEACHER RESPONSIBILITIES:
ARTISTIC AND AESTHETIC EDUCATION

Up to the present, the author has never encountered a serious educator who expressed satisfaction at the quality of artistic and aesthetic education offered to the *average* pupil in the public education system of his or her country. On the other hand, almost all national education curricula pay at least lip-service to the goal of providing pupils with an opportunity to develop their own artistic talents and to appreciate the artistic creations of others. Faced with difficult choices, some countries deal with art and aesthetic education the same way that, in the recent past, one dealt with access to education generally – by providing it only for a relatively few pupils chosen, when possible, on the basis of their outstanding aptitudes and interests. Undoubtedly, given the scarcity of resources, this is likely to remain the case in many countries with respect to formal instruction in many branches of art and aesthetic appreciation.

On the other hand, it is clear that teachers can assume, and often express willingness to assume, a more dynamic role in promoting artistic and aesthetic education. In interviews they often express regret at their own lack of preparation, a matter of concern in the context of teacher training. In addition, they point out three major constraints: (a) official timetables which may provide little opportunity for teaching on topics other than basic academic disciplines; (b) preoccupation of pupils and parents with examinations on academic topics which do not include artistic or aesthetic concerns; and (c) lack of material resources. In spite of the serious constraints they face, schools are sometimes able to achieve remarkable results in developing artistic and aesthetic education, largely by promoting linkages between the school and the community. In order for such a strategy to be effective, the teaching aims must be adapted to the capacity of the community resources being mobilized. Thus, if artistic education is inter-

preted solely in the narrow tradition of fine arts, it may exclude participation from a surrounding community which still has a living artistic
tradition; but accepting that artistic understanding can be developed
through other forms of expression leaves the door open to making use of
talented individuals with skills in crafts and other aspects of popular
culture.

The dichotomy which classifies popular artistic expression as folklore or
craft rather than art, tends to rule out strong linkages with communities,
whether in traditional or industrialized societies. In how many countries
does one find a curriculum of art appreciation which includes study of arts
and decorations made by rural dwellers? How often does one encounter a
secondary school curriculum of literature which acknowledges the oral
traditions of the country in which it is taught? How many schools are
willing to acknowledge or study the vast outpouring of so-called popular
music that occupies a major portion of the leisure time of youth today?
When great painters, great authors and great symphonies become the focus
of the curriculum definition of culture, they exclude the decorative creativity of the local artisan, the deep wisdom of popular story-telling, and the
melodic genius of a self-taught musician who uses traditional instruments
to play music that may date back more than a thousand years. One is
reminded of the UNESCO Associated Schools Project in Bulgaria which
sent students into remote rural areas, where they collected not only large
amounts of local folklore but even a manuscript of ancient songs that had
been previously unknown. How many other cultural treasures of pedagogical and sometimes historical value remain untapped outside the doors of
our schools, waiting for young minds to search them out?

TEACHER RESPONSIBILITIES:
COMMUNITY CULTURAL DEVELOPMENT

Many national systems of education promote efforts to ensure that schooling assists in the cultural development of local communities – defined
either geographically as the people living in an area or socially as one or
more cultural (or ethnocultural) communities served by a given school. In a
rather general sense, expanding educational opportunities for a community constitutes a means of community cultural development. But such a
broad definition is more or less meaningless. What we are discussing here is
the relationship between what the school does, or can do, and the living
fibre of human communities. Does one contribute to the other? How can
its contribution be improved?

The relationship between school and community depends in large measure upon the extent to which the objectives of schooling are congruent with the cultural antecedents of the community. As a Canadian, the author is familiar with one extreme, a negative one: there are many cases where the development of formal schooling to serve indigenous peoples in our country had an opposite effect. Rather than developing their communities, schooling had the effect of promoting the disintegration of the traditional social and cultural underpinnings of the community without providing an adequate replacement. Another example is becoming more well known as schooling penetrates into rural regions of the world. The rapid development of literacy is seldom accompanied by efforts to preserve oral literary and cultural traditions, which may die out within only one or two generations, leaving no trace. And one cannot help but be moved by occasional newspaper articles describing how linguists in some corner of the world are recording the words of one of the last speakers of a language which, after their death, will no longer exist.

Unfortunately, despite occasional attention from media or politicians, most indigenous cultures of the world are being submerged by the invasive culture of modern consumer societies, often aided by the role of formal schooling. Contemporary observers often view this cultural displacement as an inevitable price of progress and development. The propagation of universal public education as a foundation for development has acquired the status of an acknowledged dogma of all efforts at development. Yet there remains a logical contradiction in assuming that development of peoples should imply the eradication of their culture. In fact, many countries have experienced failure and frustration when the development of schooling has failed to be a stimulus for economic development or even to be effective in promoting literacy among indigenous peoples and among communities whose culture is widely divergent from the national norm. A plausible case can be made for the proposition that public education – including certain literacy programmes – is an ineffective means of promoting national development if it is imposed as a unicultural monolith whose role is to eradicate or replace the pre-existing cultures of communities.[9] Conversely, serious consideration should be given to the value of a national school based upon accommodating community cultures in a relationship of cultural duality, i.e. the acceptance that learners all have a culture which must be respected within the framework of schooling.

The examples just given do not deny the value of modern education but rather draw attention to the need for a sensitive interrelationship between the cultural activities of the school and the social framework from which its clienteles are drawn. All industrialized nations can point with pride to the

145

contribution made by widespread public education to their current cultural development. Yet, at the same time, most of them also face entirely new challenges of school/community relationships, such as those in inner-city and industrial environments where there may be acute alienation between schooling and youth. Many nations have experimented with projects aimed at bringing educational processes closer to the concerns of urban youth, sometimes based on recognizing 'youth culture' as a basis for understanding the aspirations of learners and using such culture as a basis for motivating students. The many partial successes of such experiments point to the need to extend them and pursue them, but the difficulties all projects encounter point to a parallel need to extend responsibility for supporting learning so that it is not limited to teachers and schools, but rather involves close contacts with the workplace and extends to later phases of life. Just how to achieve such a transformation in the 'culture of the workplace' remains a matter of intense debate with major practical significance. The workplace, too, is a community in need of cultural development.

Each national cultural setting, whether industrialized or not, faces its own challenges. Adapting the school's conception of culture in ways that make it possible for it to contribute to general strengthening of social cohesion in the surrounding community represents an unending challenge to teachers and every level of the education system supporting their efforts. Yet, this aspect of education is usually given short attention, if any, in teacher training and may occupy little or no place in the formal curriculum guidelines or regulations of a country. To a large extent, each schooling situation is unique, and the need for adaptation of its content to local needs reposes upon the shoulders of individual teachers and school administrators who often must work with very limited material resources.

TEACHER RESPONSIBILITIES:
INTERCULTURAL EDUCATION

Intercultural education refers generally to educational experiences that promote better understanding of different cultures. Except in a few countries whose populations are culturally and ethnically very homogeneous, such education has two different aspects, one 'foreign' and one 'national'. In one case the students are called upon to show understanding for the cultures of other countries; in the second case, the idea is to promote understanding between different cultural or ethnocultural groups within the same country. Not surprisingly, developing positive attitudes is sometimes easier to do with respect to cultures in distant countries than with nearby ones, particularly if the cultural differences involve also ethno-racial, linguistic, religious or social class divisions.

The opportunities for teachers to develop intercultural education are determined in large measure by curricular and social conditions over which they have little control. The openness of official curricula to the goals of intercultural education is highly variable. At one extreme, the teacher may be constrained by a highly nationalistic curriculum in a setting where public opinion is mobilized to emphasize national goals – as in the case where the country is militarily involved in dealing with an external enemy – or in a setting where internal ethnocultural rivalries are perceived to be an immediate threat to the existence of the nation or the prevailing social order. Fortunately, most education occurs in a much less polarized atmosphere, and the curriculum regulations or guidelines of many countries express support for respect of different cultures and value systems. Thus, in most countries in the world, intercultural education is possible, if not always encouraged. In some countries, such education is actively promoted on an official basis in order to promote, particularly, the better integration of linguistic and cultural minorities into the mainstream of society through more effective schooling. We shall return to this point shortly and to evolving definitions of intercultural education in education policy.

In most education systems there exists a tension in teacher responsibilities. Both official curricula and prevailing opinion tend to stress what we have called a national cultural heritage, often defined as involving only one dominant cultural viewpoint. Teachers themselves often share in much of the prevailing opinion and, in promotion of cultural understanding, must seek to overcome the limitations of their own outlooks as well as dealing with the task of stimulating young minds to look at the world in fresh and unbiased ways. At the same time, curricular materials such as textbooks evolve very slowly, with the result that many of the available resources may be presenting negative stereotyped images of different cultures and cultural groups.

One of the most effective means of support for the teachers' task in intercultural education is to provide a collaborative school environment where intercultural education goals are a shared concern of multiple teachers. The author has personally observed this in many UNESCO Associated Schools in different countries, as well as in other schools where internal initiative has set up an atmosphere where teachers can co-operate on intercultural education. Where such schools are supported by national authorities, they can become effective demonstration centres, nodes in a

147

communication network that promote diffusion of better teaching methods to teachers in other schools. The UNESCO Associated Schools demonstrate that, with a minimum of central support, the goals of better intercultural understanding, both at the national and international levels, serve as strong forces motivating teachers to undertake additional tasks and to experiment with better teaching methodologies in their own classes.[10]

At present, only a small handful of countries in the world have made preparation for intercultural education an integral part of pre-service teacher training. For the foreseeable future, the development of teacher skills in this field will depend upon in-service training systems and upon the type of mutual assistance that is integral to innovation methodologies used in schools such as the Associated Schools. At the same time, strenuous efforts must be made to bring these concepts into the teacher training colleges and faculties of education that prepare new generations of teachers.

TEACHER RESPONSIBILITIES:
TEACHING SPECIAL POPULATIONS

In every country of the world, certain citizens have some form of cultural difference from the dominant or mainstream culture of schooling which sets them at a disadvantage in terms of how well they succeed in public education systems. We shall refer to these groups as 'special populations', avoiding a terminology which might suggest that they are responsible for the difficulties they encounter in education.[11] In the not distant past, most countries dealt with special populations by using selection mechanisms, such as examinations, to remove them from the more prestigious types of school and, as early as possible, to leave them outside school altogether.[12] This tendency remains widespread, partly because of the integral role that examinations and testing play in the operation of teaching/learning systems. Nevertheless, major contrary tendencies have been much in evidence in the recent past, each linked to a different concept of cultural development.

Since the potential number of special populations is almost infinite, we shall limit our remarks here to discussing two types of cultural need recognition that have gradually emerged. The first concerns persons who are treated as being 'handicapped' on physical or intellectual grounds not related to ethno-cultural background: physical infirmity, perceptual handicap, intellectual dysfunctioning and similar problems. The second involves ethno-cultural differences.

148

Because 'handicap' is seldom treated as a cultural issue and the topic is only now receiving more widespread attention, we shall simply outline the parameters of the problem of culture as it is currently emerging. Many education systems have in created special institutions serving those who have been classified as profoundly handicapped; those considered as having lesser handicaps have mainly been dealt with in public schooling by creating some form of 'special education', usually involving separating students for most or all of the day from other students without the designated handicaps. For a variety of reasons, many of the more advanced industrialized countries have begun to phase out, as far as possible, the procedures for separate instruction of special populations and have integrated them into regular classrooms (called 'mainstreaming' in some English-speaking countries).[13]

The cultural implications of such changes reside mainly in the fact that they coincide with a gradual recognition of the worth of individuals, independently of handicap. Persons who must live most of their lives in wheelchairs because of motor difficulties may often benefit from regular schooling with peers who have normal faculties, provided they receive certain appropriate support. At the same time, however, viewing their lives and expectations for the future, they represent a group whose needs and future way of life is almost unmentioned in any aspect of contemporary school curricula, even in fields such as 'social studies'. It has been discovered that teachers who deal with such individuals, classed as handicapped, often adapt very rapidly to recognizing that teaching must be adapted in the light of their cultural expectations for future life. Although little noted in 'mainstream' society, it is important to emphasize that, largely through volunteer organizations, such handicapped individuals have begun to organize and to make heard their specific cultural needs. In some countries, the deaf, for example, have organized and obtained recognition of the existence of what might be called a 'deaf culture' with specific demands for modification of curricula for their instruction.[14]

Most countries in the world contain minorities of citizens who are distinguished in linguistic, cultural, religious and/or ethno-racial terms from the majority or dominant national groups. In most countries of the world, including many of those which now make educational provision for linguistic and cultural minorities, the dominant mode of public education was usually, in its early stages of development, based upon a model of a single national or regional culture transmitted via a single language of instruction. On a worldwide basis, treatment of minorities in education systems ranges from full recognition of their languages and cultures to ignoring completely all linguistic and cultural differences in the popu-

149

lation. There is, however, a long-term and apparently worldwide trend towards providing educational services that are adapted to the needs of special populations.

Few authoritative studies exist concerning the issue of how school systems deal with cultures of ethno-cultural groups of the country itself. The author has been involved with one such study, concerning more than twenty industrialized countries, which shall serve as the basis for the discussion that follows. One of the findings of the study was that almost all of the countries studied had taken steps in recent years to improve the educational opportunities of linguistic and cultural minorities in their public school systems. Almost all of them had developed policies well beyond the stage of providing simple remedial assistance to pupils of different groups to permit them to learn the main language of instruction and 'fit in' to the existing school curriculum. Instead, almost all had adopted at least a form of what is termed intercultural or multicultural education (terminology varies even for very similar pedagogical practices). The key element in the operational definition of this education for a multicultural society was the decision by policy makers to recognize that linguistic and cultural minorities often suffer from educational problems due to the difference between the school curriculum and their home culture and language. In response, the school curricula were modified to teach about elements of the culture of the minorities. In addition, many jurisdictions provided some support for the mother tongue of the minorities, such as in after-school classes. A few jurisdictions had moved, of course, to more complete recognition of the contribution of the culture of the minority group to the national cultural makeup, involving teaching of their languages as recognized subjects of study or use of the minority languages as a medium of instruction for various aspects of the curriculum. This recognition was always accompanied by an effort to ensure that the majority group(s) were given the opportunity of learning about the minority culture(s) in a way that expanded their opportunities for greater intercultural learning and understanding. The highest form of recognition occurred in countries where minorities were accorded equal status to the majority, enjoying control of their own education systems. Obviously, recognition was often linked to the length of permanency of the minority in question: the highest levels of recognition were given to those which had long been established in a given country.[15]

The responsibilities of teachers in dealing with populations of varying ethno-cultural origin vary with the type of national educational policy. The first major stage of development of such policies, which usually involves recognizing the minority culture in the curriculum and eliminating negative stereotyping in curriculum materials, can represent a near psychological revolution for teachers whose training has not prepared them for cultural adaptation. Reports from this and other studies emphasize the need for continuing dialogue not only with teachers but with all concerned communities, including the majority community.

One of the more interesting insights resulting from the study was that, as educational policies evolved towards greater recognition of the minority culture (and language), the value placed upon that cultural heritage tended to shift. Where such cultural differences are not recognized in the school, educational problems encountered by minority children are treated as stemming from a deficiency: they are seen as lacking an appropriate (majority/mainstream) cultural background and their own origins are treated as an obstacle to be removed, so to speak. But if *cultural differences* – rather than cultural deficits – are recognized as the source of educational difficulties, a shift occurs. Part of the problem is considered to be a deficiency in the school curriculum itself, a cultural 'mismatch' between teaching and pupil. Such a change tends to result not only in a recognition of the minority culture in the curriculum but also a willingness to treat the cultural background on a 'neutral' level, rather than as a purely negative factor. When educational policies reach the point of dealing with the child's own home language as a positive factor, as the root of the child's psychological and personal development, the result is usually twofold: some form of support measures to ensure, at least, further cognitive development in the mother tongue and a strongly positive value placed on the family culture in the curriculum. Further steps are possible in some countries, up to the full recognition of a minority culture as a valued part of the national heritage on a par with the culture of the majority. The use of more than one language as a medium of instruction is becoming more widespread and needs to be recognized in its own right as an important aspect of curricular decision making.

Varying degrees of recognition of minority groups in educational policy raise important issues with respect to teachers' responsibilities. Recognition of minority cultural differences in the majority classroom or school can be accomplished by teachers belonging to the majority cultural group, at least within certain limits. On the other hand, most countries with such policies appear to give priority also to ensuring that members of the minority groups are recruited as teachers or as teacher-aides. Obviously, use of the minority child's mother tongue for instructional purposes requires a native speaker in most situations.

The range of minority cultural differences to be accommodated depends upon the populations involved in a given situation, including an estimate

151

of their permanency as well as their relative numbers. It is entirely different to accommodate a single refugee child in the classroom of an industrialized country and quite another to deal with tens of thousands of refugees intermingled with the local population of an African city or a concentration of refugees making up more than 50 per cent of some classrooms in major immigration centres.[16] From his contacts with situations of this nature in different parts of the world, the author would tend to summarize the situation as follows: it is in the interest of educational authorities to review regularly their own national situation, to determine the extent to which the educational needs of their own minorities are being met adequately by current measures. The official recognition of an unmet educational need of a minority is the first step toward defining a policy to deal with it. In this process, the teaching profession should play a key role, providing information on educational needs and being consulted on appropriate responses, including the means of shaping the responsibilities of the teaching profession in a way that does, indeed, provide a means of adapting education to meet varied cultural requirements.

SUPPORT MEASURES FOR TEACHER RESPONSIBILITIES

The discussion of teacher responsibilities for cultural and intercultural aspects of education raises the issue of measures to support their work. As noted earlier, teachers' classroom roles and activities as facilitators of cultural development have two related aspects: (a) the curriculum and administrative framework within which they carry out their duties; and (b) their own autonomous efforts to adapt their instruction to teach students of widely varying cultural backgrounds and levels of academic aptitude. In the following, we discuss briefly the measures that may be taken by national authorities[17] to facilitate the role of the teacher as facilitator.

Given that teachers' example and outlook in everyday teaching behaviours plays a major role in determining how cultural learning occurs, steps to strengthen their effectiveness obviously require: first, a collaborative approach that recognizes teachers' basic role in promoting better education and, secondly, development of effective measures to support their assumption of new and more broadly-defined responsibilities.

As stated earlier, the issues to be dealt with by national authorities to promote cultural and intercultural education cannot be limited to the sole area of curriculum or to declarations of broad objectives. In some situations, purely symbolic declarations can serve to legitimate the actions taken by individual teachers to promote cultural objectives or to combat cultural prejudice. For example, a national leader may seize an appropriate occasion to speak out strongly before the media in support of racial tolerance – an action which may have a large symbolic value in determining how individuals interact. But large-scale effective changes in education require a co-ordinated approach to provide resources and leadership that support the individual responsibilities of teachers. For example, to give greater emphasis to cultural development – in the general objectives of the school – would be meaningless if the emphasis were not accompanied, for example, by measures to reflect this in the approved courses of study or in appropriate teaching materials. The definition of new or expanded roles for teachers in relation to cultural development and intercultural education requires that specific decisions be made to ensure co-ordinated action at all levels of the education system.

The most important decisions regarding cultural development involve: (a) modifying the curriculum, including teaching materials; and (b) providing assistance to teachers in their tasks and to facilitate their own evolution in applying the curriculum effectively.

The major aspects of *curriculum modification* are easy to enumerate, but the modifications themselves are complex activities requiring serious resources and sustained attention from senior authorities. The main aspects to be dealt with involve changes to:

1. The officially approved *objectives of schooling and the contents of syllabi* for specific subjects to ensure that sufficient weight is given to cultural aspects of teaching, both in terms of ensuring coverage of topics that are deemed culturally relevant and in terms of permitting necessary adaptations by the teacher to meet different learning needs and capacities of students.

2. Officially *approved or sanctioned textbooks* (and other resource materials), particularly in order to *include* the topics specified in the curriculum but also to *remove* those elements that run counter to cultural goals – for example, in promoting inter-group understanding and to combat racism, it would be important to remove negative stereotypes based upon race, religion, language or ethnic origin.

3. *Examination systems* to ensure that their operation does not run counter to the objectives set for cultural development – for example, failure to include culture-related issues in examinations may, in many environments, so devalue them that parents and students will essentially consider them of little practical relevance.

4. *Instructions given to school administrators* that encourage initiatives supportive of the teachers' role as facilitator, such as promotion of

153

linkages between the school and the surrounding communities, use of community resources in schooling, and the involvement of parents and families of students (particularly for disadvantaged groups) in school activities.

5. *Criteria for school inspection and teacher evaluation* that give due weight to cultural objectives.

Whereas most educational authorities have extensive experience in curriculum modifications to deal with traditional topics of instruction, promotion of cultural development can be strongly assisted by making use of other institutions outside the normal educational administration bureaucracies. *Specialized institutions* can be very helpful in promoting meaningful change. The following are examples of typical institutional roles that can be developed:

1. Use of research and university institutions in the process of gathering information on the educational needs to be met with respect to special populations.
2. Building linkages with non-governmental organizations in the cultural field, such as in performing arts, fine arts, literature, and popular arts and crafts to bolster and extend the necessarily limited resources available within the education systems.
3. Recourse to independent review mechanisms to study instructional materials and other resources to identify and eliminate excessive cultural bias and negative stereotyping of cultural or national groups.
4. Development of inter-school linkages similar to those promoted by the UNESCO Associated Schools Project, in order to ensure that better methods of dealing with cultural and intercultural aspects of education are experimented with and then made known on a widespread basis.[18]
5. Identifying strategies that are relevant and suited to national situations to strengthen the ties between schools and their surrounding communities.

All such curriculum change requires that *teacher training* should itself recognize cultural development goals. This implies, therefore, that two parallel courses of action be pursued:

1. Basic programmes of pre-service training should be revised, in particular to introduce requirements in certification procedures for teachers that will show due weight to cultural development.

2. Programmes of in-service education for teachers need to be designed so as to support evolution in teaching practices among those who are already in the profession. Because experienced teachers are the 'number one' influence determining how newly trained teachers will adapt to their profession, it is important to give especial emphasis to programmes of education that involve practising educators in reviewing their own practices. 'Surface' shifts in educational practice may be accomplished by administrative measures, but in-depth changes in attitudes are rarely achieved except through voluntary measures where groups of educators work together on a collaborative basis to develop their awareness and sensitivity to cultural issues.

CONCLUDING REMARKS

In reviewing the role of teachers as facilitators of cultural development, we have emphasized primarily those aspects where the teaching profession interacts with the official curriculum prescribed for schooling, including the resources used in teaching, i.e. the areas where fruitful collaboration between national authorities and the teaching profession can lead to positive change. The examination has been primarily guided by the viewpoint of teachers in terms of their work, based on the premise that their roles and responsibilities in facilitating cultural development will best be exercised in an environment where the realistic needs of their difficult roles are given appropriate consideration as a basis for long-term change. Developing the roles of teachers is a joint responsibility, shared by the teaching profession and educational authorities.

NOTES

1. Schools supported from private funds but whose teaching content is formally regulated by the State are, therefore, included; but post-secondary education and informal, unregulated education is excluded. The educational roles of families, the media, and para-public or private institutions are, therefore, not the focus of the article. However, the reader should note that in most of the discussion that follows, the author uses the word 'school' in the abstract sense to refer to any teaching/learning situation. The remarks thus apply to informal educational situations (i.e. outside formal school buildings) provided that they fall within the criterion of being State regulated – such as literacy campaign in rural areas.

2. It is common to talk of 'sub-cultures' to refer to the variety of cultural groupings found within States or localities, as if each one were derived from a single over-arching culture, using terms such as sub-culture of poverty, youth sub-culture, working-class sub-culture and so on. I prefer to view each individual as being a participant in multiple communities of persons with varying degrees of shared (cultural) traits. For example, family identity is usually at the centre of individual cultural affinity and the family is, in this sense, a cultural community. It is also possible to speak of a school culture to refer either to the specific ambience of an individual school or collectively to the type of cultural framework provided by schools of a given type: the school culture of a vocational school may be different from that of an elite secondary school.

3. 'Western' sociological literature has dwelt extensively upon the analysis of culture in relationship to schooling and the school process. There are few authoritative syntheses of the many diverse schools of thought that have emerged in the last three decades. cf. Jean-Claude Forquin, *École et culture : le point de vue des sociologues britanniques*, Bruxelles, De Boeck, 1989, a synthesis which, though focused on one country, provides insights into theoretical developments that are widely shared in other countries.

4. In this discussion, we shall refer to all such forms of teaching adaptation as 'intercultural' and shall keep the adjective 'multicultural' as a neutral descriptive term to refer to a country or situation/school where multiple cultures are present.

5. Artists were often hard-working, but in a European society where the vast majority of the population were peasants or farmers and the small urban populations consisted mainly of working and service classes who performed manual or craft labour, 'fine art' was a distinctly upper-class phenomenon, at least in terms of the consumers of the finished products. Although many women practised fine arts, their labours were rarely considered worthy of serious public consideration as art. Cloth products rarely achieved status as art, except for tapestries from workshops such as Gobelins, in France, where overall designs were furnished by a small number of male artists; the execution of the design and the detailed selection of colours, on which the artistic effect actually depended, was done by other persons whose work was perceived to be inferior and, therefore, a craft (*artisanal*).

6. Cf. the early work of Paulo Freire, *Pedagogy of the oppressed*, New York, Seabury Press, 1968.

7. Following usage in UNESCO and other international bodies, all education authorities within a given Member State are referred to as national authorities. In many member countries, decision-making on education may be distributed between authorities ranging from a central national ministry through various intermediate levels of administration and elected officials down to the school and the individual teacher. The reference here to 'national educational authorities' is to all of those authorities who make decisions on what should be taught and how it is taught, thereby setting guidelines for teachers' activities.

8. In most countries, attempts to use such media as a major vehicle for teaching ordinary subject areas are usually confined to limited populations taught in some form of distance education; widespread use of such media for a significant portion of the day in the 'average' schoolroom remains a distant utopian suggestion in most countries, but its advent would imply not a new approach to what is called 'media education' but a fundamental restructuring of schooling as it now exists, including all aspects of the teaching role.

9. Literacy programmes are rarely perceived as being intended at cultural replacement or displacement. However, when combined with other forces at work in society, they may serve as the medium through which additional stress is placed upon traditional cultures

and life-styles. The fact remains, as well, that literacy programmes are often pursued to promote literacy in languages which the intended learners do not speak as a mother tongue and may not understand well or at all.

10. An inventory of typical models for using school-based curriculum development for stimulating new approaches to intercultural education is provided in: S. Churchill, 'Teaching about world issues in UNESCO Associated Schools', *in*: Robert Harris, ed., *The teaching of contemporary world issues*, Paris, UNESCO, 1986. The reader should note that such approaches can easily be adapted in schools that are not members of the Associated School network.

11. The terminology is borrowed from an OECD study: 'The Finance, Organization and Governance of Education for Special Populations', cf. *The education of minority groups. An enquiry into problems and practices of fifteen countries*. Centre for Educational Research and Innovation, Organisation for Economic Co-operation and Development. Aldershot, UK, Gower, 1983.

12. Melvyn I. Semmel, Jay Gottlieb & Nancy M. Robinson, 'Mainstreaming: perspectives on educating handicapped children in the public school' *in*: David C. Berliner, ed., *Review of educational research* (American Educational Research Association), 1979, no. 7, (Washington, DC), p. 223-79.

13. Ibid.

14. In Canada, for example, organizations of the deaf have carried on major campaigns for recognition of their linguistic needs, resulting in changes in the type of sign language that is taught in some institutions.

15. I summarize very briefly a highly complex situation. See: Stacy Churchill, *The education of linguistic and cultural minorities in the OECD countries*, Clevedon, UK, Multilingual Matters, 1986.

16. For educational considerations see: Isabel Kaprielian-Churchill and Stacy Churchill, *The pulse of the world: refugees in our schools, a guide for educators*, Toronto, OISE Press, in press (1994).

17. The reader is reminded that 'national authorities' is used here generically to refer to all *responsible authorities* from the level of school principal/headmaster up to the national level.

18. See remark in note 14 above.

CHAPTER VIII

The role of education in cultural and artistic development

Kees P. Epskamp

Roughly speaking, there are two ways in which people are mapping and ordering their social and physical environments, and attaching meaning to this self-made order. This is the way, for instance, that people create their own social and physical reality, which in the final resort turns out to be nothing more than a social construction. The first way to map out the world is the logical and causal approach. The other one is the more associative approach.

Inventories, lists, separations, classifications and models based on a logical/causal way of ordering the environment take as their point of departure a cause/effect relationship – if A then B – in which there is always a time aspect playing an important role. First there is the cause, and later there is the effect; there is always 'sooner' and 'later'. In using this form of classification people strive for an absolute mutual distinction between the categories used. This is one of the reasons why people use terms and concepts which are opposite to each other in meaning and significance. In fact, one is using oppositions with a clear binary character.

This situation is quite different with the more associative approach. In classifying the world through an associative approach distinctions are made through the similarities and differences between objects, plants, animals, people, etc. Even today, these associative classifications of the environment are still important within society, not because they have been proved by empirical tests to be infallible, but because the community or the individual using them has confidence in them. This is a domain where truth and make-believe lie very close together.

In the associative approach to analysing and explaining the world, objects and ideas are brought together because the 'explorer' feels emotionally that they belong together, even though a more logical approach may suggest that they have absolutely nothing in common, perhaps being completely different in time and place. At the beginning of this century some Western anthropologists labelled the associative approach to ordering and analysing the world the 'primitive mentality', typical of people living in remote African, Asian and Latin American countries, in other words, people who were supposed to be incapable of thinking in a logical/causal way, as people living in the North Atlantic world have learned to do.

Theories about 'primitive mentality' have now lost their meaning. The idea about the 'primitive way of thinking' was later picked up by Lévi-Strauss in his ideas about the 'savage mind'. According to Lévi-Strauss (1978, p. 13) we have to make a distinction between the scientific way of thinking and the 'logic of the concrete', a distinction between those who prefer to communicate mainly by using images and symbols and those who have respect for and use the data which are mainly collected directly by the senses.

However, all terminology like 'primitive mentality' or 'savage mind' supports the image of the noble savage living in his world and looking at his surroundings through the eyes of a naive child. And this imagery goes even further, because we tend to associate such exotic cultures with a pure and unspoilt way of life very close to and in harmony with nature.

This naive way of perceiving the world is not only synonymous with a so-called 'primitive' or childlike environment, but is also typical of the world that artists create for themselves within society. In fact, by using the associative potential the artist is supposed to project an 'image' of the world (his or her own world) onto the mind of the public. He or she transforms a piece of wood or stone, a blank canvas or an empty stage into a work of art.

For a very long time this way of perceiving and analysing the world in an associative way has also been considered typical of women, because women – by their 'nature' – were supposed to have a much more emotional approach to their surroundings than men.

Thus, in general, women, children, primitive people and artists are supposed to have a different view of life than the average North Atlantic adult male, whose trademark is to approach the surrounding world in a logical and causal way. This is the way of thinking, analysing and ordering the world that made it possible to achieve modern technology, without which most countries on the Northern hemisphere would be still poor agricultural nations.

ART EDUCATION AND THE TRAINING OF ARTISTS

Most learning is hierarchical. The process evolves one step at a time. Certain things have to be successfully accomplished before new things can be learned. It begins with the most simple learning and ends up with the understanding of very complex matters. There are various ways to differentiate this step-by-step learning process. First of all children learn to discriminate signals and to respond to them. Then one learns the connection between a stimulus and the given response. After that, children learn to perceive a relationship between more than one stimulus/response relationship. They 'chain up' several of these relations into a 'field'. Then the child slowly starts to learn all sorts of visual and oral discriminations followed by verbal associations. Slowly the meaning of rules and (abstract) concepts is taught and, finally, the child is confronted with learning how to solve problems.

This clearly shows that the learning process starts at a simple level and becomes more and more complex. The same is true of the following taxonomy of learning packages taken from Schramm (1977, p. 72): attitudes, motor skills, verbal information, cognitive strategies and intellectual skills. In this context cognitive strategies are the managerial skills which we learn in order to manage most effectively our learning experiences and our intellectual luggage. Here also there is a kind of hierarchy in learning goals and achievements. In both taxonomies the development of intellectual skills is in fact the last stage of a successful education. Most education systems begin in elementary school with the teaching of simple motor and mental skills, and ending with the ultimate level of mental skill training at university. Art education and the training of artists follows more or less the same path.[1]

The training of artists is not the same thing as art education. The training of artists has to do with the development of a science of the concrete concerning the materials one is working with. It has also to do with the development of motor skills about handling the technical devices to work and re-work the raw materials. First and foremost the artist-to-be learns craft-skills. He/she also receives training in using the senses to perceive and analyse the materials he/she is working with.

Art education is a more intellectual exercise forming part of the curriculum in the formal education system. According to Goblot (1973, p. 434), art education as we know it today at the secondary school was introduced at the end of the last century. Its foremost purpose was to educate middle-class children about the general cultural heritage. One of the objectives of art education is to make children 'culturally literate' and to introduce them to elementary practical skills in dealing with the arts, including, according to Tohmé (1992, p. 21), music, theatre, dance, art in general and literary expression.

Following the ideas of Bourdieu, cultural literacy or even 'art literacy' was something the middle-class art consumers were lacking. Confronted with a work of art, every individual among the public will experience something very directly, but not necessarily because the work of art appeals to his/her feelings. First of all, says Crego (& Groot, 1985, p. 224), one looks at a work of art as a puzzle, trying to find significance in it by comparing it with other works of art one knows or with things in one's daily experience to which the work of art might refer.

Enjoying art brings along the necessary knowledge and skills to evaluate it. And there are several ways of evaluating it. One approach is to find indications about the period when the work of art was produced. Another is to find out more about the 'school' or movement to which the artist belonged or, on the contrary, did not belong. Or one might compare it to works of art by other artists from the same period and see if there are similarities in style or theme. After some training this makes it possible to come to a genre evaluation.

Schooling, training and a positive attitude towards art in the home environment are of great help in learning to evaluate works of art. Those unfamiliar with art, such as the 'man in the street' who rarely goes to a museum or a theatre, will recognize and interpret a work of art by reference to their regular daily life. Realism and recognition are important evaluative criteria for them.

As is already clear from this statement, differences in art appreciation are directly connected with social differences. In short, knowledge of culture and art is related not only to social environment but also to social class. To be able to talk about the meaning of works of art becomes a symbol of distinction in itself. And this is partly what art education is meant for: to train a new 'aristocracy' of well-educated art lovers with a taste for distinction.

Another aspect of art education is the practical side. Some art techniques – like drawing, painting, sculpture, music, drama and dance – form part of the art education curriculum at primary and secondary school levels. This practical skill training is not meant to make the students into artists. It is meant to introduce them to artistic skills, according to Bateson (1973, p. 439), combining many levels of mind – unconscious, conscious and external – to make a statement about their combination.

In the Dutch education system, art education is divided into three disciplines: visual arts, theatre and music. According to Demirbas and Rabbae (1990, p. 13), art education in the Dutch formal education system aims at the development of a stronger personality, the development of creativity and the transfer of knowledge to contribute to an optimal functioning in societal and cultural life. This fairly matches the three general main objectives of the Dutch education system: personal development; societal and cultural development; and an orientation and preparation for the labour market, including the artistic one.

There are differences – some people say – between arts and crafts. According to Wollheim (1968, p. 54), when speaking about crafts, we are talking about efficacy: getting started and achieving an end product. Talking about crafts, one can make a distinction between planning and execution. Planning demands some prior knowledge about the desired result and a sort of rough calculation about how this result is going to be achieved. Most often, the arts have to do with the final product, while the crafts are related to the working process, the making of art. This means that, during his/her training, the artist becomes familiar with several crafts which, later on, he/she will need for creative art work. Of course, there are people who use these same skills – like woodcarving – for non-artistic purposes. Craftsmen, for instance, use them to make utensils for use in daily life.

Although the training of artists nowadays forms part of the formal education system, in former days this training was of a much more informal nature. In some societies, children were confronted with the arts on a permanent basis in their daily existence. The arts were present and children picked up the relevant skills in a playful way. A really talented child would get extra training on a personal basis by some experienced grown-up artist, be it as a drummer, a dancer, a woodcarver or puppeteer.

However, in societies with a more elaborate social organization and a differentiated rural and urban environment, this personal counselling became part of the training process. Craftsmen organized themselves into guilds or associations, and also took care of training. Young and talented boys and girls became the apprentices of a 'master'. These guilds and associations had a monopoly in the production of their works of art. They were set aside as special social groups within society. In some societies they even developed as separate castes.

In societies with a fixed aristocracy, there existed the system of royal patronage. Noblemen not only functioned as the main sponsors of art, they also established the first formal art schools or academies. In the European feudal society of mediaeval times, as also in other societies with a strong monasterial infrastructure, such as in South-East Asian Buddhist societies, the 'temple' also sponsored the arts.

According to Williams (1981, p. 60), the emergence of the secular art schools was marked by two historical developments: the declining importance of the church and the court as the main patrons of the art; and a further differentiation between 'arts' and 'crafts'. The master/apprentice relationship developed into one between the professor and the student. Although there still existed an emphasis on the personal relationship between the teacher and the pupil, more and more students received training in a classroom situation.

Of course, there still were the informal academies which were related to a special artist – painters and sculptors – like those in Florence, for example, which were visited by Michelangelo at the end of the fifteenth century. However, these 'schools' were still financially supported by a duke or other noblemen. But they soon achieved a more independent status, especially since the upper levels of the 'bourgeoisie' became interested in possessing art as objects of prestige.

Academies organized exhibitions and a new kind of middleman developed, the art 'broker', nowadays better known as the art dealer. Instead of guilds, artists now started to organize themselves into professional societies. Academics, such as historians, started to take a special interest in art and the arts were a subject of 'research' among professors at the university level. What was formerly known as a specific conglomeration of artists being educated at a specific academy, now became known as a 'school' or 'movement'. Among artists and art historians, the word 'school' achieved a double meaning. Following Williams (1981, p. 63), a 'school' could be literally, in the modern sense, an institution in which there was a master and pupils, whose work can be recognized by typical characteristics. However, for some art historians a 'school' was more or less identified with a particular 'master', without being directly related – in an institutional way – to the products of his supposed pupils.

At the beginning of this century artists and art historians started to talk about (their) art as 'movements' created by the historical flow of ideas opposing or influencing each other. These currents or tendencies became labelled by several '-isms', like Impressionism or Expressionism.

BACK TO THE BEGINNING

According to Nketia (1975, p. 59-60), so far there is no evidence that art education in Africa South of the Sahara in pre-colonial times was organized in a formal, systematic manner; it was not organized on an institutional basis. Learning took place by social experience in which children were exposed to music, dance, masquerades, etc. Training by organized apprenticeship learning was not highly developed. A drummer or singer would

163

sometimes be sent to a master. But, in the first instance, the children themselves learned some basic artistic skills by observing and imitating.

In daily life, the African child was hardly ever deprived of these experiences. From the cradle, it was familiar with the mother's singing and dancing. Later on, music, dance and performance formed an important part of the informal education among the various peer- and age-groups the child and adolescent was passing through. Because specialization in musical instruments tended to run through families or households, children were encouraged to start learning these skills at a very early age.

The child was often corrected in his 'homework' in a physical way. The master drummer, for example among the Akan (in Ghana) would tap the various rhythms the child was learning on his shoulder blade to obtain the motor feeling involved in working on a talking drum (Nketia, 1975, p. 61).

This physical way of teaching is also well known in dance education on Bali (Indonesia). According to Bateson (1973, p. 87), teaching by muscular rote, in which the pupil is made to perform the correct movements, is most strikingly developed in the dancing lessons. Schechner (1985, p. 213-14) described the way a teacher on Bali 'manipulated' his pupil:

I've watched Kabul, the dance guru of Batuan, Bali, as he stood behind a young girl, maybe 8 years old, manipulating her wrists, hands, and shoulders with his hands; her torso with his body; her legs with his knees and feet. He used her as a puppet transferring directly his own body-sense of the dance. [. . .] In this method of 'direct acquisition' by manipulation, imitation and repetition, there is the paradox that the 'creativity' of the performer comes only after he has mastered a form by rote learning.

Thus, creativity, in the sense of personal expression in a work of art, is only permitted once the craft has been mastered. In this context craftsmanship is understood as the skill to use the tools, whereas expression is the ability to communicate, to 'say' something to the public or the wider community. Learning these skills is not only achieved by manipulative techniques but also by developing a better understanding with the students, by teaching them how to observe carefully the performance techniques of adult artists within the community. This leads to control, which, according to Grallert (1991, p. 262), is an instructional concern in any children's training programme, where making a finished, polished product is considered the most important outcome.

This refers especially to the context in which the learning process is becoming more and more formalized, a training process in which exercises are carried out on a regular basis, in which the underlying 'logic' of performing is learned by doing, and followed by some years during which the student is enabled to find out for himself/herself what he/she is working on, while experimenting with the arts is a domain reserved for the very experienced, the wise and old masters. These are the only ones entitled to make changes to the cultural heritage passed down from one generation to the next.

This is quite opposed to the contemporary Euro-American tradition in which creativity and originality are highly prized among young artists. As Schechner (1985, p. 229) says, critics in the North Atlantic societies are keen on new interpretations of old texts. Thus, says Schechner (ibid), 'a new interpretation is a way of uncovering the progressive tendencies in an apparently old (= outdated, of no more use) text.'

And this reflects the different attitude towards the role of the teacher in various 'living' cultures. As Schechner (1982, p. 40) has stated, many Asian theatre artists support themselves by teaching, which serves three functions: (a) supporting the artists in their personal development as a performing artist; (b) transmitting performance knowledge; and (c) 'educating' the audience. The main difference in attitude to the teacher between the Euro-American and the 'Southern' traditions is that in the former the teaching of past traditions is often looked down on: 'Those who cannot perform, teach'. While in most Southern societies beyond the North Atlantic world teaching is the crowning achievement of the artist's career (Schechner, 1985, p. 255).

This says something about the societal perspective used to show respect for masters of the arts. Pupils are not expected to ask questions. Expressing one's doubts about the craft is regarded as disrespectful. It is only in the North Atlantic world that pupils who want to become artists are expected to state their expectations about their teacher. And according to Barthes (1977, p. 197), the pupil expects the teacher: (a) to be of help in following qualified professional training; (b) to fulfil the traditional role of a scientific authority, a knowledgeable, didactically qualified source; (c) reveal the techniques and secrets to become a future master by helping the pupil to pass his final initiation (e.g. exams); (d) perform as an instructor (a guru) in reflection; (e) represent a 'movement of ideas', a 'school', an intellectual heritage; (f) initiate the pupil into the complexity of the professional language and terminology; (g) make understandable the rules which have to do with the final proof of ability; and (h) be of help in writing application forms, requests for sponsorship or writing a reference to a potential future employer.

STRENGTHENING THE CULTURAL IDENTITY

'Culture is the soul of our people. Without a soul, without art our people cannot exist,' says Proeung Chhieng, director of the dance department of

165

the School of Fine Arts in Phnom Penh (Cambodia) in an interview with Van Vegchel (1990, p. 10). Although for more than twenty years people in Cambodia have not experienced peace, this conservatory in the capital city of the country functions as the host for some 600 students in dance, music and visual arts.

In former days, patronage of Cambodian artists was in the hands of the aristocracy, monasteries and the landed gentry. However, with the coming of Pol Pot not only were the majority of Cambodian nobility murdered, but also their functionaries and proteges, such as artists. Thousands of artists were arrested, put in camps, tortured and killed. Costumes and instruments were destroyed, as well as scripts, books and performance scores. For that reason, at the conservatory in Phnom Pen old dances and pieces of music are literally being 'restored'. Only a few people survived the Khmer Rouge violence, and without any written reference or visual documentation they are trying to recollect those performing scores they remember and transfer them to younger generations of performing artists.

But most of the dance pieces are irretrievably lost. Of the more than twenty dances in the repertory, explains Proeung Chhieng, the women have only been able fully to reconstruct three, and only an hour or two of many five-act ballets that traditionally started at 7 p.m. and lasted until dawn (Blaustein, 1989, p. 44).

Eradicating the soul of the people by destroying part of their cultural heritage has also been carried out systematically during colonial times and is still a major problem in situations of political oppression and ethnic conflicts, as many indigenous people are still experiencing today. To keep up their old traditions more and more ethnic groups are taking the initiative by organizing their own art education institutes.

Among the various Canadian Indian groups, an initiative has developed to set up a native theatre school as a programme of the Association for Native Development in the Performing and Visual Arts (ANDPVA), a non-profit-making organization which seeks to promote 'the arts' as a means of preserving native traditions by developing some of these traditions into a contemporary art form, and communicating to natives and non-natives alike an awareness of the Indian heritage and concerns in an ever-changing society.

Not only are non-governmental organizations setting up art education institutes, but elected governments are also paying attention to this matter. An example of this might be Papua New Guinea. At the beginning of the 1980s, this country had an outspoken cultural policy, which was reflected in the State budget. In an interview with Berman (1984, p. 26-27), the former Prime Minister of Papua New Guinea, Michael Somare, had a clear vision on this matter. In a country with as many as 717 different ethnic groups, the cultural policy and the policy concerning art education is to come to a part of the national identity. In a country where traditional wooden works of art and contemporary art might both be made by one and the same woodcarver, the only possibility to strive for this national identity was to set up a consistent, nationwide art education system.

The Expressive Arts curriculum takes the Papua New Guinean culture as its point of departure. This art education curriculum consists of several subjects which in other countries might be taught separately, such as, for example, drawing and painting, manual skills and music. The Expressive Arts curriculum has been designed by the National Education Board to create a more flexible educational approach towards the arts. This was based on the fact that in the traditional Melanesian society there is no real separation between the manufacturer of a drum and the musician who plays it, between the carver of a wooden mask and the bearer, between the costume-maker and the dancer, between the composer and the singer, etc.

To create qualified teachers in this area there was a need for art education at the tertiary level. In 1975 the National Arts School was called into being in Port Moresby. It was the first Pacific artistic training centre at the level of higher education. According to Thompson (1989, p. 48-49), although there is more and more formal training, there is still a refreshing quality about a lot of the work. Most of the people undergoing education still have one foot in the past and one in the future. For that reason 'contemporary art' at this training institute is synonymous with continuation, and a contemporary artistic evolution is an ongoing process.

Unlike Papua New Guinea, most developing countries have not opted for an unconventional arts education curriculum. One of the reasons for this is that their curriculum is still a reproduction of the colonial education system introduced in former times. This in fact goes for most education systems in the North African countries, such as Tunisia, Algeria and Morocco. Music schools in Morocco fall under the jurisdiction of the Ministry of Culture. The curriculum and the teaching methods resemble the European way of teaching.

However, the music school in the *medina* of Fez has a different way of teaching music. Here the traditional way of teaching music is still preferred. The school is a public school. It does not have any religious affiliations. Most teachers teach the way they were taught, via the oral tradition with a strong emphasis on memory training using mnemonic devices to learn the various rhythms. According to Loopuyt (1990, p. 6), the students come together three times a week. The training sessions last two hours. At the first session the student is supposed to know the lines of an eighteenth century poem by heart. Collective reciting, in fact, is a warming-up exercise for the voice and the mind. This is done in a very effective way, through the *iqa* in which (hand) clapping and reciting are brought together. Step by step the training programme goes on.

After having learned *iqa*, the students are taught to handle the small accompanying drum. And after two years the students are allowed to learn the techniques of playing instruments required for the melody line. However, from the beginning to the end in this music training programme the training of the voice is dominant. Although all students are very acquainted with the melodies they know from childhood onwards, they are not allowed to sing until their education has been finished.

MUSIC EDUCATION IN A MULTI-ETHNIC SOCIETY

A lot of people from Morocco and Turkey came to The Netherlands at the end of the 1960s as foreign industrial labourers, mainly living in the bigger Dutch towns. From those who started to live permanently in the country, the second and third generation of children attended Dutch primary schools. The children were expected to learn Dutch as a second language and were confronted with Dutch expressions, values and attitudes. Art education in the visual or performing arts, in drawing, music or drama emphasized the Dutch definition of things, such as 'beauty' or 'perfection'.

In the meantime there has been a growing tendency to strive for intercultural education in general. The reason for this is that, although the multi-ethnic nature of those living in the Netherlands may be evident, the willingness of the Dutch people to accept and participate in this multi-ethnic community is still minimal (Dors, 1990, p. 28). One of the ways to change this attitude is by starting to make children aware of cultural differences and to create a sense of mutual understanding. This means not only paying attention in the classroom situation to cultural differences but also to aesthetic experiences.

It is for this reason that more and more attention is paid to intercultural education in the Dutch education system at all levels. In basic education especially the subjects in the field of art education (music in particular[2]) are dealing with a more common understanding of the mutual experience and appreciation of each other's ethnic art forms. At the higher education level, teacher training (including that for drama) has developed a special focus on intercultural education. In the out-of-school educational programmes at music schools, children nowadays are offered the possibility of learning to play musical instruments other than the usual well-known European ones.

As we have seen, music forms a lively integrated part in the upbringing of many children, especially in those cultures where music is used to demarcate the daily and seasonal events of public life. In the North Atlantic world the consumption of live music on such occasions has been reduced to a minimum. There are still brass bands which are called for on important public occasions, like sports matches, agricultural fairs or royal events, etc. There are still church bells to remind the general public about the time of day or about their religious obligations. There is 'muzak' in supermarkets and airports. However, the consumption of music in the North has become differentiated into groups according to age, taste and ethnic background. This has been made possible by the media. Contrary to music consumption in communities in Africa South of the Sahara, people in the North started to consume music as a solitary activity by radio, stereo or walkman. The only public music events left are concerts.

In the formation of musical perception, rhythm plays an important role. It appears as a support and impulse to the child's musical memory, being consolidated long before consciousness of melody. In spite of the fact that the child responds to rhythm accurately with his body, he does not become conscious of rhythm per se until he has developed his consciousness of melody. The child cannot distinguish the rhythm from accompanying movements. This is possible only at a subsequent stage between six and seven years of age and this seems to depend not on the development of musical perception, but on the evaluation of his thought (Suliteanu, 1979, p. 210).

To make children minimally 'literate' in at least their own musical tradition, music must form part of the basic education curriculum. However, most primary schools, at least in the big cities in the Netherlands, are of a multi-ethnic nature. This makes it hard to decide in which musical tradition the children should be made 'literate'. However, during the 1980s among policy makers and teachers an ongoing debate resulted in the first experiments of intercultural musical education at primary schools.

CONCLUDING REMARKS

More and more attention is being paid within the various basic education curricula all over the world to arts education. This has been done for at least two reasons: (a) to give children a general cultural background and under-

169

standing of art in general – in theory as well as in practice; and (b) to provide children with the opportunity to discover their preferences and talents in the arts and to prepare some of them for future artistic education at a higher educational level. In this way arts education within the basic education curriculum functions as a form of 'discovery learning'. It enables children to undertake a step-by-step discovery of various ways of thinking and thus to acquaint themselves with a more associative approach of ordering their social and physical environment.

A side effect of including the visual and performing arts into the basic educational curriculum is that this kind of teaching might strengthen the cultural (ethnic) and/or national identity. In countries making a big effort in favour of national identity, like for example Papua New Guinea, emphasis in arts education is laid upon the common traits among the aesthetic traditions of the more than 700 ethnic groups in the country. In the North Atlantic world, where there is a growing awareness about being a multicultural society, emphasis is put on developing a tolerant attitude among children towards differences in experiencing the arts.

In this context, music seems to be an appealing subject for children. Music forms an integrated part of culture to which children become acquainted at a very early age. The development of different rhythms is among the first things a child learns. Only at a later stage in its development will the distinctive experience of various melodies become explicit, about the age of 6 or 7, corresponding to the age of entry into the basic education system. It is at this age that the child is very flexible in learning to discriminate and appreciate the various rhythmic and melodic cultural differences, especially when this is related to singing and movement.

Of course, there are other institutions in society which are helpful in developing a positive attitude among children towards unfamiliar cultural and artistic expressions.[3] Several ethnological museums have developed an educational department together with a special display area for children. The Royal Tropical Museum (Amsterdam) created a special children's museum in which they are actively introduced to other ways of life. Children are enabled to walk through a village in Bali and (under professional guidance) to touch and play with the things available to create a Balinese feeling of their own, playing the musical instruments available and trying out the first dance steps.

NOTES

1. See V.S. Sobkin and V.A. Levin with their article 'Artistic education and aesthetic upbringing' in *Soviet education* (now *Russian education and society*) (Armonk, NY), vol. 33, no. 4, 1991, p. 67-82, referring to the situation in the former USSR. See also: Seyyed Hossein Nasr and his article entitled 'The teaching of art in the Islamic world', which was published in *Muslim education quarterly* (Cambridge, UK), vol. 6, no. 2, 1989, p. 4-24.
2. See: D.J. Elliott's article 'Muziek als cultuur: naar een multi-cultureel concept van kunst-zinnige vorming (1)', published in *Kunsten & Educatie: tijdschrift voor theorievorming* (Utrecht), vol. 3, no. 3, December 1990, p. 33-39.
3. See the article by H. Kakebeeke and J. Letschert: 'Het god'lijk licht en een blik toffees; gesprek over kunst, educatie en de rol van musea' published in *Onderwijs en Opvoeding* (Baarn, Netherlands), vol. 37, no. 3, 1985 .

REFERENCES

Barthes, R. 1977. *Image, music, text.* Glasgow, UK, Fontana/Collins.
Bateson, G. 1973. *Steps to an ecology of mind: collected essays in anthropology, psychiatry, evolution and epistemology.* St Albans, UK,, Paladin.
Berman, M. 1984. Cultuur- en kunstonderwijs slaat brug tussen traditioneel en modern; Papua New Guinea ende kunst van het overleven. *Overzicht* (The Hague), vol. 14, no. 2, p. 48-49.
Blaustein, S. 1989. The Khmer renaissance; Hun Sen's government seeks legitimacy as the preserver of the nation's culture. *Far Eastern economic review* (Hong Kong), vol 145, no. 38, p. 44-46.
Crego, C.; Groot, G.1985. Pierre Bourdieu en de filosofische esthetica; aantekeningen bij het nawoord van La Distinction. *Algemeen Nederlands Tijdschrift voor Wijsbegeerte* (Assen), vol. 77, no. 1, p. 21-35.
Demirbas, N.; Rabbae, M. 1990. Intercultureel onderwijs en kunstzinnige educatie. *Kunsten & Educatie, tijdschrift voor theorievorming* (Utrecht), vol. 3, no. 3, p. 8-16.
Dors, H.G.1990. Kunstzinnige educatie in multi-etnisch perspectief.*Kunsten & Educatie, tijdschrift voor theorievorming* (Utrecht), vol. 3, no. 3, vol. 24-32.
Engelen, P. van. 1991. Drama: een volwaardig onderwijsvak. *Speltribune*, September, p. 24-27.
Goblot, E. 1973. Cultural education as a middle-class enclave. *In:* **Burns, E.; Burns, T.**, eds. *Sociology of literature and drama.* Harmondsworth, UK, Penguin Books, p. 433-44.
Grallart, M. 1991. Working from the inside out: a practical approach to expression. *Harvard educational review* (Cambridge, MA), vol. 61, no. 3, p. 260-269.
Lévi-Strauss, C. 1978. *Myth and meaning; five talks for radio by Claude Lévi-Strauss.* Toronto, University of Toronto Press.
Loopuyt, M. 1990. De muziekschool in Fez; Marokko. *Wereldmuziek* (Amsterdam), vol. 1, no. 5, p. 6-7.
Nketia, J.H.K. 1975.*The music of Africa.* London, Victor Gollancz Ltd.
Schechner, R. 1982. *The end of humanism; writing on performance.* New York, Performing Arts Journal Publications.
—. 1985. *Between theatre and anthropology.* Philadelphia, PA, University of Pennsylvania Press.

Schramm, W. 1977. *Big media, little media; tools and technologies for instruction.* Beverly Hills, Sage Publications.

Suliteanu, G. 1979. 'The role of songs for children in the formation of musical perception.' *In*: **Blacking, J.; Kealiinohomoku, J.W., eds.** *The performing arts; music and dance.* The Hague, Mouton Publishers, p. 205-19. (Series: World Anthropology)

Tohmé, G. 1992. *Cultural development and environment.* Geneva, International Bureau of Education (IBE).

Thompson, L. 1989. A foot in the past, a foot in the future. *Pacific islands monthly*(Suva, Fiji), no. 59, p. 48-49.

Van Vegchel, J. 1990. Het herstel van de Kambodjaanse cultuur. *Internationale Samenwerking*, no. 10, p. 10-11

Williams, R. 1981. *Culture.* Glasgow, Fontana/Collins.

Wollheim, R. 1968. *Art and its objects.* Harmondsworth, UK, Penguin Books.

CHAPTER IX

Cultural development through the interaction between education, the community and society

F.M. Bustos

PRELIMINARY CONSIDERATIONS

This chapter tries to explore the possibilities and potentialities that schools have to promote cultural development for the benefit, first, of the local communities and then for the whole society. As is clearly expressed by the chapter heading, it is assumed that certain kinds of interaction are possible for cultural development in both directions: from the school to the community and society, and from them to the school.

What are these interactions and what are the possibilities of increasing them? What is their character and what factors make them possible or limit them? These are some of the questions that are intended to be answered in the following pages.

The relationships between education and culture, between educational and cultural development, between cultural agencies and educational institutions, and between cultural and educational activities is a subject whose interest and importance has been on the increase during recent years. Evidence of this is the fact that the forty-third session of the International Conference on Education (ICE, Geneva, September 1992) was devoted to the analysis and examination of this theme, and to proposing worldwide actions.

Several factors seem to underlie or determine to a greater or lesser extent a new approach to interaction in cultural development between educational institutions and communities, especially at the local level. Among others, the following can be considered:

First of all, the most obvious and perhaps the most determining phenomenon is the profound demographic, economic, political and social changes that have occurred in society in a relatively short period, especially as a result of the extremely rapid advances of science and their technological applications. These changes and the speed at which they have taken

place have modified the world's scenery, our social relations, our organizations – the State, among them – and even the values and behaviour of
human groups and individuals (King & Schneider, 1991).

The demographic transformations, have already been described in
Chapter I. Another important factor to be considered, resulting from the
rapid advances of technology, is the growth, diversification and penetration of the mass media, which has had obvious implications – both negative and positive – on cultural development. In a later section of this
chapter we will deal with this aspect in more detail.

In economic terms, it is important to note that culture has now acquired
the dimension of merchandise that can be bought, sold, used to make a
profit and provide employment. In fact, the cultural 'worker' has become
an occupational category.

From a socio-political point of view, it is worth remarking the progress
that has been achieved regarding the recognition of some universal human
rights, the reduction of different kinds of discrimination, the recognition of
social and individual liberties, and the acceptance of democracy as a form
of political organization. All of this has had positive effects on the cultural
field, such as the recognition of multi-culturalism, respect for the cultures
of ethnic minorities – especially indigenous peoples – and the recognition
of culture as a social good and as a right of peoples and individuals.

These changes or transformations occurring at present in society have a
number of typical characteristics.

ACCELERATION

Both in quantitative and in qualitative terms the pace of progress has been
quickening. This has posed serious problems for its appropriate assimilation by people. It has also had a negative effect due to the ever-widening
technical-scientific gap existing between industrialized and developing
countries. In educational terms, the main effect is a lack of synchronization
between the speed of changes in society – including some cultural ones –
and the ability of education systems to adapt (Gozzer, 1990). The negative
effects have been suffered most directly by the poorest social groups and
countries.

These rapid changes occurring in different sectors of society have
brought about progress in certain aspects of culture. In fact, society's
opinion has gained more influence in the formulation of cultural policies
and in the allocation of State resources, has been more widely diffused
through the mass media, and has also carried more weight through the

involvement of enterprises, non-governmental organizations and even individuals. In general, culture has significantly widened its coverage. Technological progress in the production of materials and equipment has led to improvement in quality – of image and sound, especially – and has also provided previously silent cultural sectors with better opportunities to express themselves.

THE GLOBAL VILLAGE

The globalizing and interdependent character of these changes at a world level appears as another evident characteristic. Not only have the problems tended to become more planetary, but so also have their solutions.

In cultural terms, this globalization of society has positive and negative effects. Among the positive ones, easy access to other cultures' experiences and their rapid intercommunication and diffusion can be highlighted, which contributes to our knowledge and appreciation of closed or not-well-known cultures. Among the negative aspects, it is worth drawing attention to the risk of global standardization and of imposing certain cultural patterns, values and behaviours typical of the so-called 'central' countries, which threaten the identity of the peripheral cultures. To all of this, the already conspicuous risk of the 'banalization of culture' and the generation of 'stereotypes' should be added. The greatest challenge facing educational and cultural systems in all countries is finding a way to participate and interact in the world's cultural movements while preserving their own cultural identity.

WOMEN'S RIGHTS

The continuous progress made by women with regard to their rights and their participation in most human activities appears as another element related to changes in society. In particular, their presence and active participation is remarkable in education and culture. However, in some countries there is still a long way to go, especially in rural areas.

MACRO-SOCIAL CHANGES

What is also typical of these changes is the significant difference in their pace, depth and extension from one context to another. While in the industrialized countries these changes have been rather homogeneous, in the developing countries they have been slower, more peripheral and less effective. In this sense, there are phenomena which could hardly have been imagined some decades ago, such as European union or the unexpected economic emergence of some South-East Asian countries, accompanied by some implicit cultural factors which have not yet been acceptably explored or analyzed.

Parallel to these macro-social changes, other phenomena, some of a circumstantial character and some of a structural nature, have been appearing, which, no doubt, are associated with or will have some influence on the future development of society, with direct or indirect impact on culture and educational development. Recent changes considered to have the most impact are the following:

– The collapse of the Communist Bloc and of planned economies in Eastern European countries, which has had obvious implications for the future of these countries and of Europe as a whole;

– The reappearance of nationalism of an ethnic character, especially in the old countries of Eastern Europe, and the appearance of racism among youngsters in some Western European countries;

– The destruction of nature and the increasing deterioration of the environment as a result of the exploitation of natural resources and of uncontrolled industrialization;

– The likely scarcity, in the medium and long terms, of energy resources associated with industrialization at a world level;

– The burden of foreign debt (especially in Latin America), which has had a direct impact on economic development and the provision of social services;

– The appearance of new diseases, such as AIDS, the aggravation of some others, such as cardiovascular ailments, and the appearance in poor countries of some diseases previously considered to be practically exterminated, such as cholera;

– The increasing migratory currents from poor to rich countries of people in search of employment and a better way of life, which has contributed to the generation of new outbreaks of racism and ethno-cultural conflicts;

– The strengthening and almost total monopoly of economic neo-liberalism and political conservatism, which might lead to a greater concentration of wealth and to wider social inequalities and, ultimately, to weakening the role of the State.

To these changes occurring in society, which have contributed to increase the value of cultural development and the role played by education, some other factors of a positive character can be added, mainly the following:

– The creation of a specialized organism of the United Nations – UNESCO – whose task is to enhance and strengthen these dimensions of development. With the presence and influence of this organizataion, it has been possible to register some progress in the fields of theory, policies and achievements during the second part of this century.

– The institutionalization, in almost all countries, of Ministries of Culture or other high-level organisms responsible for the orientation and formulation of cultural policies and for giving an impetus to plans, programmes and projects. This, to a greater or lesser extent, has made it possible to give institutional bases to cultural activities, as well as to articulate policies and to allocate resources. To some degree, and here again, according to the socio-economic and political conditions applying to each country, this institutional circumstance has served to enhance cultural action at a combinatory and basic level, to mobilize and co-ordinate some resources, and to strengthen and preserve expressions of multiculturalism.

– The development of various international meetings – at a world and regional level – in which the participating countries have expressed and recommended principles and policies, and accepted programmes for multilateral and bilateral co-operation.

It is worth pointing out two events the outcomes of which can be taken as the framework for cultural and educational development at the international level.

The *World Conference on Cultural Policies* (Mexico, 1982), the Final Declaration of which incorporated the main approaches of almost all the countries in the world and stated that 'culture constitutes a fundamental dimension of the development process and helps to strengthen the independence, sovereignty and identity of nations' (para. 10). This conference was preceded or followed by regional conferences and meetings.

The *World Conference on Education for All – Meeting Basic Learning Needs* (Jomtien, Thailand, 1990), whose World Declaration, taking into account the progress made, the experiences acquired and the needs yet to be met, formulated a set of principles, objectives and guidelines to make real the right to education for all – men and women of all ages throughout the world.

Another important landmark was the decision by the forty-third General Assembly of the United Nations to proclaim the period 1988-97 as the

World Decade for Cultural Development. This decade, whose goal is 'to promote an awareness of the fundamental importance of culture in the life of human beings and society, as well as of the fruitful interactions that relate culture and development', has been structured around four basic objectives leading to a Programme of Action conducted under the supervision of UNESCO.

Similarly, a significant step forward was the decision to discuss 'the contribution of education to cultural development' at the forty-third session of the International Conference on Education. The Recommendation of this meeting issued some guidelines to strengthen the development of education and culture in the framework of the emerging new societies.

THE EDUCATION OF CHILDREN AND YOUTH
FOR ACTIVE PARTICIPATION IN CULTURAL LIFE

As described in the previous paragraphs and as stated in the Mexico Declaration, 'the world has undergone profound changes in recent years. The progress of science and technology has changed man's place in the world and the nature of his social relations'. These rapid transformations make themselves felt in the form of trends that may lead to crises in society, in the sub-systems that make it up, in the institutions that implement these trends and in the human growth that makes them necessary (Mesarovic & Pestel, 1974).

Today's children and adolescents have been born, have grown up, have been living and are being educated in new settings, with new values and under new paradigms. While they have been experiencing the effects of the changes occurring within society, especially in terms of values and behaviours (family, nationality, work, sex, art), they have also been prisoners of rigid, immobile education systems permanently out of tune with the changes occurring in the rest of society.

In the industrialized countries – those of Western Europe and North America, Japan and Australia – the major needs of the greatest part of the younger population, those related to health, food, home education and recreation, appear to have been satisfied. However, some sections of the population in these countries, such as ethnic minorities and the children of immigrant workers (as was expressed during the movement of the French *lycées* in 1990) may feel that these needs are not sufficiently satisfied. There are, on the other hand, some worrying events in an important number of developing countries, such as the persistence of high rates of unemployment and the ever-increasing use of drugs.

By contrast, in the Third World, beyond the universal trends that affect them directly or indirectly, there are particular conditions governing life in each country or social group. These conditions include, among others: a low standard of living for many families with children and infants; the lack of any hope in the future for many marginal groups; uncritical and unconscious assimilation of values and behaviours coming from industrialized countries transmitted by the mass media; low or non-existent political participation; extreme forms of violence; drug trafficking; and the tendency for talent to emigrate to developed countries. To these factors, it is necessary to add the narrow pedagogic, economic and organizational infrastructures prevailing in their education systems, which reinforce the social inequalities and contribute to isolate young people from the scientific and social transformations taking place elsewhere.

Taking these internal and external factors as a framework, we shall now establish the scope of the actions taken in educational institutions to help children and adolescents assume their active role in the cultural development of their immediate community in particular, and of society in general.

As was pointed out by the team preparing the theme of the forty-third session of the ICE, 'it is the task of the school to develop different and multiple functions to promote cultural development, especially at a regional level' (International Bureau of Education, 1992). This does not exclude the impact that the school can have on the cultural development of society and vice-versa. In fact, it is possible to suppose that the school exerts or could exert certain direct and immediate cultural influences on the community in which it is immersed and mediate a long-term influence on society in general. This criterion to some extent expresses the concern of the ICE not to attribute to the school any responsibilities that properly belong to other sectors of society.

With a descriptive and analytical intention, we can distinguish and differentiate the following forms of interaction between the school and the community for cultural development.

FORMATIVE ACTIVITIES THROUGH THE FORMAL
CURRICULUM

This refers to those disciplines of the formal curriculum of a general character, that is to say those whose objective is the development of the student's analytical skills and understanding of the world, processes of constructive critical thought, capacity to observe phenomena, and spiritual

179

and moral values. Both in the survey conducted by the IBE prior to the ICE and in the discussions at the session, some disciplines were listed that can have a greater impact on participation in cultural development.

Languages, especially the mother tongue. The language of a country or of a cultural group is one of the qualities inherent to its cultural identity. It is, at the same time, a means of diffusion and socialization, and a way of obtaining knowledge and appreciation of other cultures.

In those countries where one language is predominant, as is the case in almost all the industrialized countries and in Latin America, its articulating role between education and culture is less complex and occasionally less expensive. The predominance of an official language in countries where there are minorities with their own languages (Spain, Canada and those Latin American countries with relatively strong indigenous groups) does not exclude a total or partial use of second languages at school. This kind of situation depends on the policies of each country and the framework of its national sovereignty.

In countries with two or more official languages, the problem of selecting one of them for educational and cultural purposes is more complex. This situation is especially serious when dealing with adult education and basic education for children.

On the other hand, the grammatical construction of many of these languages has not yet been written down, which calls for important efforts by researchers in linguistics, cultural anthropology and pedagogy, before teaching materials can be designed and produced.

This implies high costs which poor countries cannot afford, especially when the problem involves small, scattered and nomadic groups or floating populations whose existence is directly related to certain periods when work is abundant, such as the harvest. In these cases, the options are very limited and, when available, they do not resolve the fundamental problems. One of these options is to carry out some school activities – mainly extracurricular ones – with the objective of publicizing the cultural expressions of these minorities through dances, music, theatre, exhibitions of craftsmanship and art, sports, etc.

Learning to speak a second language of a universal character to benefit from its economic and cultural opportunities, such as English, constitutes another challenge and need of the present society. In fact, although predominance of a few languages, tends to monopolize science and culture, it constitutes an alternative means to begin studying and acquiring knowledge of other cultures.

History is considered as one of the main ways of knowing about, understanding and appreciating one's own culture. It is also the most expeditious way to get acquainted with and appreciate cultures and other universal trends of human thought and spirit. The importance and pertinence of teaching history nowadays is more evident since the world map is assuming new forms and also because localized conflicts cast worrying shadows on the future of society. Of course, this implies giving scientific rigour to the teaching of history, and trying to circumscribe belligerent conflicts, exaggerated nationalism and patriotism arising from the particular circumstances of certain peoples.

For this, it is necessary that teachers should have a solid formation and an open mind about the phenomena and facts related to present society in general and to local communities in particular. One idea is to take into account the recommendation of the ICE regarding the celebration in schools of certain historical events – for example, the Meeting of Two Worlds, 1992 – in which several cultures have taken part. These are also actions which have been the outcome of joint efforts by several peoples in order to promote and guarantee international tolerance and understanding, such as the Universal Declaration of Human Rights.

Among the most frequently mentioned other disciplines used in the service of cultural development are *philosophy, ethics and religion*. Their significance and contribution to the education of children and adolescents, and to the development of knowledge, attitudes and values are obvious. They can contribute to the development of desirable moral and spiritual attitudes and dispositions, such as respect for human rights and solidarity among countries, human groups and individuals. In fact, the internationalization of society, the weakening of national frontiers through the creation of large economic blocks and the penetration of the mass media, leading to a reduction in times and distances, require a broader consideration of the world, which could be provided through these disciplines.

Aesthetic and artistic education are not confined to those disciplines or activities that are part of the formal curriculum and whose objective is the development of an aesthetic and artistic awareness. The training of artistic skills and the encouragement of creativity also have important educational and formative effects. Through them, it is possible to inculcate a balance between the cognitive processes of reasoning and the creative processes of imagination and the growth of the spirit.

As one of the paragraphs of the ICE's Recommendation expresses, 'artistic education should promote access to a variety of cultural events, be they of local, national, regional or universal scope, encouraging appreciation of the diversity of values and meanings inherent in them. It could constitute a stage in further training for the artistic professions' (para. 18).

In developing countries, incorporating these activities into the curriculum – as is typical of industrialized countries and for the wealthy classes of poor countries – becomes a very difficult and complex matter, because of a lack of proficient teachers and suitable didactic materials, with the possible exception of activities of a local, folkloric type. Given these conditions, their educational value is limited.

A frequently mentioned choice – but one whose implementation is really difficult (except in some countries) – is the participation and involvement of professional artists from the region in the artistic activities of the school. An alternative that is frequently mentioned is the possibility of using premises, personnel, materials and equipment belonging to local organizations or groups for educational purposes.

Complementary or supportive cultural activities are actions to reinforce the formative work carried out in the classroom which help pupils to obtain an understanding and appreciation of the cultural inheritance. Among the most enriching activities are visits to museums and historical, cultural and/or scientific sites, guided by the corresponding teachers or tutors of the curricular disciplines. The pedagogical value of these activities, in the sense of bringing the students into contact with the facts, is obvious.

The limitations or difficulties facing these activities have to do with their appropriate organization, the transportation of big groups of students – especially when poor, isolated schools are involved – and the very capacity and availability of these cultural institutions to receive large groups.

EXTRA-CURRICULAR ACTIVITIES

Extra-curricular and/or out-of-school cultural activities and programmes can be distinguished from the formal curricular ones mentioned in previous paragraphs.

- They are not part of the formal curriculum, therefore, they are not programmed, executed or evaluated as part of the official activities of the school;
- They do not have a strictly educational purpose but one of that complements or extends formal school activities;
- Although most of these activities may be carried out in the school, some of them take place outside it;

- While some of these activities only involve the school and its pupils, many of them reach out to the local community and parents;
- In many of these activities the community's role is not only that of audience but also that of provider of resources and/or a participant playing a role in them;
- These activities do not always have a regular timetable; some of them are occasional or haphazard;
- Usually, these activities are not compulsory either for students or teachers; they may be offered on the initiative of voluntary groups.

The main characteristic of these activities is their diversity, depending on the available resources and the degree of relationship with the educational institution. The most frequently used are:

- *Adult education*: in addition to their educational value – which is frequently questioned – these activities have an important social impact not only on the users, but especially on the students, since they strengthen their sense of social solidarity and responsibility.

- *Basic education for children from poor areas*: this is a less common activity whose results could be more effective if carried out in a systematic and organized way involving teaching by students from higher levels of education.

- *Artistic/musical activities*, such as orchestras, bands, choirs, dancing groups and ballet. The music employed may be that of the region, the nation or even of the world.

- *Artistic/aesthetic activities*, such as painting, sculpture, ceramics, craftwork, from the most simple to the most complex forms, and from the most local to the most universal of themes.

- *Literary activities*: such as literary and poetic contests, literary and history clubs, recitations, theatre groups, periodicals, school magazines and newsletters.

- *Scientific activities*: such as conferences, contests, exhibitions, and science and technology weeks. All of this not only has a high educational value in the communication of scientific knowledge, but also constitutes a means to popularize science.

- *Sportive/recreative activities*: such as sports clubs, school games championships, scientific excursions, and school trips with a recreational and educational character.

The list could be longer since it is the motivation, creativity and organizational capacity of the school and the community which play the most important role. The various forms, the degree of involvement, the continuity and the coverage of these activities depend on factors such as the organizational capacity and the resources of the institution, the level of interaction with the community, and the real and potential support that can be offered by the schools.

In the present-day world, especially in rural areas, there are factors that contribute to the development of these activities, such as the availability of modern equipment and sophisticated materials, the support provided by the mass media, and the recreative requirements and demands of the population itself.

It is these activities which, given their diversity, flexibility, accessibility and even their direct and immediate impact, permit the establishment of more direct and wider forms of interaction between the school and local communities in the interest of cultural development. These activities frequently have direct and collateral effects, such as strengthening, appreciating and preserving the community's cultural inheritance, as well as experiments and innovations which may lead to an increase in it. A second outcome directly favours the school, not only in relation to its appreciation and social relevance, but also fostering the educational processes through contact between the children and their surrounding reality. These cultural activities become a convergent point for joint action between the schools and local communities. At the same time, they become a means to strengthen social participation, mutual co-operation and human solidarity, values greatly appreciated in our present society. Furthermore, they give the schools an opportunity to benefit from their own educational potential and to give adequate direction and optimize non-conventional resources.

In poor countries, in impoverished rural and isolated areas, and in marginal urban zones, this kind of activity constitutes, at the present time, probably the principal mechanism of cultural interaction between the school and the community.

The appropriate implementation of the activities and programmes mentioned above offers the challenge of action to the educational and cultural institutions, as well as to communities. From my own point of view, the most relevant benefits are the following:

– The interdisciplinary perspective these activities give to the formal curricular educational activities of children and adolescents is a valuable part of their education for active participation in the cultural development of their communities, instead of an isolated or inarticulate division of the cultural dimensions acquired from a few disciplines. It is not a question of adding new disciplines to the curriculum. What must be done is to reformulate the approach and content of the existing ones, incorporating cultural objectives. In addition to the educational aspects of this interdisciplinary vision – harmonizing and articulating the confluent elements – it can contribute to the rationalization of resources and time.

- The incorporation of the cultural component into the formal educational process (pre-school, elementary, secondary and higher education). At each level, the component has specific connotations and goals and can be expressed through different actions and programmes. In fact, as higher educational levels are reached, the school's cultural activities get wider, more diverse and complicated.

- Harmony and complementarity between the educational activities of the formal curriculum and extra-curricular activities since they provide mutually enriching experiences. Without each other, they are both incomplete.

- The effective involvement of people in these activities, from the point of view of both users and participants, and of individuals with different limitations, such as the handicapped, the illiterate, immigrants and refugees.

- The active and increasing participation of women in these activities, as users and contributors, not only for reasons of social equity but also because they are in a strategic position to inculcate and transmit worthy values to their children.

- Given the present trend to destroy nature and degrade the environment, it is necessary to give to some of these cultural activities an ecological perspective in the medium and long terms in order to make life on Earth safer and more rewarding.

To sum up, the school has not only the responsibility but also a wide variety of possibilities of promoting, strengthening and enriching the cultural development of its immediate neighbourhood and society in general. Obviously, conditions vary in each geographical, economic and political context, which means that it is not possible to suggest common strategies and variations, but only some general trends and practices.

THE SCHOOL AS A CULTURAL CENTRE FOR THE LOCAL COMMUNITY

The school has been traditionally portrayed and criticized as a rigid, closed type of institution. The anti-school movement conceived the school as 'an

185

institution where students of a specific age, regularly, and during a number of years, receive some instruction transmitted in classes, centred on a teacher, in order to learn a graded curriculum, in which it is necessary to go through certain low stages to reach higher levels' (Illich, 1971). This criticism levelled at the traditional school has not led to any significant changes, but it has given rise to theories concerned with more flexible curricula, greater recognition of informal and out-of-school education, development of active methods centred on the student and the learning process, and to approaches which link schools more directly with the needs and problems of the environment and community life.

One strategy – the one that seems to produce the best results – is to grant the school its role as the cultural and activity centre of the community. In this respect, there are a variety of forms for these activities, according to the geographic, demographic as well as the social context. In isolated, poor environments, such as rural communities in the majority of developing countries, the school – especially the primary school – is still a meeting place for the community, and the school-teacher, despite the social deterioration of his/her social image, is still a prominent community figure. Cultural rather than purely educational activities provide a centre of attraction, a meeting place and a cultural link between teacher, adults and children.

The situation in developing countries

Up to now, the cultural activities of the school, both regular or formal and extra-curricular, have been limited and simple. The teachers' educational and socio-economic circumstances have limited their contribution to rare reading/writing lessons, generally reproduced directly from primary school practices. The teacher's attitude is often that any activity that does not follow the formal scheme of teaching is not his/her responsibility and has no educational value.

The problem is even more serious when the teacher does not live in the community, and therefore the degree of identification is very weak. Added to this are the limitations due to lack of space and suitable furniture in schools, the scarcity and even the total lack of didactic materials, the long distances to reach the school which may be poorly located, the passivity of children and the poverty of the rural marginal populations.

Under such circumstances, cultural interaction between schools and the community may be limited. A strategy used in some countries is to try to make the curriculum more flexible and to adapt it to take into account the concerns or problems of the local community.

This strategy requires a good attitude and capacity on the part of teachers to achieve a balance between the theoretical concepts and the realities observed. Of course, it also implies going beyond a pedagogical model of isolated disciplines towards an interdisciplinary one.

Another frequently used strategy is to involve the parents in the educational processes. In some poor countries and areas, the mothers' participation is encouraged during the pre-school and elementary period.

In rural areas with a greater density of population, and where the economic activities and forms of production are more modern, the opportunities to carry out cultural activities in the schools with community support are frequently better for several reasons: more proficient teachers; better facilities and materials; and higher socio-economic status of the population. In these areas, the cultural activities of schools and their interaction with the community are more fluid, diverse and dynamic.

Here, the most important cultural activities can be those related to artistic expression, sports and occasionally formal curricula. Similarly, the possibilities of the community to be involved in different ways may be greater than those of scattered or isolated rural populations. In fact, education in these environments can have a greater social and economic value and sometimes is considered as the door leading to emigration to urban areas.

The schools' situation and its cultural role in the indigenous regions of most developing countries is even more complex than in other rural areas. In these communities, the socio-economic conditions are often very deficient as regards economic production, family income, health, housing, nutrition, and supplies of drinking water, sanitary services and schools. In some cases people live widely dispersed in isolated jungle areas, and lack transportation and means of communication – as is the case in Amazonia. In other cases, they live among a dominant ethnic group, but under conditions of discrimination and even subordination, usually on land with poor productive capacity.

Their schools, if they have any, are inadequate and frequently copied from urban models. Even the limitations exhibited by their native tongues, i.e. no written grammatical structure, make it difficult for them to respond to their needs and cultural patterns. In addition to their poor physical facilities, trained teachers and suitable didactic materials are often lacking.

But these communities possess several positive resources: a sense of community; of cultural unity; of individual and collective interdependence; and an awareness of having inherited organizations and services belonging to the community's structure. In this context the relations

187

between school and community, culture and education are frequently solid, clear and articulate.

Nevertheless, they are also vulnerable to cultural penetration and domination, especially by the mass media which they have often already experienced, as well as by the affluent life-styles of settlers and neighbours from nearby towns.

Very often, the most advanced or more urbanized cultures consider the cultural expressions of these groups as exotic or quaintly folkloric. Nevertheless, indigenous movements whose goal is to preserve and strengthen their culture, with support from the school and through it, have begun to gain importance in several parts of the world. Among their claims are the preservation of language and customs, and the creation of schools capable of satisfying their needs directly.

In those younger developing countries – as is the case of Latin America and Africa and, perhaps, some countries of Asia – there is a marked difference between the economic, social, educational and even cultural situations affecting rural and urban areas; within these regions conspicuous differences occur, with obvious implications for possible articulations between school and community for cultural purposes. An attempt to describe this situation is as follows:

In those suburbs or zones of developing countries where high-income groups live, their living conditions, behaviour and even values do not differ significantly from those of more affluent people in industrialized countries. Their children attend private schools of an exclusive character, endowed with adequate facilities, teachers and didactic materials. Frequently, the teaching language is that of an industrialized country, such as English or French. Here, local cultural activities – both formal and non-formal – are very limited; the cultural activities proposed by both the formal curriculum and extra-curricular activities are more often drawn from foreign cultural patterns.

A second category of urban educational services is provided by areas in which the middle classes (of various kinds) live. This population is made up of independent technicians and professionals, owners of shops and small businesses, civil servants in State enterprises and organisms and sometimes even successful artists.

Here the interaction between school and community for cultural development tends to be more regular and frequent, through both formal and non-formal activities. Educational services here are provided partly by the State and partly by the private sector.

A third category consists of urban areas made up of low-income families – labourers, small shopkeepers, medium and low-skilled categories of employees – whose living conditions are often close to the subsistence level. In these areas the most predominant school institutions are of a State character and their pedagogical and physical facilities are barely acceptable.

In these areas, cultural interaction between the school and the community does not exhibit any definite features, although extracurricular activities predominate. The community's participation tends to be limited due to different sorts of difficulties: in some cases, time and resource limitations; in others, a low appreciation of culture; and in still others, no motivation, leadership and dedication on the part of teachers.

A fourth category is the type of area considered as marginal or inadequate from the housing, income, public services, health, nutrition, etc., points of view. These areas are inhabited principally by people who have recently migrated from poor rural areas. In some large cities they may make up about one-third of the total population. Educational and cultural services tend to be scarce and insufficient to meet the population's needs. Here, cultural activities are necessarily limited, mainly for economic reasons and questions of survival. Extra-curricular activities, such as sports and recreation, seem to be the only realistic possibility of cultural interaction between the school and the community.

In small towns of the Third World, socio-economic and cultural conditions tend to be more homogeneous. The interaction between school and community is more frequent and direct, especially through out-of-school activities, although there is an increasing tendency to articulate the formal school processes to the reality and cultural character of its context.

The situation in developed countries

The interaction between school and community for cultural purposes in industrialized countries is quite different from that in developing countries. While in the former, in general terms and with some exceptions, growth has been a gradual process, in the latter expansion has been vertiginous, due to the natural growth of the population but particularly because of migratory currents from the country to the city. In this sense, even the smallest cities in developed countries preserve a certain degree of social, economic, architectural and cultural harmony. In them, the interaction between educational institutions and community is more homogeneous and institutionalized, given the fact that their education systems have a greater tradition and solidity, and are articulated to the cultural development of their peoples. In them, culture and its different manifestations have passed through slower evolutive stages, have been more deliberately studied, organized and institutionalized, and have benefited from the backing of the State in terms of policies and resources.

In these contexts the school has been a product of the community's cultural evolution and, at the same time, one of the axes of its preservation, development and enrichment, both via the formal curriculum and through extra-curricular activities, though to a lesser degree. On the other hand, schools do not exhibit the stresses experienced by developing countries.

Some Asian cultures, such as China, Japan and India, have experienced a similar evolution of education and culture regarding the cultural role of the school.

One of the most important problems faced today by major cities in industrialized countries regarding their education and cultural relation with the community, and even with society, is the presence in the school of large numbers of immigrant children from developing countries. This situation constitutes a challenge that schools cannot easily solve.

The dilemma is how to integrate these children and young people into the new culture without losing their roots and links with the original cultures. Another complication is the recent manifestations of racism emerging within certain groups of young people in some countries. There have been two tendencies: to integrate groups of immigrant children and youth into traditional schools; or to create bilingual schools specifically for these groups with the objective of progressively integrating them into the new culture. This has been the case in some parts of the United States, especially in those states with a high level of Hispanic migration.

STRATEGIES

Within this generic framework of areas that, from a demographic, cultural and administrative point of view, make up the 'local communities', what strategies can contribute to promote and strengthen cultural development as an interaction process between educational institutions and communities? In general terms, we could point out some that have already been tried and that were mentioned during the ICE. They are definitely not new or unique formulae or recipes, nor do they call for blind or mechanical implementation. They are rather 'processes' that can be progressively tried out, refined and consolidated.

Social participation by educational participants

The participants involved are school directors, teachers, students and administrative personnel. The intensity, form and degree of participation of each of them depend on factors such as the type of activities to be performed, availability, and the competence and motivation of each person.

There isn't any doubt at all that motivation and interest play important roles. It is equally true that cultural activities constitute one of the points of convergence where the activities and motivations of the 'school community' can occur more expeditiously. Furthermore, this participation contributes to strengthening the sense of 'institutional development' and thus in attaining the objectives of the educational process.

From the 'local community' perspective, participation tends to occur through the formally constituted community organizations (parent/teacher associations or councils; trade union, professional and civic organizations; non-governmental organizations; private enterprises; State agencies and/or enterprises; sports, artistic and scientific clubs, etc.). This participation can also occur through a personal interest or initiative (artists, scientists, technicians, etc.).

The main forms of participation and co-operation are the following:

– Material and economic aid (money, premises, facilities and materials);
– Technical and professional contribution (artists, scientists, technicians and other specialists);
– Logistic support (equipment and technical aid);
– Institutional support (museums, cultural centres, theatres and exhibitions).

Intersectoral and inter-institutional co-ordination

One expression of formalized and institutionalized participation is the co-ordination of institutions around cultural activities. This co-ordination between agencies of a single sector, for instance a grouping of schools, or of various sectors, such as educational agencies and cultural agencies, constitutes one of the primary conditions to widen, strengthen and give intimacy to the activities of community cultural development. This co-ordination supposes the capacity to organize, negotiate and reach agreement, personal and institutional leadership, clarity in objectives and means – in a few words, a wide vision of what community development is.

This co-ordination leads to the creation of institutional and programme 'networks' in which the institutions, through the conduct of their own activities, contribute to the development of other sectors and support the total infrastructure. This 'synergy' of human and material forces increases the creative and productive potential of institutions.

Projects

Planning and management of cultural activities between schools and communities can take place through the launching of projects. Such initiatives lead to the setting of clear objectives, the identification of resources and the assignment of responsibilities. In addition, it permits monitoring and evaluation mechanisms to be established.

Institutional leadership

Dynamic and continuous cultural development between schools and communities presupposes a great deal of institutional leadership. This leadership permits motivations to be developed, interests to be oriented, individual and group capacities to be identified, and resources to be provided. This leadership can also produce a beneficial competence and provide a stimulus to less dynamic institutions.

The previous considerations do not try to exaggerate the role and responsibilities of the school in the cultural development of a community or society. In other words, the school should not assume all the responsibilities, since some of them rightfully belong to other sectors of society, especially the family and the State. Our purpose is to emphasize the school's role and potential in cultural development and how it may be harmonized with the surrounding community. This need is more evident in societies still in formation and in those where other community development agencies are scarce or non-existent.

To sum up, the different ways in which the school and the community can interact for cultural development can produce benefits and multiplier effects in a double direction: in the school, by enriching the teaching/ learning processes and accentuating the higher objectives of individual development and a social conscience and in the community, by enriching the cultural inheritance and strengthening human solidarity and social cohesion.

THE MASS MEDIA AND COMMUNITY CULTURAL DEVELOPMENT

The mass media's impact upon society is one of the most important events of the modern world. One controversial issue concerns their impact on childhood and adolescence, the psycho-educational effects and their educational potential. This phenomenon has been widely studied and debated in industrialized countries, with sometimes conflicting conclusions.

Given the fact that the media themselves are an element of culture and a most efficacious vehicle for diffusing cultural information and values, they must have an effect on young people, not only from a strictly cultural point of view, but also from an ethic-social, scientific and humanistic point of view.

It is evident that the mass media constitute an instrument which it is possible to use in a positive or negative way, according to the particular objectives being sought.

Advantages

Some of the most frequently mentioned advantages are:

– *The speed and timeliness* with which scientific or cultural information is communicated can be contrasted with the slow process of updating curricular content in schools. This is particularly evident in marginal urban or rural areas of developing countries. This imbalance between the speed of changes and society's corresponding reaction time – especially in scientific-technical fields – has widened the gap between rich and poor countries, and between rich and poor social groups in any country.

– Each day the technological advances in telecommunications shorten the distance and time required to *gain access to information* coming from research centres and networks.

– *The diversity and quality of images, colours and sounds* used to display the facts, phenomena and discoveries in an attractive and easily comprehensive way.

– *Their coverage.* The mass media can easily reach large human groups living in remote and isolated places, scattered populations and people from the same group located in different sites. This phenomenon is one of the most significant for the cultural and educational processes.

– *The diversity of means, programmes and activities* permit multiple uses and access not only to one's own culture, but also to that of others.

– *The diversity of the mass media.* They come in a bewildering range of sizes, technologies, levels of sophistication, coverage, types of service and programmes. This enables them to be used for a multitude of cultural and educational goals. Some of them represent multinational corporations with world-wide coverage: radio and television broadcasting stations; data and scientific networks; and journals and magazines (of both a general and specialized character). They are, in a sense, expressions of the scientific and cultural domination of the industrialized countries, the only role being left for developing countries is that of the passive user.

Some of these mass media are available to schools and, indeed, have been used by some educational institutions, especially universities and research centres. However, poor and isolated schools in developing countries are far from having the opportunity to have access to them and exploit them adequately. There have been some attempts to use radio and television for cultural and educational activities, as we shall see later.

Disadvantages

The use of the mass media for educational and cultural purposes implies several kinds of problems, such as:

– The high costs of acquisition and maintenance.

– Problems due to lack or inadequacy of infrastructures for their operation and/or maintenance (for example, electricity supplies and the technical competence needed to make adjustments).

– The availability of spare parts and supplies for their operation.

– Technical capacity and motivation among teachers for their appropriate use in the classroom. This implies more pedagogical and technical training in their appropriate use.

– A further question implied by the relative complexity of the mass media has to do with the extent they can be used in poor areas and at lower cost.

As a matter of fact, even the poorest countries have experimented with some of these media in the educational and cultural fields, especially radio, television, cinema and printing. They have been used for all levels of education, including adult education, in both exclusively educational and cultural situations. The results have been varied.

– In some cases a close loot at their cost/benefit ratio has drawn attention to the high cost of their installation, materials and programmes.

– In other cases, the impact of programmes that reproduce the methods and practices of traditional schools have been minimal.

– Last, but not least, serious questions have been posed about the effect of these technologies on children's and adolescents' behaviour.

In any event, these media are having a greater determining influence on the way in which knowledge, information, cultural values and behaviour are transmitted. Some of these media, telecommunications for instance, have given rise to new extended educational forms, such as 'distance education', which, in some cases, has become a real and important alternative to traditional education. Their applications tend to have more impact on higher education, not only for reasons connected with coverage, but also because of the students' learning efficiency. In this respect, in recent years remarkable theoretical, methodological and instrumental progress has been made. Everything tells us that future progress will be even greater, both in both concept and application.

A point in question and at the same time a challenge for poor and isolated schools and communities is the possibility of using simpler, easier, cheaper and more accessible media. Some of them may permit a more local and restricted use. Through close co-operation between schools and communities, it is possible to make better use of printed media (periodicals, magazines, bulletins), local radio stations, scientific and cultural video-clips and films in general. Their use is becoming more widespread, even in remote places.

In this sense, it is also necessary for educational institutions to look more closely at the advantages and possibilities provided by the mass media, not only for their intrinsic value – technological, educational and cultural – but also because inevitably they will be present in social, family and individual life.

However, we cannot overlook their limitations and risks. The most frequently mentioned of which are:

- Their power to mediate knowledge and information by filtering and sometimes distorting them;

- The priority of commercial criteria over the common good;

- The indiscriminate transfer of cultural values and behaviour patterns foreign to the national culture;

- The strengthening of passive and receptive attitudes in the user with a negative effect on intellectual development and reasoning powers;

- The risk of losing one's cultural identity;

- The risks of ideological and political manipulation by the owners of the media;

- The superficiality of popular messages and information, to the detriment of a scientific vision, constructed through study and research.

The negative impact of the mass media and how to limit their effects could be the subject of an international conference. In fact, this is one of the most worrying matters for international leaders, parents, teachers and community workers. Although studies on this matter are abundant in industrialized countries, in developing countries they are scarce, which hampers a more precise estimate of the advantages and disadvantages.

With the purpose of taking advantage of the potential of these media and of reducing the negative impact, in recent years emphasis has been place on the necessity of including in the formal education curriculum lessons which show pupils how to analyse and reflect on the nature, impact and limitations of the mass media. It is intended that children and adolescents should obtain a clearer vision of the real value of these media in individual and social life.

This applies not only to students. Teachers and parents too have the responsibility of educating themselves in this respect, from an ethic-social, pedagogical and cultural perspective. For parents, this represents a new dimension in their social responsibility towards their children.

But the State must also have clear policies and norms regarding this matter. Those who own these media and those who design and make the programmes cannot escape their responsibility. Today, the mass media are agents of education and culture, and in the future this will be even more so. It is the task of the educational and cultural institutions and of the community, to benefit from and supervise their appropriate use.

REFERENCES

Coombs, Philip H. 1985. *The world crisis in education: the view from the eighties.* New York, NY, Oxford University Press. 353 p.
Gozzer, Giovanni. 1990. School curricula and social problems. *In: Prospects* (Paris, UNESCO), Vol. XX, No 1, (73).
Illich, Iván. 1971. *Mensaje.* Santiago de Chile.
King, Alexander; Schneider, Bertrand. 1991. *The First Global Revolution: a report by the Council of the Club of Rome.* New York, NY, Pantheon Books. 259 p.
Mesarovic, Mihajlo; Pestel, Eduard C. 1974. *Mankind at the turning point: the second report of the Club of Rome.* London, Hutchinson. 210 p.
International Bureau of Education. 1992. *Communication.* International Conference on Education, 43th session, No. 5, Geneva.
— 1992. *Statistical document on education and culture.* Geneva, September. (ED/BIE/CONFINTED 43/Ref.1)
— 1992. *Main working document: 'The contribution of education to cultural development'.* Geneva, September, 1992. (ED/BIE/CONFINTED 43/3)

CHAPTER X

Education and the survival of small indigenous cultures

G.R. Teasdale

INTRODUCTION

This chapter is addressed to educational policy makers and administrators in those countries where small indigenous cultures still exist. In all parts of the world small cultures are threatened; they are being eroded by the persistent spread of modern industrialized societies with their emphasis on individualism, competitiveness, consumerism and technological change. For some small cultures it is already too late. The damage done to their values and symbols – the nuclei on which they depend both for their internal development and for their relationships with the wider society – has been irreversible. The consequences, as León-Portilla (1990, p. vii–viii) has pointed out, are 'various types of trauma, marginalization, and the dissolution of the culture's very being'. Elsewhere, however, cultural groups are resisting erosion by pressing for the right to self-determination and survival. Education can play a crucial part in this process.

The chapter is written by a non-indigenous person for a non-indigenous audience. It does not presume to tell indigenous peoples how to manage their affairs: too many outsiders have imposed their 'solutions' on small cultures with disastrous results. Rather, it suggests how managers of education systems might support members of small indigenous cultures as they seek to develop their own survival processes. Examples and case studies are drawn from Australia, New Zealand and the Pacific, reflecting the author's own range of experience. The issues addressed in the chapter do have global relevance, however, and should be considered with care by all who are engaged in education at the interface of industrialized and indigenous societies.

Indigenous peoples are defined as the original occupants of a particular land or territory. The concept of 'smallness' is introduced to help differentiate two categories, both of which are considered in this chapter:

(i) Indigenous minority groups at present comprising a non-dominant sector of a larger society; Cobo (1987, p. 29) defines such peoples as

197

having 'a historical continuity with pre-invasion and precolonial societies that developed on their territories, [and who] consider themselves distinct from other sectors of the societies now prevailing in those territories, or parts of them'. Examples include the Polynesian peoples of Hawaii and New Zealand, and Aboriginal Australians.

(ii) Indigenous communities or nations, numerically small by world standards, that have suffered considerable cultural disruption as a result of colonialism, and that continue to be assaulted by powerful forces of cultural standardization emanating from dominant industrialized societies; most South Pacific island nations fall into this category. Although indigenous peoples may be dominant both numerically and politically, their cultural values and traditions are under threat, and signs of anomie are increasing, especially amongst young people.

In discussing the survival of small indigenous cultures it is important to stress that culture is not being viewed in a static way, as in a museum. Rather, culture is recognized as a living, changing, dynamic entity. The dilemma for small cultures is not the fact of change, but the pace of it, and the sheer strength of the forces of standardization.

ALTRUISM OR MUTUALISM?

Why should we be concerned about the survival of small cultures? Altruism is the wrong motive. Too often it leads to a perpetuation of unequal relationships. If we are to stand alongside indigenous peoples, we need to acknowledge that our need is at least as great as theirs. The survival of small cultures is equally as important to modern industrialized societies as it is to indigenous peoples themselves.

It is ironic that, at a time when scientists are pointing humankind back to metaphysical and even mystical explanations of our existence (Hawking, 1988; Reanney, 1991; Davies, 1992), many of the dominant industrialized societies are facing a crisis of spiritual and moral decay. They appear to have moved so far along the road of capitalism, with its emphasis on competition, the consumption of goods and services, and the exploitation of the world's non-renewable resources, that they are losing their deepest roots. As I have noted elsewhere:

Symptoms of this appear in the breakdown of family relationships, the loss of a sense of community, and the selfishness and greed that are so apparent in people's relationships with each other. Fundamentally, the problem is caused by decay of the deep social, spiritual and moral values that have underpinned our societies in the past. Many of the world's small indigenous cultures, with their essentially spiritual value systems, have retained lifestyles based on interdependence, family solidarity and harmony with the natural environment. The western world needs these small cultures as never before. It needs them to point the way forward to a more human, caring and harmonious way of life. The world cannot afford to lose them (*Voices in a seashell*, 1992, p. 1).

Our challenge, then, is to work with indigenous groups in relationships of equality and mutual respect, recognizing that our own long-term survival may well depend upon our capacity to learn from their wisdom. The global difficulties created by modern societies are unlikely to be resolved by more information and greater technological capacity but rather, as Stanford University ecologist Paul Ehrlich argues, by 'quasi-religious' solutions. He believes the problems of the West are inherent in the way we perceive our relationships with the rest of nature, and the way we perceive 'our role in the grand scheme of things' (cited by Knudtson & Suzuki, 1992, p. xxiv). Indigenous peoples, with their essentially holistic and spiritual world views, have much to teach us in this regard. From an environmentalist perspective David Suzuki agrees: 'My experiences with aboriginal peoples have convinced me [...] of the power and relevance of their knowledge and world view in a time of imminent global ecocatastrophe' (Suzuki, 1992, p. xxxv). A similar argument could be supported from social, political or even economic perspectives. But if we are to learn from indigenous cultures we must ensure their survival before it is too late.

FINDING A STARTING POINT

How can education contribute to the survival of small indigenous cultures? During 1992 a UNESCO-sponsored seminar for the Australia-Pacific region was held in Rarotonga, in the Cook Islands. The seminar brought together representatives from indigenous groups in Australia, New Zealand and the island nations of the South Pacific to explore the role of education in the development of small cultures. One overwhelmingly strong theme emerged. It was expressed most clearly in the preamble to the seminar recommendations: 'If "Education for cultural development" is to have meaning, the question of who controls/owns the education system is crucial [...] *indigenous cultures must own all aspects of the education of their people*' (*Voices in a seashell*, 1992, p. 6).

It is a hard lesson for non-indigenous people to learn. Dominant cultures, at both national and international levels, find it difficult to relinquish control. For too long they have wrongly assumed the superiority of their own systems and processes. Yet, if indigenous peoples are to have genuine freedom to revive, maintain and develop their cultures, they must be given full and authentic control over all aspects of their lives, and their children's lives. Effectively this requires recognition of their prior rights, as original occupants, to ownership and control of their lands and territories; for educational self-determination is bound up with wider questions of political control, land rights and financial autonomy. This was reflected in the recommendations of the Rarotonga seminar which speak of the sharing by all people of 'the nation's rights, responsibilities and resources in a just and mutually beneficial manner', and elsewhere of the need for indigenous cultures to have an 'absolute guarantee that no veto be exercised by any other cultural group' (Teasdale, 1993, p. 6-8). As a starting point, then, the survival of small cultures depends on their members having full ownership and control, not only of education, but of all other social, political and economic processes that directly effect their lives.

THE IMPORTANCE OF LANGUAGE

Language and culture are interdependent, having an almost symbiotic relationship. Erosion of one almost invariably weakens the other. This is particularly true for those small indigenous cultures that have no tradition of written language and thus rely exclusively on oral language for the transmission of cultural knowledge. Harris (1990) notes that, in these circumstances, language death can occur in as little as three generations after significant contact with a dominant culture, or roughly sixty to ninety years. 'This', he suggests, 'is alarmingly sudden'. He goes on to point out that the 'crucial matter in language survival is whether the children are both learning the language and using it among themselves' (Harris, 1990, p. 72).

What can educational policy makers and administrators do to support indigenous language maintenance? This is a complex and much debated question. The Australian and New Zealand experience, however, is that 'top down' solutions do not work. The motivation and determination must come from indigenous peoples themselves. Even then, the school can play only a secondary role. The primary responsibility lies with families and communities to foster spontaneous, everyday use of the vernacular in the home and the village. Fishman (1985) has pointed out that nowhere in the world have programmes of language maintenance, revival or revitalization been successful if their major emphasis is on the school rather than on other, more primary social processes. He goes on to say:

[...] the school will have its role to play in the overall language maintenance design, but it will do so by serving a vibrant and purposeful community – a community with a modicum of

Education and the survival of small indigenous cultures

economic, political and religious power of its own – rather than being called upon to do the impossible: to save the community from itself (Fishman, 1985, p. 374).

An exciting example of the power of community action was given by Maori participants at the Rarotonga seminar. They spoke with deep fervour about the *Kohango Reo* Movement that has spread throughout New Zealand during the past decade. Translated literally, *te kohango reo* means 'the language nest'. And this is exactly what the Maori people have created – 'nests' where the fledgling child is nurtured in Maori language and culture. The basic concept is one of immersion of children during their first five years of life in early education programmes based exclusively on the Maori language. In 1982 five pilot centres were established. Parents, grandparents and children came together, generally in the *marae* (the meeting place, or spiritual and social centre of the community), in a shared process of cultural renewal.

Iritana Tawhiwhirangi, referred to by many in New Zealand as the 'mother of *te kohanga reo*', described the birth of the movement to seminar participants in the following way:

In the last ten years Maori people have taken responsibility themselves for strengthening their language, culture and traditions. We have not depended on government because we realized in 1982 that in order to move as we culturally desired we would have to bring our own people together and take collective responsibility. So we began with five pilot schemes that immersed the children in Maori language for eight hours a day from the time they were born. Why did we succeed? Because Maori people owned the programme and made all decisions about its operation. It was based on the principle of ownership, of Maori people being able to drive their own canoe (Tawhiwhirangi, 1992, p. 1).

The movement celebrated its tenth anniversary in the latter part of 1992. By then it was supporting no less than 680 centres throughout New Zealand, and was still growing. Central to its ethos is the concept of collective responsibility. The movement places power back in the hands of parents, families and communities.

The *Kohanga Reo* at Green Bay in suburban Auckland is typical of most. The following vignette provides a brief account of its salient features.

The achievements of the *Kohanga Reo* Movement are impressive. Essentially, it demonstrates the effectiveness of community-initiated language programmes in enhancing the cultural identity of indigenous peoples. It has shown that indigenous minority groups can take power into their own hands and develop autonomous programmes that affirm the value and significance of their own language and culture.

So powerful and successful has the movement become that it has acted as a catalyst for a major government reform of primary and secondary schooling in New Zealand, particular emphasis having been given to the

THE *KOHANGA REO* AT GREEN BAY, AUCKLAND

Young children were still arriving with their parents and/or grandparents as we approached the marae. We waited to be invited formally into the large, warm, carpeted room used for the Kohanga Reo. Removing our shoes we were traditionally called into the room by the teacher and some of the older children. The first activity of the morning was 'welcome time' and we watched as the young male teacher greeted each child in turn, and by name. The greeting was both verbal and physical. The child and the teacher conversed quietly in Maori, rubbed noses, and hugged. As visitors, we were treated in a similarly inclusive manner. After the greetings the children and teachers sang us a song of welcome and then entertained us with a number of action songs.

The 'nest' was simply and sparsely furnished, both inside and out. One noticed the absence of clutter. There were relatively few books and toys, playground equipment was basic and functional, and there was little of the busy, crowded atmosphere of the typical Western preschool. Instead we were aware of people. The community had not been forewarned of our visit. This was an entirely normal day. Yet around the room were seated grandparents, elders, mothers (some with babies at the breast), fathers, friends, and a few teenage girls who were no longer attending school and had come to help. All were conversing and sharing in the Maori language, both with each other and with the children, thus providing a warm and language-rich environment for all who were present.

Informal socialization of the children was constant, facilitated by the high ratio of adults to children. There was clear evidence of the quiet and unobtrusive shaping of the children's behaviour as they were inducted into the mores of Maori society. Direct cultural teaching also was taking place. Story-telling and action songs absorbed the children completely, even some of the youngest ones. The delight and pleasure of the children was very evident. Small boys emulated the male teacher as he led them in a dance involving facial expression, hand movements and bodily rhythm. Here was an obvious example of traditional skills being learned by observation and imitation.

No English language is spoken in the Kohanga Reo. Although some children are exposed to very little Maori language in the home, the level of warmth and acceptance within the 'nest' allows them to adapt and learn quickly. It is hoped that by providing these young children with such a firm and positive beginning they will remain strong in Maori language and culture throughout their lives. It also is hoped that the participation of parents and community members in the Kohanga Reo will reinforce their own knowledge of the Maori language and encourage its wider use in the everyday activities of the home and neighbourhood.

As we took our leave from the Kohanga Reo, replacing our shoes and walking past the garden with its food producing plants, we were left with the strong impression that here was a vibrant centre that was making a significant contribution, especially through its emphasis on the use of indigenous language, to the cultural identity of a new generation of Maori children.

(Adapted from Teasdale, 1993, p. 8)

teaching of the Maori language. To its credit, the New Zealand government has allowed the Maori people to affirm their autonomy and make their own decisions about language programmes. It also has been prepared to respond (although perhaps too slowly for some) to requests for financial support for community-initiated language programmes, thus giving practical expression to its philosophy that:

Toi te kupu   The stronger the language

Toi te mana   The stronger the *mana* (the power or prestige of the culture)

Toi te whenua The stronger the nation (*Tihe Mauri Ora!*, 1990, p. 10).

RECONCEPTUALIZING EDUCATION

The concept of the school is a Western invention that had its origins in the European Enlightenment, the rise of modern science and the Industrial Revolution. It is a concept that has imprinted itself on most other cultures around the globe with remarkable strength and pervasiveness. Yet it does not necessarily provide the most effective means of transmitting contemporary scientific knowledge, let alone the knowledge and values of small indigenous cultures. It is important, therefore, that educational policymakers allow indigenous groups the freedom to reconceptualize schooling within their own cultural parameters. To suggest that conformity to the European idea of the school is a precondition for effective learning in either the dominant or the indigenous culture is quite inappropriate. Various Aboriginal Australian groups have been developing alternative patterns of education for a number of years, initially with significant opposition from the government. There is much we can learn from their experiences.

YIPIRINYA SCHOOL

In the arid centre of Australia lies the town of Alice Springs. Dissatisfied with the lack of cultural support in mainstream schools, Aboriginal parents in the town established their own primary (elementary) school in 1978. Despite the refusal of the Northern Territory government to register and fund the school, and the threat of Supreme Court action to force its closure, parents persisted, growing firmer and ever more determined in their struggle (Teasdale & Teasdale, 1986). In 1983 the intervention and financial support of the federal government ensured its long-term survival. Since then Yipirinya has grown strong as a fully Aboriginal-owned and controlled school. As it has grown, it has evolved into what is best described as an all-age community education centre where Aboriginal people participate at every level of the teaching/learning interface. It incorporates childcare and pre-school facilities for children from birth to 5 years of age. At the primary and secondary level, four language groups each go to a separate teaching area for language and cultural studies, coming together during part of each day for a curriculum based on Western knowledge and skills. There is a teacher education programme where Aboriginal people can gain a formal qualification in teaching. Post-school and adult education programmes operate on demand. A literature production unit ensures a steady supply of attractive and culturally relevant literacy materials in each of the four languages of instruction. What began as a primary school has become a unique centre where *all* members of the local Aboriginal community can share together as both teachers and learners in an environment that affirms their language and culture. The following vignette offers further insights into this vibrant institution.

YIPIRINYA SCHOOL, ALICE SPRINGS

This is the country of the caterpillar dreaming. It is not until visitors take to the air and look down on the ancient, weatherbeaten land in the centre of the continent that they become aware of the giant, caterpillar-like formations of the Macdonnell Ranges that stretch across this arid landscape. Yet they have held deep spiritual significance to the Aboriginal people of this region for many millennia, and Yipirinya itself takes its name from this particular dreaming.

It took immense determination to establish the school in the face of government opposition, but eventually, after a change of national leadership, Yipirinya was formally registered and became eligible for government funding. Today, after capital grants of over 3 million dollars from the Australian government, a sensitively designed school sits in the folds of a rugged hill on the outskirts of Alice Springs, melding into the landscape in quite a remarkable way. Aboriginal culture derives its meaning from a spiritual one-ness with the earth. Yipirinya, in its form, colour and location, gives the appearance of having grown out of the earth on which it sits, thus endowing the buildings themselves with an almost spiritual quality.

Why did Yipirinya begin? Aboriginal elders and parents in central Australia saw the children losing their Aboriginality – their sense of identity and self-esteem –as they were forced by law to send them to monocultural state schools

---

that made minimal concessions to the languages and cultures of their indigenous students. In these schools very few Aboriginal students were able to cope, let alone succeed. They were ill at ease socially and culturally, and failure was the norm in a curriculum entirely focused on Western knowledge and Western modes of knowledge transmission. Most Aboriginal children therefore attended school irregularly, and dropped out as soon as possible in their teenage years. Petrol sniffing, vandalism, violence and other social problems were rife. All of this was the catalyst for Yipirinya's development.

If you visit Yipirinya now, it quickly becomes apparent that it is much more than a school in the conventional sense. It can best be described as an all-age learning centre, but these are sterile words that fail to capture the vibrancy of a place where babes in arms and toddlers learn alongside grey-haired grandparents. It is a school that affirms and strengthens the use of Aboriginal languages, so much so that it has classes in four languages – Walpiri, Central Arrente, Western Arrente and Luritja – and its literature production unit publishes reading materials to support vernacular literacy in all four. Within the school a process of 'two-way learning' is central. The aim is to provide Western knowledge in such a way that Aboriginal children can access the dominant culture without losing the deep roots of their Aboriginality.

Within the primary and secondary classes a significant proportion of each day is set aside for the teaching of Aboriginal languages and cultures. Bush trips are a regular feature, led by elders who use the country around Alice Springs as a huge open air classroom where they share spiritual, social, legal, ecological, nutritional and other cultural knowledge with the children. The literature production unit is a source of many new and innovative books and teaching resources based on the Aboriginal languages and cultures of the region. Storytellers and other custodians of the culture provide information which is written down and illustrated in a culturally appropriate way. Some books have been recognized nationally with significant awards, and teaching materials are sought by Aboriginal communities throughout the central desert area. Importantly, some non-Aboriginal educationists are starting to use resources produced by Yipirinya in cross-cultural teaching programmes in mainstream schools.

The Aboriginal people of Alice Springs obviously feel a great sense of empowerment from all they have achieved at Yipirinya. Most importantly, they see their children and youth slowly but surely regaining pride in their Aboriginality. The extent to which Yipirinya has enhanced the sense of cultural identity of children and adults alike is inestimable. Yipirinya is also showing non-Aboriginal people something of the richness of Aboriginal culture and its importance to the entire Australian nation. (Adapted from Teasdale, 1993, p. 31-32).

HOMELAND CENTRE SCHOOLING

Throughout central and northern Australia during the past twenty years Aboriginal people have been moving out in small extended family groups to reoccupy traditional lands. This dispersal from larger communities has become known as the 'outstation' or 'homeland centre' movement. As well as reaffirming spiritual ties to the land, the movement has allowed a return to a more traditional lifestyle (Downing, 1988). It has also resulted in less-formal patterns of schooling.

One of the earliest examples comes from Hermannsburg in central Australia. Parents requested that non-Aboriginal teachers based in the main community visit each outstation for two hours per day, their responsibilities being limited to the teaching of English language, literacy and numeracy. Teaching was carried out in the open air, or in some form of temporary shelter. All other forms of education were provided by family members within the informal setting of the camp.

In other places family groups have accepted full responsibility for the education of their children, relying on weekly, fortnightly or even less-frequent visits from peripatetic teachers to provide curriculum resources and support. Overall, there are wide variations in the way kin groups are arranging for the education of their young, but in almost every case there is clear evidence that homeland centre education is playing an important role in the maintenance of language and the renewal of cultural identity. A clearer picture of an outstation school is provided in the accompanying vignette. To preserve the anonymity of the family group involved the name and location of the homeland community is not identified.

In both of the vignettes, Aboriginal Australian groups have reconceptualized the schooling process in quite significant ways, achieving a synthesis between their traditional, informal patterns of education and the more formal, structured approaches of industrialized societies. In recent years the Australian government has been increasingly supportive of such initiatives; it has provided Aboriginal groups with funding for capital developments and resources in ways which affirm their freedom to choose schooling models that enhance language and cultural development.

Reconceptualization of schooling is relatively straightforward in settings where all students are from similar cultural backgrounds. But what of interactive settings involving students from two or more different cultures? Here it becomes more complex. Yet it can be achieved, as demonstrated by the quite remarkable changes that are taking place in many schools in New Zealand.

OUTSTATION SCHOOL, NORTHERN TERRITORY

As we approach the tiny airstrip hacked out of scattered eucalyptus forest we are aware of the isolation of this small community set beside a running creek and almost hidden from sight by the trees. It helps us to appreciate the strength of the spiritual ties which bind Aboriginal people to their country. Why else would a group of people choose to come and live in such a remote and inaccessible place? Yet here, seemingly in the middle of nowhere, an extended Aboriginal family, under the patriarchal leadership of the group's senior male, has re-established its roots in its own homeland.

By the time our small charter plane touches down several people have come to meet us and accompany us back to the school. Apparently our arrival is surprising as a twin-engined aircraft has not previously landed at the strip.

We immediately feel the pleasure that this community has in its school, and their acceptance of our visit to it. The building has been provided recently by a government grant, and comprises one classroom and a small room the visiting teacher from the hub school can use for overnight accommodation when she visits two or three times a term. It is clear that the facility has been keenly sought and has met with acceptance and considerable success. Importantly, through the school, the community now feels it has control over the education of its children, with parents taking direct responsibility for day-to-day teaching.

Twelve primary and seven secondary students are receiving their education in this tiny school. It is certainly an improvement on the tin shed and bough shelters which were formerly used. The children enjoy the shady verandah, the large blackboards, and the shower and toilets that have contributed significantly to improvements in the health of both the children and the community. The traditional leader of the community, a quiet man possessed of a rare sense of dignity and certainty, assures us that student attendance, learning and sense of well-being are better because of the new school. The community also uses the building for meetings, health visits, video nights, and as a pleasant spot to come and read books and magazines. Outside the school a well-used trampoline and volleyball net suggest plenty of physical activity. A small, well-tended plantation of tropical fruit trees nearby shows another dimension of the school's programme. Inside the classroom the children show us their written work. It appears of comparable standard to that of children in the hub school.

As we return to the airstrip we talk more with children and parents, once again forming an impression of an integrated community with a strong sense of identity. Perhaps the words of one of the parents sum up their feelings: 'We can now live on our own traditional land. We have a school, running water, showers and pit toilets. We now live away from the problems of the big community. No more alcohol, no more violence'. (Adapted from Teasdale, 1993, p. 30-31).

In 1988 a major transformation of the New Zealand education system was initiated by the then Minister of Education (Lange, 1988). The essence of the reforms was the devolution of responsibility for education to local communities. The bicultural nature of New Zealand society was emphasized; the reform documents urged cultural sensitivity within a 'partnership of equals':

Partnership implies incorporating the organizational styles and procedures of other cultures in the day-to-day work of the institution. [...] The effects of lack of cultural sensitivity can be considerable. Learning institutions have been largely inimical to cultural values outside the mainstream – and without a sense of security about the worth of their culture, individuals can suffer a personal and social dislocation that makes learning difficult, if not impossible (*Administering for excellence*, 1988, p. 4-5).

As well as emphasizing local autonomy, collective responsibility, and cross-cultural understanding, the reform documents also acknowledged the rights of Maori parents to have their children educated in the Maori language within the State school system. This led to the development of a Maori Studies syllabus with the dual goals of supporting the maintenance and development of Maori language and culture amongst the Maori children of New Zealand, while also providing Pakeha [European] children with a deeper knowledge of and respect for Maori language and culture (*Tihe Mauri Ora!*, 1990). Significantly, the new syllabus stresses that Maori language and culture is not simply another subject to be taught, like mathematics, art or geography, but a way of life to be shared and experienced. In other words, Maori Studies is taught as process, not just as content. The syllabus refers to *taha Maori* as the underlying philosophy of the school curriculum. The term implies that all aspects of the life of the school will reflect a Maori dimension or perspective. One teacher expressed it this way:

The school ethos should be based on good relationships and open communication. Good relationships between teacher and teacher, between teacher and child, and between child and child will reduce tensions and minimize violence. This is basic to *taha Maori*. In the past our schools have been modelled on the British system. They have been administered on a 'top-down' basis. Now they are becoming indigenous New Zealand institutions. We have adapted our teaching and learning processes to take account of the multicultural ethos of this country (cited by Teasdale, 1993, p. 17).

The syllabus places strong emphasis on *taha Maori*, noting that it should permeate all aspects of school life: 'Maori values such as *aroha* [love and concern], *manaakitanga* [hospitality], arriving at decisions by consensus, allowing each person the right to voice an opinion, and respecting the contribution of each, are given emphasis' (*Tihe Mauri Ora!*, 1990, p. 12). It then goes on to outline how this can be achieved in practice:

Architecture. It is suggested that *taha Maori* can be reflected in the architecture and environment of the school; e.g. by using woven panels or wood carvings, by planting native shrubs and trees in the grounds, or by developing a *marae* as a place for ceremonies and greetings.

Open Door. School organization and management should provide support, encouragement and hospitality to all newcomers and visitors. This should begin in the staff room and extend to the classrooms. It should also incorporate an open-door policy between the school and its community.

Timetable. If it is to reflect *taha Maori*, a school's use of time should be flexible, and this will have implications for timetabling. The curriculum document includes the following important statement:

> For Maori people time has no beginning and no end. Unlike some other perceptions of time, it is not linear: it moves in a circle. The present and past are sometimes close and sometimes apart. This implies that courses of study should be seen as cyclical, and that teachers should revisit what has gone before, then move on to some yet unexplored aspect until, at last, the whole is complete (*Tihe Mauri Ora!*, 1990, p. 12).

Co-operative learning. This should be a feature of all schools that adopt *taha Maori.* Provision should be made for students to work co-operatively in groups of varying size. Teachers should acknowledge and reward group rather than individual success within a non-competitive ethos. All individuals within a group should have their contributions recognized and valued.

Holistic learning. The Maori approach to learning is holistic. The new syllabus therefore has implications for the total curriculum within each classroom, since Maori language and culture need to be integrated with all other subjects. The curriculum document stresses, however, that this integration should occur naturally and appropriately as the opportunity arises.

Changing attitudes. For effective implementation, schools need to become steeped in *taha Maori.* Management practices and day-to-day organization should incorporate the underlying philosophies of *taha Maori.* In this way students will experience Maori culture as a living entity, thus developing more positive attitudes which in turn will lead to a deeper understanding.

These bold and innovative statements sound impressive, but the real test is whether they are feasible in practice. Certainly their implementation would require high levels of patience, cross-cultural understanding, and commitment, but even so, is it possible for a school to achieve this kind of deep biculturalism? One successful example is Tikipunga High School in

209

Whangarei, in the north island of New Zealand. This large secondary school of approximately 1,000 students, with almost equal representation of Maori and Pakeha, has been totally restructured into a non-hierarchical, democratic institution in which students take full responsibility for their own learning. The following vignette provides clear evidence that *taha Maori* can be achieved in practice.

TIKIPUNGA HIGH SCHOOL, WHANGAREI

We joined the staff early on Monday morning for their regular but brief time of information sharing. Individual teachers quickly and succinctly conveyed their messages, concerns and commendations to the assembled group. The atmosphere was open, positive and well-laced with banter and good humour. In fifteen minutes the meeting was over and teachers were away to classes. A new week had begun.

A Maori parent and some Maori students were introduced to us and became our 'minders' and 'interpreters' for the spectacular Maori ceremony of welcome that we were about to experience. Outside a chilling winter wind made us shiver, but not a tremble was evident amongst the dozens of young Maori and Pakeha students dressed in traditional Maori clothing who awaited our approach in the *marae atea* (the open space outside the school assembly hall). With incredible precision of movement and facial expression a young Maori 'warrior' moved towards us brandishing a spear. A little distance from us he threw down a challenge in the form of a sprig of leaves from a particular tree. Three times we were challenged. Only after the correct acceptance of this challenge could we proceed. Slowly we moved forward with eyes cast down. Nearing the *marae* we paused to remember the dead, those who had trodden the earth before us. Then to the seats of honour and the oratory, turn upon turn of strong, poetic, evocative speeches in the Maori language. Speakers included Maori elders and parents, Maori and Pakeha students and teachers, and visitors. All were drawn together into this communal activity of welcome – incorporating speeches, singing, dancing, laughter and togetherness. We felt as if we now legitimately 'belonged', as we were accepted by and into the school community.

First and foremost this school has only one rule, that of non-violence. This means that no member of the school community, staff or student, shall commit an act of physical or verbal violence against him or herself, against any other person, or against any school property. Any conflicts between members of the school community are dealt with supportively by small committees of mediators. When these conflicts occur between staff and students or students and students the mediating committee always includes student members. The aim is to put in place a philosophy of peace and cross-cultural understanding in *all*

---

settings and relationships at Tikipunga, regardless of the age, gender, culture, social class, physical status or intellectual capacity of the individuals involved.

The school gives relatively limited emphasis to the development of teaching aids, curriculum materials and library resources. Rather, the emphasis is on internalization of ideas, values and behaviours, and the ability to live them out. For Maori students the involvement of the *whanau* [the extended family], the *kaumatua* [elders], and other members of the Maori community in the day-to-day activities of the school has been pivotal to their full participation in the life of Tikipunga High. Truancy, vandalism, fighting, dropping out and resistance to learning are fast diminishing. All staff and students are encouraged to care, to share, and to enjoy their school experience. Most do! Staff morale is exceptionally high; student morale not far behind.

Probably the most innovative development at Tikipunga has been its radical approach to curriculum implementation. The hierarchical and compartmentalized curriculum of New Zealand secondary schools seemed quite inappropriate to the needs, aspirations and expectations of most students and their families. There was a major dislocation between the formal, examination-oriented and subject-driven national curriculum and the needs of young school-leavers in the bilingual/bicultural community of Whangarei.

Accordingly, the staff developed a totally new curriculum structure based on a modular approach. The aim was to develop a system that was responsive to student needs, respected students' personal autonomy as learners, offered a more relevant and holistic approach to school learning, and reflected the bicultural goals of *taha Maori*. Essentially, all teaching and learning in the school is done in modules of six-week blocks of four hours per week. Students enrol in six modules at a time. Each module has precise learning outcomes and assessment is criterion-based. The end-of-year report of Tikipunga High for 1991 spells out the reasons for the change to a modular system:

(i)   To enable students to work at their learning level rather than their chronological level. (The system is both multi-level and multi-grade.)
(ii) To offer integrated and comprehensive learning opportunities for students with special needs, such as those with special abilities and those requiring remedial teaching.
(iii) To try to close the learning gap between middle-class students and those whose learning is affected by factors of class, ethnicity or gender.
(iv) To offer a wider range of learning areas while continuing to offer students a free choice of modules.
(v)   To enable the school to respond quickly and appropriately to community needs and interests.

The modular system is supported by a carefully planned approach to student guidance and counselling, co-ordinated by staff members who are appointed as deans of students for each year level. Each year students receive a book containing clear descriptions of every module offered. A computerized data-base helps staff to monitor progress and keep track of each student's individ-ualized programmes.

A short descriptive account such as this can never do full justice to a school as rich and as complex as Tikipunga High. A whole web of interlocking factors has contributed to its success in living out the philosophies of *taha Maori*, and in achieving the kind of deep biculturalism referred to earlier. Certainly, the principal herself has made a remarkable contribution, inspiring the staff, and providing effective 'bottom up' rather than 'top down' leadership (as she herself has expressed it). Other key elements include:

(i) The consistent emphasis on affirmation and empowerment of all mem-bers of the school community in a non-competitive environment. This is reflected in the frequent use of celebration and ceremony to recognize and nurture the individual talents and achievements of all staff and students. (At the end of each year, for example, the school holds a *praise* giving, rather than a *prize* giving ceremony, that celebrates achievements – no matter how small and seemingly insignificant – in curricular, extra-cur-ricular and community activities.)

(ii) The fact that the school operates on a philosophy that each cultural group should function efficiently in the other's culture; that conflict resolution is the responsibility of *all* members of the school community; and that non-violence is emphasized at all times.

(iii) The emphasis on respect for the individual; on strong parental and com-munity participation; and on supportive human relationships within and between all groups – children, teachers, ancillary staff, parents, commu-nity leaders, elders.

(iv) The effectiveness of the school's approach to curriculum implementation stressing the individual autonomy and responsibility of the learner; the holistic nature of knowledge; and the need for learning to be useful and relevant to the lives of the students. Thus, students are expected to be self-disciplined and to monitor their own learning. The use of achieve-ment-based assessment is also important here. Its aim is not to find out what students do *not* know, but to identify and document learning out-comes in a constructive and affirming way.

(v) The non-hierarchical and democratic management structure of the school, based on the philosophy of *taha Maori*, stresses decision making by consensus, negotiation, co-operation, and respect for each individual's contribution(Adapted from Teasdale, 1993, p.18-22).

The example of Tikipunga High School demonstrates that reconceptualization can be effective in a bicultural setting. It requires open and effective
dialogue between the two cultural groups and a willingness to compromise
in order to achieve outcomes that are culturally acceptable to both. Perhaps
the most important lesson from Tikipunga, however, is that Maori culture
has permeated the whole structure and ethos of the school, effectively
becoming a 'way of life' for Maori and Pakeha, for staff and students, for
parents and children. It is not only having a profound impact on the
cultural development of the local Maori community, but is adding important integrative and interdependency dimensions to Pakeha education.

THE PROBLEM OF PROCESS

Assuming that members of a small indigenous culture have established full
ownership and control of education, successfully developed their own
community-based language programmes, and reconceptualized education
within their own cultural parameters, they are still faced with one of the
most daunting questions of all, that of process. In fact, some observers
argue that differences between indigenous and modern processes of knowledge acquisition diverge so widely that they appear incompatible. Most
small indigenous cultures rely on informal processes, with learning taking
place in the context of everyday activities. It is largely an unconscious
process of observation, imitation and role playing, in contrast to the formal
verbal instruction of modern industrialized societies. Traditionally, children in most indigenous cultures learn through real-life performance in
concrete situations, through successive approximations to the mature end
product, and by persistence and repetition. This contrasts with modern
learning which takes place in the contrived setting of the school, involves
practising artificially-structured activities as a means to a future end,
places significant stress on the sequencing of skills and the practising of
individual components, and requires emphasis on analysis and efficiency
(Harris, 1984, 1990; Teasdale & Teasdale, 1992).

The question of process has received considerable attention in Australia.
The cultures of traditional Aboriginal Australians and those of contemporary industrialized societies are probably as unlike as any in the world.
Paramount to the Aboriginal world view is the coherence of land, people,
nature and time. Meaning lies in wholeness and relatedness. The spiritual
dimension acts as an integrating force, pervading all aspects of life. As
Christie (1985, p. 11) points out:

213

[...] all Western notions of quantity – of more and less, of numbers, mathematics and positivist thinking – are not only quite irrelevant to the Aboriginal world, but contrary to it. [...] A world view in which land, spirit beings, people and trees are all somehow unified does not lend itself to scientific analysis.' In such a system all questions of truth and belief have been answered already in the law and the 'dreaming'. This has profound implications for learning processes:

Aboriginal learners are not expected to analyze or question the basis of belief, even when dissonance exists. Theirs is a 'closed' system with cause and effect relationships having a religious rather than a 'rational' explanation. This contrasts with the openness of Western thought that encourages a scientific and analytical approach aimed at resolving dissonance between conflicting sets of beliefs. Where Westerners seek logical harmony in their explanations of reality, Aboriginal people have a tolerance for ambiguity; what they believe is more important than what they understand. Knowledge therefore is not queried or challenged, especially by young people, and from an early age curiosity in children is deliberately discouraged (Teasdale & Teasdale, 1992, p. 445).

In the light of the above, it appears almost certain that the use of modern processes of teaching and learning in schools for Australian Aboriginal children will be destructive for at least some traditional values and beliefs. Aboriginal culture is clearly vulnerable when confronted by the world view of modern industrialized societies emphasizing quantification, individualism, positivism and scientific thought. To a greater or lesser extent the same problem applies to other small indigenous cultures that are forced to co-exist alongside dominant industrialized societies. It may therefore be helpful to examine attempts currently being made in Australia to resolve the dilemma posed by incompatibilities between the two learning systems.

Increasingly, it is being recognized that the only effective solutions will be those developed from within Australian Aboriginal communities, not those imposed from without. Nevertheless, curriculum advisers and managers of education systems can facilitate the search for solutions. Their first task should be to examine their own prejudices and presumptions, particularly in relation to modern scientific knowledge.

Built into the hidden curriculum of most schools is the assumption that such knowledge is indispensable to the progress of the human race – that somehow it is superior, more powerful and more valid than any other form of knowledge. Speaking to non-Aboriginal teachers in Aboriginal schools, Harris cautions them to:

[...] guard against Western value aspects of the hidden curriculum. [You] would do this mainly by making the hidden curriculum explicit, emphasizing that Western skills are being learned so that Aborigines can function effectively in the Western domain – they are not learning these skills because such ways are better. Thus the Western content and skills [...] would be a kind of giant role play – to be learned but not believed in as necessarily representing the best way to live. [...] When an Aboriginal child learns consciously to put on and take off Western roles, almost like a set of clothes, these roles can more easily be kept external to their most personal Aboriginal identity. Teachers [...] have the responsibility to tell the children that this is how Westerners do things, and that they don't have to agree with it or believe in it (Harris, 1990, p. 16 and 64).

NEGOTIATED MEANING

Teachers, advisers and managers also need to recognize that their role in indigenous societies is not to dispense knowledge, but to share it. They should be co-learners. Their minds need to be open to learning as much – if not more – from the other culture as they offer from their own. One way of sharing is to use a negotiated meaning approach in which incompatibilities between the two learning systems are identified and analyzed. Crawford (1986), for example, developed a process of negotiated meaning in the field of mathematics with Aboriginal adults enrolled in an on-site teacher education programme in Pitjantjatjara communities in central Australia. She entered into a complex process of exchanging mathematical meanings that allowed participants to achieve a deeper understanding of modern systems, while reaffirming their own cultural knowledge and identity. Crawford reports that this process of comparative analysis and negotiation was a slow and exhausting one, but ultimately deeply enriching both for her and the participants, the latter also reporting that they felt more confident to interpret and explain contemporary mathematical concepts to children in their schools. The concept of negotiated meaning has also been developed at Yirrkala school, Wunungmurra (1988) comparing it with the traditional negotiation of meanings that takes place between moieties in some Aboriginal cultures. He stresses that negotiation must take place under the influence of *Rom* (law) and respect for the role of elders.

TWO-WAY SCHOOLING

The Aboriginal search for solutions to the problem of process is centred around the concepts of 'two-way' or 'both ways' education, and 'two-way learning'. The latter concept has evolved in Catholic schools in the Kimberley region of Western Australia, and now underlies all of their curriculum planning and development. It emphasizes the need for children to learn 'both ways of life' – the Aboriginal and the contemporary Australian – through 'sharing and exchange between the two sides' (*Two-way learning*, 1988, p. 5-6). This is achieved through Aboriginal decision

215

making, close integration of school and community, the strengthening of teaching/learning relationships between older and younger members of the community, and the development of flexible school structures. At Warrmarn (Turkey Creek), for example, most members of the grandparents' generation spend the first hour of each school day with the children teaching Kija language and culture, and many then stay on at school to participate in various learning activities. Essentially they control the school and play a strong and active role in its two-way learning processes.

The concept of the 'two-way' or 'both ways' school has developed mainly in Arnhemland. Harris (1990, p. 12) cites Yunupingu, the principal of the Yirrkala school, writing in 1987: '[We] began working towards a Both Ways curriculum last year. If you have control of both languages, you have double power. The emphasis should be put on Yolngu [Aboriginal] language and culture so they are respected equally [with English]'. Another teacher at Yirrkala, Wunungmurra (1988, p. 69), has written: 'It is through an exchange of meanings that we can produce a 'two-way' curriculum which will give our children the flexibility to live in both Yolngu and Balanda [European] worlds. To live in both worlds we need to achieve a high standard in [European] education but to keep our identity'. Wunungmurra (ibid., p. 69-71) then goes on to describe the major features of a two-way school:

– Aboriginal ownership of the school programme is recognized;
– community members take the initiative in shaping, developing and implementing the curriculum;
– clan elders come in to the school to teach, thus re-affirming relationships between younger and older generation levels;
– children are organized by clan (or kin) groups for instruction, not by age, and boys and girls are taught separately;
– flexible structures and routines allow for the recognition of traditional ceremonial obligations, especially during initiation;
– equal respect is given to Aboriginal and Western knowledge; the exchange of knowledge is stressed.

A particularly clear and compelling account of how a two-way school operates in practice was given at the Rarotonga seminar by Elizabeth Milmilany, an Aboriginal teacher-linguist in training at Milingimbi in northeast Arnhemland. It is presented below, providing some clear examples of the features identified by Wunungmurra.

THE DHANARANALA MURRURINYDJI GAYWANANALA (DMG) PROGRAMME AT MILINGIMBI

Milingimbi is a small island off the Arnhemland coast in Northern Australia, 300 miles from Darwin. It has a population of about 1,000 people. In earlier times, Aboriginal people spoke their own tribal languages. There are about eighteen different languages spoken in Milingimbi, but even though they are dialects we understand each other. Not many traditional Aboriginal languages are spoken today. The languages used in Milingimbi are divided into two main moiety groups: Dhuwa and Yirritja.

At Milingimbi, the school is run under the Northern Territory Education Department's policies and curriculum. The department expects all teachers, both Yolngu (Aboriginal) and Balanda (European), to abide by the policies for all schools, whether they are Aboriginal or Balanda schools.

In 1973 the Australian Government officially granted bilingual education [status]. Milingimbi is a bilingual school so most of the staff get together to develop their own school-based curriculum and policies. The curriculum development policy is put together by Curriculum Committees which are a combination of Balanda and Yolngu staff. The work of these Committees also helps the other teachers in the school to see which level children are in and what types of learning skills they have had in the past. The main aim for developing the curriculum document is to look at the school resources and choose what is best to achieve for our school. The purpose of the education in this school is to have appropriate aims and to take into consideration what the community thinks is important for the children to learn at the time. Most of the subject areas have a school-based curriculum and it covers the Northern Territory core curriculum.

The Milingimbi Bilingual Programme began in 1973 as one of the four pilot schools in the Northern Territory. The decision was made by the community that the Gupapuynu language would be used in the school for the Bilingual Programme. Milingimbi school gained provisional accreditation during 1985, then in 1988 Milingimbi Bilingual Programme was fully accredited.

REASONS WHY DMG STARTED

The purpose of developing school-based bilingual curriculum and policies is because Milingimbi is a Yolngu school. Yolngu people want to control decision making and be able to develop relevant programmes based on 'two-way' education.

We decided to have our own way of structuring our curriculum plan, to help the Yolngu and Balanda teachers plan together in a way of team planning and not individual planning.

Yolngu teachers know their background and have an extensive range of knowledge about their environment. They already know when to gather foods and when is the right season to hunt for certain foods such as turtle, fish, shellfish, crabs, mangrove worms and bush foods. They understand the Arnhemland environment and seasonal changes.

The Yolngu teachers also know the attitudes of the children and their backgrounds, who each child's parents are and what they are like. The kinship system is also fundamental to children in the classroom – whom to avoid and whom to talk to. The Yolngu know who are the traditional landowners and what their attitudes are towards certain areas of significance, and they know the religious and spiritual aspects of ceremonies and when they are to be held. They know when the boys are required to attend certain ceremonies as demanded by the Elders for their cultural knowledge.

Therefore we decided this knowledge would be a good basis for a Yolngu language programme. All this knowledge can be used to create new language texts with the children. In the DMG programme we are continuing to collect other stories, arts/crafts and different traditional language for different clan groups, as well as other knowledge available to us so that teachers can plan activities together in reading, recording, listening and speaking for the development of our children's language skills.

While we have developed curriculum in the areas of art, social science and language, many of the lessons for the curriculum are the same. We call our DMG Programme 'Dhanaranala Murrurinydji Gaywananala', which is a name from the Dhalinybuy homeland centre. It relates to the central authority which brings people together and governs the conduct of all ceremonial and other traditional situations. This name was suggested to us by one of the Wangurri clan leaders, who gave us permission to use it for this language curriculum. We thought it was a good name because this curriculum is based on our traditional lifestyle.

TEACHERS, STRATEGIES AND AIMS

The long-term content goals of the DMG programme are generally determined by the responsible co-ordinator, so that the teachers can carry out the teaching strategies in the classroom situation. Teachers have an important role to play to develop children's knowledge.

The most important people, when it comes to developing the curriculum for Aboriginal people, are the Aboriginal teachers. They receive help in preparation and with lay-out of the materials from their Balanda counterparts. Important strategies for the programme come from thinking of curricula that will work in the classroom environment. This programme will also enable students to engage in practical experience outside the classroom in a variety of literacy skills.

Parents are encouraged to become involved from the beginning. The students will be encouraged as they will be required to participate with a new and creative approach to the curriculum. This will give them a sense of responsibility to assert control over their own lives, so they can actively participate in creating a positive and productive future.

The programme is run by the Yolngu staff, co-ordinated by the school teacher-linguist and teacher-linguist-in-training. The Yolngu staff are responsible for ten weeks of planning and teaching the programme with the help of community members. The community and Yolngu have decided to have 50 per cent Yolngu curriculum and 50 per cent Balanda curriculum. The former takes place daily from 10 a.m. to 12:30 p.m. The children are grouped according to the needs of the subjects taught into moiety, gender or age groups.

Similarly, the lessons take place according to the subjects taught. For example, in language lessons children are kept in the classes, where they are taught by community members, and sometimes they are taken out for excursions to see and experiment directly.

The aims of the programme are to teach the children to read and write in their own language and to learn cultural aspects of Yolngu knowledge. One of the strategies to teach the children how to read and write is to surround the classroom environment with written materials, posters, big books, audiovisual materials, etc.

The subjects taught are always from a cultural perspective and the children learn by watching, listening and recording. The children learn to write by watching and copying the models. The children learn many aspects of cultural knowledge and their own language, and most importantly they have the opportunity to understand Balanda culture through their own cultural heritage.

REACTION AND PARTICIPATION OF THE COMMUNITY

The Milingimbi Community feels that it is important for Yolngu youths to be literate in their own language and to be able to maintain, develop and appreciate the significance of their distinctive culture which is a rich and important part of the nation's living heritage.

Today, this new initiative is being carried out by Yolngu staff with some Balanda teachers, to make sure that children are not receiving too much emphasis on modern technology, and are well-equipped in traditional education.

The DMG programme takes place within the school on aspects of traditional knowledge and it is not only integrated into the school-based curriculum but, and most importantly, in liaison with both the community council and community members. Parents and knowledgeable people are asked to advise and to collaborate at all stages from the beginning to the implementation of the Programme. The community council is interested and keen to see this programme operating. After several meetings with the members of the Council, they realized the importance of a Yolngu curriculum and support and encourage the programme.

(This account was prepared by Elizabeth Milmilany, teacher-linguist-in-training at Milingimbi.)

THE GANMA CURRICULUM

The use of metaphor as a tool to facilitate understanding is widely used by some Aboriginal groups. At Yirrkala, a coastal community, the people have extended the notion of two-way schooling using a metaphor based on the *ganma* process. Within their language (Gumatj), *ganma* describes the situation where fresh water from streams and rivers encounters salt water from the sea and the two flow together and engulf each other: 'In coming together the streams of water mix across the interface of the two currents and foam is created at the surface so that the process of *ganma* is marked by lines of foam along the interface of the two currents' (Yirrkala Community School Action Group, 1989, p. 7-10). *Ganma* curriculum theory deals with the processes of drawing together the two streams of knowledge – Aboriginal and modern – and recognizing that they can be mutually enriched by their interaction, while still retaining their separateness. The *ganma* curriculum process operates within legitimate Aboriginal knowledge-producing procedures and under the authority of clan elders, and is directed towards full Aboriginal control over all curriculum decision-making. It therefore has become a powerful tool for defining curriculum content and process in both the hub and homeland centre schools at Yirrkala.

LAND, IDENTITY AND EDUCATION

The Pintupi people of Walungurru, a remote community in the Western Desert, 520 kilometres West of Alice Springs, have confronted realistically the contradictions between their own knowledge and its modes of transmission, and the content and processes of education imposed upon them by the dominant society. Central to the educational philosophy they have evolved is the concept of *Nganampa manta lingkitu ngaluntjaku*. The primary implication here is one of actively grasping and holding on strongly to their land and looking after it. As Keeffe (1992, p. 21) notes, however, the image of holding the land forcefully is intended 'to convey a larger message about holding on, especially through education, to that which comes from the land. In an Aboriginal view, this includes law, language and culture'.

Despite its status as a government institution, the school at Walungurru is firmly under the control of the local community, and visitors quickly become aware of the underlying strength of Pintupi language and culture. In 1989 the school's Aboriginal staff represented their philosophy of schooling visually in a large painting in the Western-desert acrylic genre.

They presented the painting and its underlying concepts at a national curriculum conference in Canberra. There they explained how they had begun formulating curriculum content and processes that centred on a Pintupi sense of self, and on core values such as connection to the land, relationships within the extended family and community, and spiritual knowledge from the 'dreaming'. Keeffe (1992, p. 29) notes, however, that the Wa*l*ungurru people do not claim to have achieved the balance that they seek between '*yan*angu [Aboriginal] knowledge from their parents and grandparents, and *walypala* [white-fellow] knowledge and power'. He continues:

They see their way, from the perspective of their history, to a point in the future where they will be able to balance the processes of cultural retrieval and restoration on one hand, with the many demands (especially economic and employment demands) of their current location within a modern and developed nation-state on the other hand. Getting to that point is a difficult and conceptually tangled task [...] (Keeffe, 1992, p. 29).

SUMMARY

It is clear that the problem of process is a complex one for indigenous peoples. Aboriginal Australians have probably moved further than any of the other small indigenous cultures in the world in dealing with the problem both in theory and practice. The writings of the Yirrkala people and the visual representations of the Wa*l*ungurru people, for example, represent particularly sustained and sophisticated attempts to theorize about the two knowledge systems and their modes of transmission. Nevertheless, most Aboriginal educationists admit that they still have a long way to go in developing curriculum content and processes that achieve an effective balance between the acquisition of functional modern knowledge and the maintenance and development of Aboriginal languages and cultures.

CONCLUSIONS

The survival of small indigenous cultures is important, and not just for the well-being and sense of identity of their own members. Embedded in their knowledge, value and belief systems, are social, political, environmental and even spiritual solutions to many of the crises facing contemporary industrialized societies. The survival of small cultures is important for all humankind. Education can play an important role in this survival, especially in settings where small cultures co-exist alongside dominant industrialized societies. Non-indigenous people do have a role to play, not by offering solutions but by changing their own attitudes and roles. Their challenge is to work alongside indigenous peoples in relationships of equality and mutual respect.

Already solutions are starting to emerge from within some indigenous cultures. Socio-cultural conditions vary widely, and approaches that work in one setting may not be appropriate in another. However, the following directions obviously are important:

1. It is imperative that indigenous peoples have genuine freedom to make their own decisions about education. They have every right to full ownership and control, not just of education, but of all other social, political and economic institutions that directly affect their lives.

2. Language is crucial to cultural survival, and full support should be given to indigenous peoples' initiatives to revive, maintain and develop their languages, especially when these initiatives are based within and nurtured by the extended family and the community, and not just the school.

3. Indigenous groups should be given freedom to reconceptualize schooling within their own cultural parameters. Resources should be made available to ensure they have full opportunity to choose models of schooling that enhance language and cultural development.

4. The knowledge systems of modern industrialized societies may be best transmitted as a kind of 'giant role play' to be learned but not necessarily agreed with, or believed in.

5. The negotiated meaning approach may be useful in sharing knowledge and dealing with some of the incompatibilities between modern and indigenous processes of learning.

6. The concept of 'two-way' or 'both ways' schooling developed by Australian Aboriginal communities offers a potentially powerful way of dealing with the dilemma posed by the fundamental differences between the teaching-learning processes of modern and indigenous cultures.

Finally, members of indigenous cultures should draw strength from the increasing evidence of global support for their predicament – the activities and interest generated during 1993 by the International Year of the World's Indigenous Peoples providing just one set of examples – and from the evidence of a new sense of cultural distinctiveness and autonomy that is emerging from within small societies. Sahlins (1993, p. 1), for example, believes that the 'cultural self-consciousness developing amongst colonialism's erstwhile victims' to be one of the most remarkable phenomena of the world's history in the later twentieth century. He sees the current emergence of 'culturalism' as a spontaneous worldwide movement of cultural defiance whose full meanings and effects are yet to be determined. Sahlins' analysis gives hope that small indigenous cultures do have the strength and adaptability to survive, and that there is a significant role for education to play in the renewal of their deepest values and symbols.

REFERENCES

Administering for excellence: effective administration in education. 1988. Report of the Taskforce to Review Education Administration. Wellington, New Zealand Government Printer.

Christie, M.J. 1985. *Aboriginal perspectives on experience and learning.* Geelong, Deakin University Press.

Cobo, M. 1987. *Study of the problem of discrimination against indigenous populations.* New York, United Nations.

Crawford, K. 1986. Bridging the gap: bicultural teacher training in mathematics education for Aboriginal trainees from traditional communities. *South Pacific journal of teacher education*, vol. 14, no. 1, p. 44-55.

Davies, P. 1992. *The mind of God.* New York, Simon & Schuster.

Downing, J. 1988. *Ngurra Walytja: country of my spirit.* Darwin, Northern Territory Research Unit, Australian National University.

Fishman, J. 1985. *The rise and fall of the ethnic revival.* Berlin, Mouton.

Harris, S. 1984. *Culture and Learning.* Canberra, Australian Institute for Aboriginal Studies, 1984.

Harris, S. 1990. *Two-way Aboriginal schooling: education and cultural survival.* Canberra, Aboriginal Studies Press.

Hawking, S.W. 1988. *A brief history of time.* London, Bantam.

Keeffe, K. 1992. *From the centre to the city: Aboriginal education, culture and power.* Canberra, Aboriginal Studies Press.

Knudtson, P.; Suzuki, D. 1992. *Wisdom of the elders.* Sydney, Allen & Unwin.

Lange, D. 1988. *Tomorrow's schools: the reform of education administration in New Zealand.* Wellington, New Zealand Government Printer.

León-Portilla, M. 1990. *Endangered cultures.* Transl. by J. Goodson-Lawes. Dallas, TX, Southern Methodist University Press.

Reanney, D. 1991. *The death of forever.* Melbourne, Longman Cheshire.

Sahlins, M. 1993. Culture and modern history'. Cited in: *The University of the South Pacific bulletin*, vol. 26, no. 6, p. 1-2.

Suzuki, D. 1992. A personal foreword: the value of native ecologies'. *In:* Knudtson, P.; Suzuki, D. *Wisdom of the elders.* Sydney, Allen & Unwin.

Tawhiwhirangi, I. 1992. Transcript of a presentation at the UNESCO sub-regional seminar on 'Education for Cultural Development', Rarotonga, Cook Islands, February.

223

Teasdale, G.R.; Teasdale, J.I. 1986. Rekindling the flame – Aboriginal initiatives in education'. *UNESCO review* (Canberra, Australia), no. 12, p. 2-4.

Teasdale, G.R.; Teasdale, J.I. 1992. Culture and curriculum: dilemmas in the schooling of Australian Aboriginal children. *In:* Iwawaki, S.; Kashima, Y; Leung, K., eds. *Innovations in cross-cultural psychology.* Amsterdam, Swets & Zeitlinger.

Teasdale, G.R. 1993. *In-depth study concerning the major questions relating to the implementation of the 1974 Recommendation Concerning Education for International Understanding, Cooperation and Peace and Education Relating to Human Rights and Fundamental Freedoms.* Bangkok, UNESCO, 40 p.

Tihe Mauri Ora! Maori Language – Junior Classes to Form 2. 1990. Wellington, New Zealand Ministry of Education.

Two-way learning: language and culture in schools. 1988. Revised ed. Broome, Kimberley Catholic Education Language Team.

Voices in a seashell: education, culture and identity. 1992. Suva: UNESCO in association with the Institute of Pacific Studies, University of the South Pacific.

Wunungmurra, W. 1988. 'Dhawurrpunaramirra': finding the common ground for a new Aboriginal curriculum. *Curriculum perspectives* (Perth, Australia), vol. 8, no. 2, p. 69-71.

Yirrkala Community School Action Group. 1989. *Interim report on the project: towards a ganma curriculum in Yolngu schools.* Yirrkala, Northern Territory.

Documentation of the forty-third session of the International Conference on Education,
Geneva, 14-19 September 1992

The theme of this *Yearbook* has been drawn from the forty-third session of the International Conference on Education and many of the texts reproduced here were presented in their original forms at the Conference. The following pages print the list of all the documentation presented at this Conference: questionnaire replies, working documents, information documents and national reports presented by the Member States of UNESCO.

The International Bureau of Education has made the complete documentation available on microfiche in its Series of International Reports on Education (SIRE). Readers may obtain further information on ordering these microfiches from:
Documentation and Information Unit,
International Bureau of Education,
P.O. Box 199,
1211 Geneva 20,
Switzerland.
The price is 2 Swiss francs per microfiche when purchasing the entire collection and 3 Swiss francs per microfiche for individual documents (bearing in mind that some documents occupy more than one microfiche).

QUESTIONNAIRE REPLIES

[SURVEY ON THE CONTRIBUTION OF EDUCATION TO CULTURAL DEVELOPMENT: REPLIES FROM MEMBER STATES OF THE AFRICA REGION]
Geneva, UNESCO:IBE, 1993. 24 documents. Replies to questionnaire ED/BIE/CONFINTED/43/Q/91. (various texts in eng, fre, spa)
DESCRIPTORS: cultural development; education and development; cultural policies; cultural background; intercultural programmes; multicultural education; modern language instruction; aesthetic education; art education; cultural interrelationships; teacher education; literacy programmes; basic education; Angola; Benin; Botswana; Burkina Faso; Burundi; Central African Republic; Côte d'Ivoire; Equatorial Guinea; Ethiopia; Ghana; Guinea; Kenya; Lesotho; Malawi; Mali; Mauritania; Namibia; Nigeria; Senegal; Swaziland; Uganda; United Republic of Tanzania; Zambia; Zimbabwe – moral education; civic education
Microfiche: SIRE/02594 (7MF)

[SURVEY ON THE CONTRIBUTION OF EDUCATION TO CULTURAL DEVELOPMENT: REPLIES FROM MEMBER STATES OF THE ARAB STATES REGION]
Geneva, UNESCO:IBE, 1993. 14 documents. Replies to questionnaire ED/BIE/CONFINTED/43/Q/91. (various texts in eng, fre)
DESCRIPTORS: cultural development; education and development; cultural policies; cultural background; intercultural programmes; multicultural education; modern language instruction; aesthetic education; art education; cultural interrelationships; teacher education; literacy programmes; basic education; Bahrain; Egypt; Jordan; Kuwait; Lebanon; Libyan Arab Jamahiriya; Oman; Qatar; Saudi Arabia; Sudan; Syrian AR; Tunisia;

United Arab Emirates; Yemen – moral education; civic education
Microfiche: SIRE/02595 (5MF)

[SURVEY ON THE CONTRIBUTION OF EDUCATION TO CULTURAL DEVELOPMENT: REPLIES FROM MEMBER STATES OF THE ASIA AND THE PACIFIC REGION]
Geneva, UNESCO:IBE, 1993. 16 documents. Replies to questionnaire ED/BIE/CONFINTED/43/Q/91. (various texts in eng, fre)
DESCRIPTORS: cultural development; education and development; cultural policies; cultural background; intercultural programmes; multicultural education; modern language instruction; aesthetic education; art education; cultural interrelationships; teacher education; literacy programmes; basic education; Australia; China; Cook Islands; Democratic People's Rep. of Korea; Fiji; India; Indonesia; Iran (Islamic Republic); Japan; Malaysia; Pakistan; Papua New Guinea; Philippines; Republic of Korea; Sri Lanka; Thailand – moral education; civic education
Microfiche: SIRE/02596 (6MF)

[SURVEY ON THE CONTRIBUTION OF EDUCATION TO CULTURAL DEVELOPMENT: REPLIES FROM MEMBER STATES OF THE EUROPE REGION]
Geneva, UNESCO:IBE, 1993. 24 documents. Replies to questionnaire ED/BIE/CONFINTED/43/Q/91. (various texts in eng, fre, spa)
DESCRIPTORS: cultural development; education and development; cultural policies; cultural background; intercultural programmes; multicultural education; modern language instruction; aesthetic education; art education; cultural interrelationships; teacher education; literacy programmes; basic education; Austria; Belgium; Bulgaria; Czechoslovakia; Finland; France; Germany; Israel; Italy; Luxembourg; Malta; Netherlands; Norway; Poland;

Portugal; Romania; Russian Federation;
San Marino; Spain; Sweden;
Switzerland; Turkey; Ukraine;
Yugoslavia – moral education; civic
education
Microfiche: SIRE/02597 (9MF)

[SURVEY ON THE CONTRIBUTION
OF EDUCATION TO CULTURAL
DEVELOPMENT: REPLIES FROM
MEMBER STATES OF THE LATIN
AMERICA AND THE CARIBBEAN
REGION]
Geneva, UNESCO:IBE, 1993. 14
documents. Replies to questionnaire
ED/BIE/CONFINTED/43/Q/91. (various
texts in eng, fre, spa)
DESCRIPTORS: cultural development;
education and development; cultural
policies; cultural background;
intercultural programmes; multicultural
education; modern language instruction;
aesthetic education; art education;
cultural interrelationships; teacher
education; literacy programmes; basic
education; Barbados; Brazil; Chile;
Colombia; Costa Rica; Cuba; El
Salvador; Haiti; Honduras; Jamaica;
Mexico; Panama; Peru; Venezuela –
moral education; civic education
Microfiche: SIRE/02598 (5MF)

CONFERENCE DOCUMENTS

IBE

The Development of education: guidelines for preparing a national report. Geneva, IBE, 28 June 1991. 3 p. (eng; also in fre, spa)
Microfiche: SIRE/02599 (1MF)

Survey in preparation for the forty-third session of the International Conference on Education on the theme: The contribution of education to cultural development, Geneva, 14-19 September 1992. Geneva, IBE, 12 June 1991. 27 p. (eng; also in ara, chi, fre, rus, spa)
Microfiche: SIRE/02600 (2MF)

The Contribution of education to cultural development. Geneva, IBE, 5 August 1992. 25 p. (eng; also in ara, chi, fre, rus, spa)
Microfiche: SIRE/02601 (2MF)

Preliminary report on the implementation of Recommendation no. 77 adopted by the 42nd session of the International Conference on Education and concerning operational policies, strategies and programmes in the areas of literacy and basic education for the 1990s. Geneva, IBE, 7 July 1992. 16 p., tables. (eng; also in ara, chi, fre, rus, spa)
Microfiche: SIRE/02602 (2MF)

[Reference documents on the contribution of education to cultural development]. Geneva, IBE, 1992. 19 documents. (various texts in eng, fre, spa)
Microfiche: SIRE/02604 (3MF)

[Information documents on the contribution of education to cultural development]. Geneva, IBE, 1992. 21 documents. (various texts in eng, fre, spa)
Microfiche: SIRE/02605 (4MF)

Final report. Paris, UNESCO:IBE, 1993.

1 v. (various pagings). (eng; also in ara, chi, eng, fre, rus, spa)
Microfiche: SIRE/02606 (5MF)

UNESCO

Statistical document on education and culture. Paris, UNESCO, 1992. ii, 53 p., diagrs., tables. (eng; also in fre)
Microfiche: SIRE/02603 (2MF)

228

NATIONAL REPORTS

Argentina. Ministerio de Cultura y Educación. *Development of the education in Argentina, 1991-1992.* Buenos Aires, Ministry of Culture and Education Press, 1992. 1 v. (unpaged), tables. (eng; also in spa)
Microfiche: SIRE/02508 (2MF)

Curriculum Corporation (Australia); Australian Education Council. *National report on schooling in Australia, 1990.* Carlton, Australia, Curriculum Corporation for the Australian Education Council, 1991. 169 p., illus., diagrs., figs., tables. (eng)
Microfiche: SIRE/02509 (2MF)

Austria. Federal Ministry of Education and the Arts; Austria. Federal Ministry of Science and Research. Kahr-Dill, Brigitte. *Austria: development of education, 1990-92.* Wien, Bundesministerium für Unterricht und Kunst, 1992. 102 p., fig., tables. (eng)
Microfiche: SIRE/02510 (2MF)

Bahrain. Ministry of Education. Information and Documentation Centre. Educational Documentation Section. *Development of education in Bahrain during 1989/90 – 1991/92/Taṭawwur at-ta'līm fī dawlat al-baḥrayn fī äl-fatra min 1989/90 – 1991/92.* Manama, Educational Documentation Section, Information and Documentation Centre, Ministry of Education, 1992. 60, 125 p., figs., tables. Bibl.: p. 59-60 (English text); p. 87-88 (Arabic text). (same text in ara, eng)
Microfiche: SIRE/02511 (2MF)

Bangladesh. Ministry of Education. *Country report: Bangladesh. Brief report on the development of education in Bangladesh during 1990-1992.* Dhaka, Ministry of Education, 1992. 22 p., tables. (eng)
Microfiche: SIRE/02512 (1MF)

Belarus. Ministry of Education; Belarus Research Institute for Education; Belarus. National Commission for UNESCO. Bondarenko, E.G.; Velichanski, I.L.; Kozulin, A.V.; Povalyaev, S.A. *Development of education, 1990-1992: national report of the Republic Belarus.* Minsk, Ministry of Education, 1992. 34 p., figs., tables. Bibl.: p. 33-34. (eng)
Microfiche: SIRE/02513 (1MF)

Belgium. Ministerie van de Vlaamse Gemeenschap. Departement Onderwijs. Centrum voor Informatie en Documentatie. *Educational developments in Belgium, 1990-1992: the Flemish Community.* Brussels, Ministerie van de Vlaamse Gemeenschap, Departement Onderwijs, Centrum voor Informatie en Documentatie, 1992. 60, xv p., tables. Bibl.: p. viii-xiv. (eng)
Microfiche: SIRE/02514 (1MF)

Institut national pour la formation et la recherche en éducation (Benin). *Rapport national de la République du Bénin.* Porto-Novo, Institut national pour la formation et la recherche en éducation, 1992. 7, i p., fig., table. Bibl.: p. 6. (fre)
Microfiche: SIRE/02515 (1MF)

Bolivia. Ministerio de Educación y Cultura. Dirección General de Planeamiento Educativo. Dirección Nacional de Programación Educativa. *Desarrollo de la educación en Bolivia.* La Paz, Ministerio de Educación y Cultura, Dirección General de Planeamiento Educativo, Dirección Nacional de Programación Educativa, 1992. 76 l., fig., tables. Bibl.: p. 74-76. (spa)
Microfiche: SIRE/02516 (1MF)

Brazil. Ministry of Education. *The Development of education, 1990-1992: national report.* Brasilia, Ministry of Education, 1992. 69 p., figs., tables. Bibl.: p. 67. (eng)
Microfiche: SIRE/02517 (1MF)

229

Bulgaria. Ministry of Education and Science. *The Development of education, 1990-1992: national report of the Republic of Bulgaria.* Sofia, Ministry of Education and Science, 1992. 18, ix p., diagrs., figs., table. Bibl.: p. 18. (eng; also in bul)
Microfiche: SIRE/02518 (1MF)

Burkina Faso. Ministère des enseignements secondaire, supérieur et de la recherche scientifique; Burkina Faso. Ministère de l'enseignement de base et de l'alphabétisation de masse. *Développement de l'éducation: rapport national du Burkina Faso.* Ouagadougou, Ministère des enseignements secondaire, supérieur et de la recherche scientifique, Ministère de l'enseignement de base et de l'alphabétisation de masse, 1992. 53 p., tables. Bibl.: p. 51-53. (fre)
Microfiche: SIRE/02519 (1MF)

Burundi. National Commission for UNESCO. *Développement de l'éducation, 1990-1992: rapport national du Burundi.* Bujumbura, Commission nationale pour l'UNESCO, 1992. 33 l., figs., tables. Bibl.: l. 33. (fre)
Microfiche: SIRE/02520 (1MF)

Cameroon. Ministère de l'éducation nationale. *Développement de l'éducation: rapport national du Cameroun.* Yaoundé, Ministère de l'éducation nationale, 1992. 59 l., tables. Bibl.: l. 54. (fre)
Microfiche: SIRE/02521 (1MF)

Cape Verde. Ministère de l'éducation. *Développement de l'éducation: rapport national du Cap Vert.* Praia, Ministère de l'éducation, 1992. 46 p., table. Bibl.: p. 45-46. (fre)
Microfiche: SIRE/02522 (1MF)

Central African Republic. Ministère de l'enseignement fondamental, secondaire et technique, chargé de la jeunesse et des sports; Central African Republic. National Commission for UNESCO. *Développement de l'éducation en République centrafricaine [et] Innovations et changements intervenus depuis 1990.* Bangui, Ministère de l'enseignement fondamental, secondaire et technique, chargé de la jeunesse et des sports, Commission nationale centrafricaine pour l'UNESCO, 1992. 21 l., tables. Bibl.: l. 21. (fre)
Microfiche: SIRE/02523 (1MF)

Chile. Ministerio de Educación. *Informe del Gobierno de Chile a la 43a. reunión de la Conferencia Internacional de Educación, UNESCO-OIE, 1990-1991.* Santiago de Chile, Ministerio de Educación, 1992. 83 l., tables. (spa)
Microfiche: SIRE/02524 (1MF)

China. State Education Commission. *The Development and reform of education in China, 1991-1992: national report from the People's Republic of China.* Beijing, State Education Commission, 1992. 44 p., fig., tables. Bibl.: p. 42-44. (eng)
Microfiche: SIRE/02525 (1MF)

Colombia. Ministerio de Educación Nacional. Oficina de Planeación del Sector Educativo. División de Coordinación y Seguimiento Subsectorial. *Desarrollo de la educación: informe nacional de Colombia.* Santafé de Bogotá, Ministerio de Educación Nacional, Oficina de Planeación del Sector Educativo, División de Coordinación y Seguimiento Subsectorial, 1992. 24 l., table. Bibl.: l. 21-24. (spa)
Microfiche: SIRE/02526 (1MF)

Côte d'Ivoire. Ministère de l'éducation nationale. Direction de la planification, de l'évaluation et des statistiques. *Développement de l'éducation, 1985-1990: rapport national, Côte d'Ivoire.* Abidjan, Ministère de l'éducation nationale, Direction de la planification, de l'évaluation et des statistiques, 1991. 68, i l., fig., tables. (fre)
Microfiche: SIRE/02527 (1MF)

Cuba. Ministry of Education. *Cuba: organization of education, 1989-1992.* Havana, Ministry of Education, 1992. 42 p., fig., tables. (eng; also in spa) Microfiche: SIRE/02528 (1MF)

Cyprus. Ministry of Education. *Development of education, 1990-1992: national report of Cyprus.* Nicosia, Ministry of Education, 1992. 49, v p., figs., tables. Bibl.: p. 49. (eng) Microfiche: SIRE/02529 (1MF)

Institute of Information and Prognoses of Education, Youth and Sports (Czechoslovakia). *Development of education, 1990-1992: Czech and Slovak Federal Republic.* Bratislava, Institute of Information and Prognoses of Education, Youth and Sports, 1992. 110 p., fig., tables. Bibl.: p. 99-110. (eng) Microfiche: SIRE/02530 (2MF)

Denmark. Ministry of Education and Research. *Development of education, 1990-1992: national report of Denmark.* Copenhagen, Ministry of Education and Research, 1992. 15 l. (eng) Microfiche: SIRE/02531 (1MF)

Ecuador. Ministerio de Educación y Cultura. Dirección Nacional de Planeamiento. *Desarrollo de la educación: informe nacional del Ecuador.* Quito, Ministerio de Educación y Cultura, Dirección Nacional de Planeamiento, 1992. 59 l., tables. Bibl.: l. 59. (spa) Microfiche: SIRE/02532 (1MF)

National Centre for Educational Research and Development (Egypt). *Development of education in Arab Republic of Egypt, 1990/91 – 1991/92.* Cairo, National Centre for Educational Research and Development, 1992. v, 153 p. Bibl.: p. 151-153. (eng) Microfiche: SIRE/02533 (2MF)

El Salvador. Ministerio de Educación. Oficina de Planificación Educativa. *Informe sobre el desarrollo de la educación salvadoreña a partir de septiembre de 1990 a la fecha.* Nueva San Salvador, Ministerio de Educación, Oficina de Planificación Educativa, 1992. 1 v. (unpaged), tables. (spa) Microfiche: SIRE/02534 (1MF)

Ethiopia. Ministry of Education. *Report on educational development, 1990-1992.* Addis Ababa, Ministry of Education, 1992. 24, 7 l., fig., tables. (eng) Microfiche: SIRE/02535 (1MF)

Finland. Ministry of Education. *Developments in education, 1990-1992: Finland.* Helsinki, Ministry of Education, 1992. 98 p., figs., diagrs., tables. Bibl.: p. 93-94. (eng) Microfiche: SIRE/02536 (2MF)

France. Ministère de l'éducation nationale et de la culture. Direction des affaires générales, internationales, et de la coopération. *Rapport de la France.* Paris, Ministère de l'éducation nationale et de la culture, Direction des affaires générales, internationales, et de la coopération, 1992. 74 p., tables. (fre) Microfiche: SIRE/02537 (1MF)

Gambia. Ministry of Education. *The Development of education: national report from The Gambia.* Banjul, Ministry of Education, 1992. 25, xxv l., figs., tables. Bibl.: l. 24. (eng) Microfiche: SIRE/02538 (1MF)

Standing Conference of Ministers of Education and Cultural Affairs of the Länder in the Germany FR. Secretariat. *Report on the development of education, 1990-1992/Bericht über die Entwicklung des Bildungswesens, 1990-1992.* Bonn, Secretariat of the Standing Conference on Ministers of Education and Cultural Affairs of the Länder in the Federal Republic of Germany, 1992. 186 p., fig., tables. Bibl.: p. 185-186. Glossary German/English: p. 99-100. (same text in eng, ger) Microfiche: SIRE/02539 (2MF)

Ghana. National Commission for UNESCO. *Ghana's country paper on development of education, 1990-1992.* Accra, National Commission for UNESCO, 1992. 40, xi l., fig., tables. (eng)
Microfiche: SIRE/02540 (1MF)

Guinea. Ministère de l'enseignement préuniversitaire et de la formation professionnelle. *Développement de l'éducation: rapport national de la République de Guinée.* Conakry, Ministère de l'enseignement préuniversitaire et de la formation professionnelle, 1992. 28 l., diagrs., figs., tables. (fre)
Microfiche: SIRE/02541 (1MF)

National Institute of Educational Planning and Administration (India); India. Ministry of Human Resource Development. Department of Education. *Development of education in India, 1990-1992.* New Delhi, National Institute of Educational Planning and Administration, Department of Education, Ministry of Human Resource Development, 1992. 54 p., diagrs., fig., tables. Bibl.: p. 52-53. Glossary: p. 54. (eng)
Microfiche: SIRE/02542 (1MF)

Indonesia. Ministry of Education and Culture. *The Development of education in Indonesia: national report from Indonesia.* Jakarta, Ministry of Education and Culture, 1992. 34, viii l., fig., tables. Bibl.: l. 33. In annex: Summary. 8 l. (eng)
Microfiche: SIRE/02543 (1MF)

Iran (Islamic Republic). Ministry of Culture and Higher Education. Institute for Research and Planning in Higher Education. *Education and cultural development, Islamic Republic of Iran: national report.* Tehran, Institute for Research and Planning in Higher Education, Ministry of Culture and Higher Education, 1992. 33 l., diagr., fig., tables. Bibl.: l. 33. (eng)

Microfiche: SIRE/02544 (1MF)

Iraq. Ministry of Education. *Development of education in Iraq, 1989/1990 – 1990/1991/Taṭawwur attarbiya fī āl-ʻirāq, 1989/1990 – 1990/1991.* Baghdad, Ministry of Education, 1992. 55, 50, ix p., illus., figs., tables. Bibl.: p. 44-45 (English text); p. 41-42 (Arabic text). (same text in ara, eng)
Microfiche: SIRE/02545 (2MF)

Israel. Ministry of Education and Culture. Senior Division for Economics and Budgeting. Sprinzak, Dalia, ed.; Bar, Ehud, ed.; Levi-Mazloum, Daniel, ed. *Facts and figures about education and culture in Israel.* Jerusalem, Ministry of Education and Culture, Senior Division for Economics and Budgeting, 1992. 93 p., illus., diagrs., figs., tables. (eng)
Microfiche: SIRE/02546 (1MF)

Japan. Ministry of Education, Science and Culture. *Development of education in Japan, 1990-1992.* Tokyo, Ministry of Education, Science and Culture, 1992. 99 p., diagrs., figs., tables. (eng)
Microfiche: SIRE/02547 (2MF)

Jordan. Ministry of Education. General Directorate of Planning, Research and Development. Jaradat, Izzat; Abusheikha, Mohammad. *The Development of education in the Hashemite Kingdom of Jordan, 1990-1991.* Amman, General Directorate of Planning, Research and Development, Ministry of Education, 1992. 55 p., diagrs., figs., map, tables. (eng)
Microfiche: SIRE/02548 (1MF)

Kazakhstan. Ministry of Education. *Development of the system of education of the Republic of Kazakhstan.* Alma-Ata, Ministry of Education, 1992. 5 l. (eng; also in rus)
Microfiche: SIRE/02549 (1MF)

Democratic People's Rep. of Korea.

232

National Commission for UNESCO. *Promotion de l'enseignement en République populaire démocratique de Corée (septembre 1990 – août 1992).* Pyongyang, National Commission for UNESCO, 1992. 5 p. (fre) Microfiche: SIRE/02550 (1MF)

Republic of Korea. Ministry of Education. *Educational development in Korea, 1990-1992.* Seoul, Ministry of Education, 1992. 85 p., figs. Bibl.: p. 84-85. (eng) Microfiche: SIRE/02551 (1MF)

Kuwait. Ministry of Education. *The Development of education: national report from State of Kuwait, 1990-1992.* Kuwait, Ministry of Education, 1992. 164 p., diagrs., figs., ports., tables. Bibl.: p. 125-126. (eng; also in ara) Microfiche: SIRE/02552 (4MF)

Lesotho. Ministry of Education. *The Development of education: national report from Lesotho, 1990-1992.* Maseru, Ministry of Education, 1992. 37 l., fig., tables. (eng) Microfiche: SIRE/02553 (1MF)

Libyan Arab Jamahiriya. al-Laǧna aš-ša'biyya al-'āmma li-āt-ta'līm. *Taṭawwur at-ta'līm fī ăs-sanawāt 1989-90-91: at-taqrīr al-waṭanī, al-Ǧamāhiriyya al-'uẓmà.* Ṭarābuls, al-Laǧna aš-ša'biyya al-'āmma li-āt-ta'līm, 1992. 51 l., figs., tables. Bibl.: l. 49-51. (ara) Microfiche: SIRE/02554 (1MF)

Luxembourg. Ministère de l'éducation nationale. *Développement de l'éducation: rapport national du Luxembourg.* Luxembourg, Ministère de l'éducation nationale, 1992. 99 l., table. (fre) Microfiche: SIRE/02555 (2MF)

Madagascar. Ministère de l'instruction publique. *Rapport national sur le développement de l'enseignement primaire, secondaire et technique malgache.* Tananarive, Ministère de l'instruction publique, 1992. 33 p.,

diagrs., tables. (fre) Microfiche: SIRE/02556 (1MF)

Malawi. National Commission for UNESCO. *Educational development in Malawi: 1990-1992.* Lilongwe, Malawi National Commission, 1992. 27, iii p., figs., tables. Bibl.: p. 26-27. (eng) Microfiche: SIRE/02557 (1MF)

Malaysia. Ministry of Education. External Affairs Division. *Malaysian country paper: development of education, 1991-1992.* Kuala Lumpur, External Affairs Division, Ministry of Education, 1992. 47 l., fig., tables. (eng) Microfiche: SIRE/02558 (1MF)

Maldives. Ministry of Education. *Developments in education, 1990-1992: Maldives country report.* Malé, Ministry of Education, 1992. 40 p., map, tables. In annex: Activities and projects for the World Decade for Cultural Development (1988-1997): Republic of Maldives. 4 p. (eng) Microfiche: SIRE/02559 (1MF)

Malta. Department of Education. Educational Planning and Post-Secondary Sections. *The Development of education, 1990-1992: national report for Malta.* Floriana, Malta, Educational Planning and Post-Secondary Sections, Department of Education, 1992. 51 l., diagrs., map. Bibl.: l. 51. (eng) Microfiche: SIRE/02560 (1MF)

Myanmar. Ministry of Education. *Education in Myanmar.* Yangon, Ministry of Education, 1992. 26, iii p., figs., maps, tables. (eng) Microfiche: SIRE/02561 (1MF)

Netherlands. Ministry of Education and Science. *Education policy in the Netherlands, 1990-1992.* Zoetermeer, Netherlands, Ministry of Education and Science, 1992. 37 p., tables. (eng) Microfiche: SIRE/02562 (1MF)

Nigeria. National Commission for

233

UNESCO. *Development of education, 1990-1992: national report of Nigeria.* Lagos, Nigerian National Commission for UNESCO, Federal Ministry of Education and Youth Development, 1992. 37 p., figs., tables. Includes the text of the Local Government Education Authority, etc. Decree 1991. (eng)
Microfiche: SIRE/02563 (1MF)

Norway. Ministry of Education, Research and Church Affairs. *The Development of education, 1990-92: national report of Norway.* Oslo, Norwegian Ministry of Education, Research and Church Affairs, 1992. 53 p., diagrs., figs., tables. Bibl.: p. 51-53. (eng)
Microfiche: SIRE/02564 (1MF)

Pakistan. Ministry of Education. *Development of education, 1990-1992: national report of Pakistan.* Islamabad, Ministry of Education, 1992. 69, iii p., figs., tables. (eng)
Microfiche: SIRE/02565 (1MF)

Poland. Ministry of National Education; Institute of Educational Research (Poland). *The Development of education in Poland in 1990-1991.* Warsaw, Ministry of National Education, 1992. 64 p., diagrs., fig., tables. Bibl.: p. 63-64. (eng)
Microfiche: SIRE/02566 (1MF)

Portugal. Ministère de l'éducation. Bureau des relations internationales. *Rapport national du Portugal.* Lisbonne, Relations internationales, Ministère de l'éducation, 1992. 139 p., figs., tables. Bibl.: p. 133-139. (fre)
Microfiche: SIRE/02567 (2MF)

Qatar. National Commission for UNESCO. *Development of education in Qatar in 1990/91 – 1991/92/Taqrīr 'an taṭawwur at-tarbiya fī dawlat qaṭar ḫilāl 'āmay 1990/91 – 1991/92.* Doha, Ministry of Education in co-operation with Qatar National Commission for Education, Culture and Science, 1992.

62, 104 p., figs., tables. Bibl.: p. 62 (English text); p. 104 (Arabic text). (same text in ara, eng)
Microfiche: SIRE/02568 (2MF)

Romania. Ministère de l'enseignement et de la science. *L'Enseignement en Roumanie.* Bucarest, Ministère de l'enseignement et de la science, 1992. 19, vi p., diagrs., fig., map, tables. (fre)
Microfiche: SIRE/02569 (1MF)

Russian Federation. Ministry of Education. *The Development of education: national report from the Russian Federation.* Moscow, Ministry of Education, 1992. 88, 46 p., tables. In annex: The State law of Russian Federation on education. (eng)
Microfiche: SIRE/02570 (2MF)

San Marino. Ministère de l'éducation nationale. *Développement de l'éducation: rapport national de la République de Saint-Marin.* Saint-Marin, Ministère de l'éducation nationale, 1992. 14 l., tables. (fre)
Microfiche: SIRE/02571 (1MF)

Saudi Arabia. Ministry of Education. Educational Development. Center for Statistical Data and Educational Documentation. *Development of education in the Kingdom of Saudi Arabia, 1410-1412 A.H./1990-1992 A.D.* Riyadh, Center for Statistical Data and Educational Documentation, Educational Development, Ministry of Education, 1992. 86 p., fig., tables. Bibl.: p. 85-86. (eng; also in ara)
Microfiche: SIRE/02572 (2MF)

Senegal. Ministère de l'éducation nationale. *[Rapport national du Sénégal, 1992].* Dakar, Ministère de l'éducation nationale, 1992. 13, i p., fig. (fre)
Microfiche: SIRE/02573 (1MF)

Sierra Leone. Department of Education, Youth and Sports. *The Development of education: national report from Sierra Leone.* Freetown, Department of

234

Education, Youth and Sports, 1992. 39
l. Bibl.: l. 38-39. (eng)
Microfiche: SIRE/02574 (1MF)

Slovenia. Ministry of Education and Sport. Board of Education and Sport. Center for Information and International Cooperation. *The Development of education in the Republic of Slovenia, 1990-1992.* Ljubljana, Ministry of Education and Sport, Board of Education and Sport, Center for Information and International Cooperation, 1992. 72 p., tables. Bibl.: p. 67-68, 71-72. (eng)
Microfiche: SIRE/02575 (1MF)

Spain. Ministerio de Educación y Ciencia. *Development of education: national report on Spain/Desarrollo de la educación: informe nacional de España.* Madrid, Ministry of Education and Science, 1992. 189, 194 p., fig., tables. (same text in eng, spa)
Microfiche: SIRE/02576 (4MF)

Sri Lanka. Ministry of Education and Higher Education. *Country report: Sri Lanka.* Battaramulla, Sri Lanka, Ministry of Education and Higher Education, 1992. 15 p. (eng)
Microfiche: SIRE/02577 (1MF)

Sudan. Wazārat at-tarbiya wa-ăt-ta'līm. Wakālat at-tahtīt at-tarbawī. al-Maġribī, Yūsuf 'Abd al-Lah; ad-Dasīs, Ibrāhīm Sulaymān; al-Ḥāğ, Āmina Ahmad. *Taqrīr as-sūdān li-mu'tamar at-tarbiya ad-duwalī, ğanīf, 1992.* al-Ḥurṭūm, Wazārat at-tarbiya wa-ăt-ta'līm, Wakālat at-tahṭīṭ at-tarbawī, 1992. 32 l., tables. (ara)
Microfiche: SIRE/02578 (1MF)

Swaziland. Ministry of Education. *The Development of education: national report from Swaziland.* Mbabane, Ministry of Education, 1992. 32 l., figs., tables. (eng)
Microfiche: SIRE/02579 (1MF)

Sweden. Ministry of Education and Science. *The Development of education: national report from Sweden.* Stockholm, Swedish Ministry of Education and Science, 1992. 47 p., fig., map, tables. (eng)
Microfiche: SIRE/02580 (1MF)

Conférence suisse des directeurs cantonaux de l'instruction publique. Secrétariat général. *Développement de l'éducation: rapport national de la Suisse.* Berne, Secrétariat général, Conférence suisse des directeurs cantonaux de l'instruction publique, 1992. 44 p., diagrs., fig., tables. (fre)
Microfiche: SIRE/02581 (1MF)

Syrian AR. Ministère de l'éducation. *Rapport national sur le développement de l'éducation en République arabe syrienne.* Damas, Ministère de l'éducation, 1992. 77 l., fig., tables. (fre; also in ara)
Microfiche: SIRE/02582 (2MF)

Thailand. Ministry of Education. *Development of education.* Bangkok, Ministry of Education, 1992. 43 p., figs., table. (eng)
Microfiche: SIRE/02583 (1MF)

Tunisia. National Commission for UNESCO. Secteur de l'éducation; Tunisia. Ministère de l'éducation et des sciences. *Développement de l'éducation en Tunisie, 1990-1992.* Tunis, Secteur de l'éducation, Commission nationale tunisienne pour l'éducation, la science et la culture (UNESCO – ALECSO – ISESCO), Ministère de l'éducation et des sciences, 1992. 104 p., tables. Bibl.: p. 103-104. (fre; also in ara)
Microfiche: SIRE/02584 (2MF)

Turkey. Ministry of National Education. *Developments in Turkish national education system, 1990-1992.* Ankara, Ministry of National Education, 1992. 91 p., diagr., figs., tables. (eng)
Microfiche: SIRE/02585 (1MF)

Uganda. National Commission for UNESCO. *The Development of*

education in Uganda, 1990-1992.
Kampala, Uganda National Commission
for UNESCO, 1992. 70 p., figs., map,
tables. Bibl.: p. 65-67. (eng)
Microfiche: SIRE/02586 (1MF)

Ukraine. Ministry of Education. Lugoviij,
V.I., ed. Development of education in
Ukraine, 1990-1991/Rozvitok osvīti v
Ukraïnī, 1990-1991 roki. Kiev, Ministry
of Education, 1992. 91 p. Bibl.: p. 45-46
(Ukrainian text); p. 90-91 (English text).
(same text in eng, ukr)
Microfiche: SIRE/02587 (1MF)

United Arab Emirates. Ministry of
Education. Planning and Evaluation
Sector. Department of Information and
Research. National report of United
Arab Emirates on the development of
education from 1989/1990 –
1991/1992/at-Taqrīr al-waṭanī li-dawlat
al-imārāt al-'arabiyya al-muttaḥida 'an
taṭawwur at-ta'līm fī āl-fatra min
1989/1990 – 1991/1992. Abu-Dhabi,
Ministry of Education, Planning and
Evaluation Sector, Department of
Information and Research, 1992. 36, 57
p., map, tables. (same text in ara, eng)
Microfiche: SIRE/02588 (2MF)

United Republic of Tanzania. Ministry of
Education and Culture. The
Development of education, 1990-1992:
national report on the United Republic
of Tanzania. Dar es Salaam, Ministry
of Education and Culture, 1992. 58 p.,
figs., tables. Bibl.: p. 41-42. (eng)
Microfiche: SIRE/02589 (1MF)

Venezuela. Ministry of Education.
Development of education: national
report on education. Caracas, Ministry
of Education, 1992. 1 v. (unpaged), fig.
Bibliography annexed to Spanish
version (unpaged). (eng; also in spa)
Microfiche: SIRE/02590 (3MF)

Serbia. Ministry of Education. Section
for Innovations and Information and
Documentation; Serbia. Ministry of
Education. Section of International

Relations; Yugoslavia (Serbia and
Montenegro). Ministry of Education and
Culture; Yugoslavia (Serbia and
Montenegro). National Commission for
UNESCO. Maksimović, Iskra.
Development of education in the FR of
Yugoslavia, 1990-1991. Belgrade,
Yugoslav Commission for UNESCO,
Ministry of Education and Culture,
1992. 68 p., fig., tables. Bibl.: p. 38-40.
(eng)
Microfiche: SIRE/02591 (1MF)

Zambia. National Commission for
UNESCO. Chinanda, F.M. The
Development of education: a national
report from Zambia. Lusaka, Zambia
National Commission for UNESCO,
1992. 8 l., tables. (eng)
Microfiche: SIRE/02592 (1MF)

Zimbabwe. Ministry of Education and
Culture; Zimbabwe. Ministry of Higher
Education. Development of education,
1988-1992: national report of Zimbabwe.
Harare, Ministry of Education and
Culture, Ministry of Higher Education,
1992. 39 l., figs., tables. Bibl.: l. 29-30.
(eng)
Microfiche: SIRE/02593 (1MF)

Canada. Council of Ministers of
Education; Canada. Department of the
Secretary of State. Education in
Canada, 1988-1992/L'Enseignement au
Canada, 1988-1992. Toronto, Ont.,
Council of Ministers of Education,
1992. 55, 54 p., tables. Parts I to III
prepared by the Council of Ministers of
Education, Canada; Part IV coordinated
by the Department of the Secretary of
State of Canada. (same text in eng, fre)
Microfiche: SIRE/02607 (2MF)

236